B78431

Helping Older People:
A Psychological Approach

Helping Older People:
A Psychological Approach

Charles Twining

Whitchurch Hospital, Cardiff

JOHN WILEY & SONS
Chichester · New York · Brisbane · Toronto · Singapore

British Library Cataloguing in Publication Data available

ISBN 0 471 91111 9
ISBN 0 471 91851 2 (pbk.)

Printed and bound in Great Britain by Anchor Press Ltd, Tiptree, Essex

To
Barbara,
Rebecca and Daniel

Contents

Acknowledgements

I wish to express my appreciation to all those who have given me the support and opportunity not only to complete this book but also to gain the experience on which it is based. This includes both those who have asked for and those who have taken part in the many talks, study days and discussions over previous years. More important still are the many older people whom I have been privileged to try to help overcome problems in late life.

I am especially grateful to my family who have done so much to ensure that this book was completed.

The cover illustration is taken from the work of M.S., a retired headmistress who took up painting in her eighties. The author is most grateful for her permission to use this material, which shows just one example of the opportunities for learning in later life.

Chapter 1

Introduction

This is a book about helping people, especially people who have grown old. Psychology is the scientific study of behaviour: what we think, feel, say and do. Included in this is the way in which our behaviour changes as we grow older. The aim here is to show how that knowledge can be of benefit in the important task of helping older people.

I have tried to take a practical approach and the ideas put forward should have implications for what we, as helpers, do and the way in which we think about those we help. In many cases this is illustrated using examples of real problems but there are also suggestions for exercises which you, the reader, can carry out. This will enable you to choose examples from your own experience which are going to be of direct relevance to yourself.

However much experience you may have as a professional carer you will certainly have plenty of experience as a person. Indeed this is the origin of what we call 'common sense'. Often this is our only guide as to how to behave towards other people and in everyday life it usually works very well. But we all know that sometimes we do not agree with others about what is the right thing to do. Even more frequently we make wrong assumptions about how other people think and feel. In this situation there is really no such thing as 'common sense'.

Psychology is based on systematic observations of behaviour. It is concerned with looking for laws or patterns which predict or explain what we do. By means of careful study we can agree on at least some of what makes people tick. That knowledge can help us as we try to support, treat, help or otherwise care for older people.

Very many different professions are involved in helping in this way. In particular those working in health and personal social services devote much of their time to this. This is true whether or not those engaged in such work are specially employed to do so. Obviously those who have taken jobs which

1

are designated as helping older people (working in an old people's home or hospital for example) expect to work for older people. However with certain exceptions (child care and maternity) so does everybody else who provides 'care'. For example, about 30% of all patients admitted to general hospital wards are aged 65 or over.

I have therefore assumed that you have at least some experience of this kind of help. For this reason the book should particularly suit those trying to improve their specific skills in helping the elderly. However I hope that it will also be of use to those training for any caring role who can expect to spend at least some of their time in such work.

Older people

Before going any further I shall say briefly what I mean by 'older people'. Phrases such as this or others including 'the elderly' are used freely but rarely accurately defined. In some ways this may be a good thing for it allows some flexibility in interpretation. It lets all of us pretend that 'the elderly' not only are, but will always remain, older than ourselves.

The notion of what is 'old' varies greatly according to context. For an Olympic swimmer or a sprint athlete being old is certainly over 30 and probably over 25. By these standards I am already old: indeed I rather think that I was never anything else. My 8 year old daughter thinks that I am fairly old but I do not. I am more attracted by Miss Brodie's notion of being in one's 'prime'. Being 'old' is at least partly a matter of perception.

Often 'the elderly' are taken to be those aged over 65 years or some other arbitrary age. This is useful because it does at least make it fairly easy to count how many people there are in that age group since there is a well-established system for administering pensions. There is nothing very special about the age itself but socially it does mark an important change between being of 'working age' and of 'retirement age'. It has always been the case that some people have continued to work beyond this age while others have retired earlier. In recent years however there have been many more taking early retirement which only emphasises how the choice of 'age' depends as much on the availability of work as on some fundamental process of ageing. Nevertheless the bureaucratic definition of ageing remains useful and is on the whole what I shall adopt here.

Studies of ageing suggest that it would be more appropriate to set a higher dividing line. This would distinguish those under 75 or 80 years from those over this age. It is convenient to refer to the latter as the 'very elderly'. There is no doubt that those in this category do stand an increased risk of suffering from some major limitation to their everyday abilities. Even so, there are very many in this age group who remain fit and active and who would with good reason feel quite offended at being called 'very old'.

Underlying many definitions of 'old' is some implication of decreased functional ability. In this regard, someone of 68 with diabetes and who has suffered a stroke may be more like our image of 'very elderly' than a fit and active 86 year old. As we shall see, it is interesting that the individual's perception of him or herself will also reflect his or her state of health. Often age in years is a rather poor measure of everything except time since birth.

It may well be that in an ideal world this book need not be written for helping *elderly* people, it could just be about helping *people*. Each individual would receive exactly the help that was required without regard to age. Age should be neither a barrier to nor a requirement for receiving any particular kind of help. It may be for this reason that there is still a good deal of debate about whether there should be specialist services for the elderly. Certainly the problems faced by older people are rarely, if ever, found only in those over a certain age. Rather it is in having many problems at the same time and in needing extra help to overcome these that older people differ. For example the process of change or recovery may be slower. Younger people often recover from illness quickly without the need for prolonged help and support. Professional help can focus on identifying the illness or other problem and applying the appropriate remedy. The client improves and the carer has both the satisfaction of seeing this and the grateful thanks of the patient. When progress is slower, we may have trouble seeing that things are changing at all.

Similarly when problems come one at a time, we can find at least some clients whose difficulties match our skills. For more complex problems we may not have the right skills. Indeed no one person may have these. This means that if we are to help the client best we must rely on combining our skills with those of others. This means sharing the burden but it also means sharing the glory.

Where older people receive help along with younger people everything works fine as long as both have the same types of problems and both make progress at roughly the same rate. Those with multiple problems or whose condition we are as yet unable to improve are less rewarding and, because carers are only human, less attention is likely to be given. This is not intended to be a criticism of those carers who I am sure will protest that they show no such bias. Rather it is an observation of the way in which we all behave and the way in which our behaviour is affected by what goes on around us. We all thrive on success and using psychology to help people means applying it to ourselves as well as to those whom we are helping. Specialist care for older people may therefore reflect a realistic approach rather than an ideal one.

Changes in ageing

There is nothing new about growing old. However we have all been made aware that something has been changing in societies around the world. The 'ageing population' is often mentioned, usually when referring to the strains that this imposes on health services, pensions and other care facilities. But in truth this change is a reflection of the progress which has been made in human survival and is good news for most people.There are two reasons for this.

First, we are now much better at keeping people alive and well so that they have the chance to grow old. This means that there is now a close correspondence between the number of people alive today and the number of children born at the relevant time in the past. Falling infant and child mortality have been the cause of this. We are now seeing changes in the number of people in their eighties which reflect the changes in the birth rate in the early years of this century. This is not very surprising but in the days when fewer people lived beyond childhood changes in the birth rate 80 years before did not have much effect on the overall population.

The biggest change happening now is in the numbers of people in advanced old age, by which I mean those aged over 85 years. The number of pensioners is not changing very much at the present. This a good example of how using this administratively convenient age limit is unhelpful. The number of young pensioners is fairly stable but the number of old pensioners is increasing. This is important because it is the very elderly who are most at risk for all sorts of illness and infirmity. Thus even though the total number of pensioners is roughly constant, the amount of help that pensioners need is increasing. This is best illustrated by considering some simple examples.

Of those aged 65–69 about 96%, that's 19 out of every 20, can manage to have a bath without help. But for those aged over 85, only 49% can do so. In this higher age group every other person needs help to have a bath. This can mean quite big changes for a population as the numbers in advanced old age increase.

As an example let us consider the changes expected in a typical district with a total population of just under 400,000 people. The figures are shown in Table 1.1. From 1961 to 1981 there was a big increase (27%) in those over pensionable age. Over the next 20 years the increase is very much smaller (less than 2%).

Table 1.1   The Changing Population: Example of one British County

Year	Total Population	Total Retired	Aged 85+
1961	380,300	53,800	2,400
1981	391,300	68,300	4,200
2001	409,600	69,300	5,800

Between the years 1961 and 1981 the number those aged over 85 rose from 2,400 to 4,200 or an extra 1,800 people. This means that there were an extra 900 very elderly people who needed help in taking a bath. Of course in the great majority of cases this help can be given not by a paid carer but by a relative or friend. But about 30% of pensioners live alone and roughly the same proportion have no surviving children so such informal care may not be easy to obtain.

Over the next 20 years, to 2001, the numbers increase again so by that time there will be a total of 2,900 very elderly people who need help in taking a bath. A similar story emerges if we look at a number of such activities. The effect is that although the number of very elderly people is not great, they do require a good deal of help and care.

Another trend, also related to better survival, is that people now have smaller families. There are thus nowadays fewer people to provide care for those older people who need this. However this balance is now fairly steady and is not expected to change over the rest of this century.

The second reason why there is an ageing population is that there is a slight tendency for people to live longer once they have reached old age. This increase in the life span is much less marked than the trends which I have just illustrated but it does mean that we now have more centenarians than we have ever had. Despite this, very few of us can expect to live to be a hundred even though very many of us can expect to live into our seventies and eighties.

How does this make you feel? Is growing older a good or a bad thing? As I mentioned a little earlier, using Psychology means looking at ourselves, our own behaviour, thoughts, words and deeds. Certainly in helping older people it is important to have some awareness of how we feel about our own ageing. What we see of somebody else's ageing depends at least in part on how we think we would feel in their shoes. Similarly what they see of *us* depends on who *they* are. This is especially important in ageing where stereotypes of 'old people' or 'the elderly' are often strongly held and inaccurate.

Ageism

By 'stereotype' I do not just mean the obvious negative image of ageing portrayed in comedy or the theatre. There is of course the ageing equivalent of the Mother-in-Law joke but I am here concerned with more subtle and pervasive ageism. Stereotypes in general are quite common and indeed can be quite useful. We all have expectations about the world, the typical this and the average that. There is so much information around us that we have to try and simplify things in order to make sense of it all. We can use these simplifications as a starting point, telling us what to expect. Thus if we are told that someone waiting at the door has come to mend the gas cooker we may be a little surprised if we find someone wearing a bathing costume: the dress would just not be appropriate to the job. However we might also be surprised if the waiting repairman were a woman. There is no 'reason' why we should be surprised except that our experience has taught us that most gas fitters are men. We therefore bring this expectation to the present instance. In this example there would be no real problem and we would let the person in and look forward to a working gas cooker. There would be a problem if we we responsible for recruiting trainee gas fitters and excluded women just because they were not men. That is sexism and as such has even received the attention of legislation. There is also Ageism.

We show Ageism when we expect somebody who is 'old' to have poor hearing, be slow to react or muddled and forgetful. The very word 'senile' is ageist. Strictly speaking it just means 'old' but by association and usage has come to imply decline and feebleness.

Of course the use of age as a shorthand or abbreviated way of describing people is often very useful. Buying clothes, toys or games for children is very much easier if you know how old they are. If somebody were to ask you to pop into the shops to get a birthday present for a nephew or niece you would expect them to tell you how old was the recipient. My daughter is 8 years old, my son 6. This tells you quite a lot about them because children of the same age tend to be like one another in many ways. In this case knowing just a couple of things about somebody enables us to predict fairly accurately a number of other things. Age is often useful in this respect, especially with children.

But what about 'the elderly'? Suppose somebody asks you 'Please buy a present for my Aunt. She's 70 next week.' How easy is this to do? Well certainly buying clothing is out because in this case age tells us nothing about size. It just would not make sense to label clothes '70–80 years'. Hobbies, interests, physical capacities and all sorts of other things vary so much between individuals of that age that the choice is bewildering and uncertain. You end up with a potted plant or some handkerchieves: trusty but hardly exciting or very personal.

This problem is not peculiar to older people, we all differ one from another. However it is one example of a special characteristic of ageing: greater variability.

As we shall see, many abilities and functions change as we grow older. Often the trend is for a slight decline, though for many purposes there may be little noticeable change. For example our ability to think and act quickly is reduced but not so much as to affect normal everyday activities. However there is a lot of difference between individuals. Some remain 'as bright as a button' even into advanced old age. Others slow up noticeably and may even have difficulty with everyday activities. The range of abilities from the quickest to the slowest is much more in older than in younger people. It is therefore more difficult to describe the 'typical' older person. We can take the average of a whole group of old people but there will not be very many people much like that.

Our own stereotype or best guess will be based on the average of the older people known to us. and on those images obtained from the ideas and experiences of other people. Television, newspapers, books and other media obviously play an important part in this. Such stereotypes may be wrong for at least two reasons. First, we may have encountered, either directly or indirectly, an unusual sample of older people. For example only about $2\frac{1}{2}\%$ of pensioners live in residential homes. On the whole they are quite a lot more disabled than those who remain in their own homes. It is that disability which has meant they have had to come into a home. If you work in a home or a hospital it is very easy to get a distorted view of growing older. Similarly the image of ageing which appears in the media may be more influenced by what makes interesting news than by what is typical. Moreover, in so far as advertisers do not see older people as attractive folks with money to spend they tend not to appear in promotions.

Second, our stereotype is like the idea of the 'average' old person. It takes no account of the fact that people, especially older people, differ so much from each other.

This fundamental problem with having *any* stereotype of ageing has not prevented these from being very common. Most famous of all perhaps is Shakespeare's pessimistic view expressed by the young Jaques in *As You Like It*. 'Last scene of all, that ends this strange eventful history, is second childishness and mere oblivion. Sans teeth, sans eyes, sans taste, sans everything.' Less often do you hear quoted another view from the same play. Adam, aged nearly 80, proclaims 'Though I look old, yet am I strong and lusty'. Who is right? The principle of variability suggests that we can find ample examples of both so that in a sense both are right. Yet if we assume either to be typical of old age then quite obviously both are wrong.

All of this is somewhat confusing unless we can re-learn our use of stereotypes. Even more than for other groups we need to see older people as individuals and to avoid making assumptions about how they think, act or feel. Including an understanding of older people as they see themselves is a vital part of this.

Life span development

One approach to the individuality of ageing is that of looking at life span development. The focus here is on the personal changes of ageing as a continuing part of each person's development. This emphasises that there may be positive changes, just as in childhood development, and that all changes must be understood against the background of individual history. This itself indicates why, in psychological matters, older people differ from one another. They have of course each had their own particular experiences, no two of which will be identical. The longer the life, the more varied are the experiences and the more individual are those who result.

Continuity is the key here. Sudden change in any individual is not the normal pattern, rather we evolve from our younger into our older selves. In terms of preparation for old age the answer is to start young, though few of us would think to do so. If we are to understand what to expect of an older person, knowing what they were like as a young person is a good start.

The most important source of this and other information about an older person is the person him or herself. Memories and nostalgia are not simply common side effects of old age, they can be a window into the making of an individual. Active listening, the process of helping somebody to talk about themselves, is a valuable skill which we must develop and I shall have more to say about this later.

However self-report is not infallible. Even in cases when memory is normal, as it is for the great majority of older people, we are all selective in what we remember. The full picture of an individual includes the views of others. We therefore also rely on the reports of family and friends to build up a full understanding. As we shall see, this is important in helping us to appreciate what is normal and to be alert to the abnormal. Since continuity is the usual, marked change is cause for concern. Often we judge what is normal by reference to ourselves. This may be deliberate or may happen without our conscious thought. The decision as to what is normal is more complex when the range is increased. We might think, for example, that someone is 'odd' or even 'mad' when in fact they have always been eccentric in this way. Conversely, we may think that someone is behaving quite normally when they have only very recently started to do so. Both errors could be to the older person's disadvantage since we could either meddle unnecessarily or fail to take appropriate action. There may be good reasons for doing nothing but failing to notice that something was wrong cannot be one of them. This principle of relying on more than self-report is not just a rule for finding out about personality or behaviour. In bodily disease older people are less likely than younger people to report symptoms (I feel pain/dizzy etc.) and we rely more on observations (he/she has a temperature/walks unsteadily etc.).

Continuity and background are especially crucial concerning cross-cultural differences. This is increasingly an issue in multi-racial societies where older people immigrated as adults, albeit a long time ago. It is also relevant in those cases where individuals have grown up in a sub-culture kept away from the more generally prevailing social customs. Language, social behaviour and many other things may be very different. It can be quite a shock, for example, to be taken to a high-technology hospital from a close-knit family and community where the role of 'nurse' has been taken on by family members rather than paid strangers. Knowing about traditions as well as language is important in understanding such a person's needs and can do much to comfort.

Thus we cannot think about ageing without considering both the individual and those with whom he or she has contact. Except for a few reclusive eccentrics, some of whom perhaps live in the Welsh hills not far from where I write, we all have some sort of social contact. I have therefore divided the material in this book into three sections.

Chapters 2 to 5 deal with ageing as it affects the individual. This covers changes in intellect, personality, emotions, reactions to physical frailty, dying and bereavement.

Of course being bereaved implies having lost a loved one and the end of a significant social relationship. The second section, chapters 6 to 8, focuses on social aspects of ageing. Ageing brings changes in the family, work and leisure. For frail elderly people it may mean having to spend all or some of the time in a situation with several other people such as a hospital, residential home or day centre. Large groups may become a big part of everyday life.

The third and final section deals with some of the issues which carers must face. Why do we take on this role, what should our aims be and how can we improve on the help that we provide?

Exercise 1.1

Identify four people aged between 70 and 80 known to you. Try to choose two whom you work with professionally and two who are family or friends.

List all the things they have in common. How do they differ?

Ask them what they think about growing old.

How old do they feel? Is it always the same?

Exercise 1.2

Describe how you think you will be when you are 75.

List five advantages of growing old.

List five disadvantages of growing old.

How do these lists compare?

Further reading

Stott, Mary (1981) *Ageing for Beginners* Basil Blackwell: Oxford

A very readable account which takes a positive yet balanced view of later life.

Nicholson, John (1980) *Seven Ages* Fontana: London

Based on a survey of several hundred people, this shows stereotypes of ageing at all ages. Useful because it covers all ages, including your own.

Section I
Older Individuals

Chapter 2

Thinking and Remembering

What aspects of mental function change most as we grow older? There is no simple answer to this, particularly as people differ so much. Nevertheless, very many people reckon changes in memory to be the most noticeable effect of ageing. Both young and old often agree that failing memory is characteristic of old age. Other faculties also change but the ability to remember events, people, appointments, messages and so on is the one most commonly complained about. But is this really true? If it is true, is it inevitable?

Certainly marked memory changes are the main feature of the most distressing and disabling mental illnesses of old age, namely the dementias. These conditions are at the heart of our notions of senility and constitute one of the greatest fears of ageing. I will say more about these very destructive conditions later. For now I want to focus on the important difference between this type of change, a progressive mental illness, and what may be considered as normal ageing.

Let us start with a quiz.

1. What proportion of people aged over 65 suffer from dementia?
   (a) 1%   (b) 5%   (c) 10%   (d) 20%   (e) 30%

2. What proportion of people aged over 80 suffer from dementia?
   (a) 1%   (b) 5%   (c) 10%   (d) 20%   (e) 30%

3. Mental exercise, keeping one's brain active, can help prevent dementia.
   (a) True   (b) False

The answers to these are cdb. A pat on the back if you were right on all three. Now think of the first two questions the other way around. What proportion of people aged over 65 do *not* suffer from dementia? Likewise what proportion of those aged over 80 do *not* have this condition?

13

It is perhaps reassuring to know that if you are fortunate enough to live into your eighties there is a four in five chance that you will show no abnormal impairment of brain function.

This is not however to say that things do not change. Memory and intellect do change but it is not a simple picture of steady and accelerating decline. That sort of decline might be what we would anticipate from a simple view of anatomy. Brain cells, unlike most other tissue such as skin or muscle, do not regenerate. Once you have stopped growing the number of brain cells does not increase but only gets less. Some sort of decline would therefore seem to be inevitable. Nevertheless there is good evidence that many people maintain full brain function into advanced old age. How can this be?

I have already noted that the explanation cannot be that they do more brain work. The brain is not like a muscle in that muscle gets bigger the more it is used. There must be some other reason.

One reason why in the great majority of cases no decline is seen is that we have so many brain cells to start with. Given a count of many millions of cells at the beginning we can afford to lose a great many before there is any real impairment, at least in everyday tasks. We have so much spare capacity that the loss does not normally become apparent. There are other organs of the body that show this phenomenon. Lung tissue and kidneys are among those that do not regenerate and which show a gradual decline in maximum capacity with age. Though this does not affect normal performance it does show up when there is some extra demand such as illness. The change is also apparent if there are other circumstances where we are required to use our maximum performance. I referred in the previous chapter to how ageing effects show up very early in such people as athletes or swimmers taking part in competitions. Such people are not prematurely old, indeed they are likely to wear much better than the majority of us. However they do discover sooner that age does bring very real changes. Olympic swimmers may have to retire from competitive swimming in their twenties but those of us content to potter up and down the local leisure centre pool do not notice any difference until very much later.

A similar picture emerges with respect to thinking and remembering. If we test people's maximum capacity we can demonstrate quite striking changes in performance, especially in advanced old age. But for normal behaviour these are not terribly relevant. In some situations they may be important and it is useful to have an understanding of this so that we neither over- nor under-estimate the abilities of older people.

I have already mentioned that the principle of increased variability applies to age changes in mental function. Thus older people differ greatly in the extent to which such functions have altered. More than this however, there are also big differences in the way that different skills are affected by ageing. Some types of intellectual function change a great deal whilst other remain much the same. The simple question 'Does mental function change with age?' takes on a whole new complexity.

This complexity is more than just a matter of academic interest. What seems to happen, to judge from many of the images portrayed of ageing, is we tend to take either illness or specific decline to be indicative of general deterioration. We then become conditioned to expect things to deteriorate and look for evidence of this both in other people and in ourselves. Like all prophets we like to be right. We therefore readily note the instances where our predictions come true and quietly ignore the times when they do not.

For example, I often hear elderly people referred to the Memory Clinic or consulting me for some other reason complain how bad their memory has become. I ask them to give me instances where they feel their memory is not what it used to be. Often the examples that they give relate to such things as having to use a diary, making out a shopping list or going upstairs to get something and then forgetting what it was they went for.

Of course these are common occurrences, especially among busy people who have lots to do and think about. After all if I do them as well they must be normal! However there is a serious point here. With respect to a function such as memory, we are all fallible and so the fact that someone shows imperfect memory does not mean necessarily that there is decline let alone disease. But it is also important that we recognise when things have changed and whether that change is normal or abnormal. Here again is an example where 'common sense' is not enough. Indeed it may well be that what most people commonly believe is wrong.

There has a good deal of systematic study of the effects of ageing on memory and intellect. This does enable us to reach some sensible conclusions about what may or may nor properly be put down to 'old age'.

Changes in intelligence

Psychologists and others have spent a good deal of time arguing about what is meant by intelligence. I hope however that you will agree to ignore this debate for the present and accept that it is reasonable to refer to 'intelligence' as a general ability to think, solve problems and learn new tasks. One of the problems is that we cannot easily measure this directly. What we have to do is give people a range of different tasks and look at their ability to perform these. Thus a typical 'intelligence test' has lots of items which cover using words, simple memory, solving puzzles and so on. These are the sorts of tests that have been used to look at the effects of ageing.

The first data which were collected to compare young and old people suggested that the pattern of change with age was much as we might have expected. They indicated a steady increase in ability during childhood, reaching a peak at around 20 years of age. There was then a brief plateau and after the age of about 30 things started to go steadily downhill. Do we really need to look further than this?

Unfortunately this fairly simple approach of comparing young and old people is not a very satisfactory way of finding out about ageing. This is not a special problem for Psychology but affects all scientific study of ageing including biology, physiology and so on. The data to which I have just referred were collected by selecting subjects in different age groups and giving all the subjects in each group the same intelligence test. So there would be subjects in age groups 30–39, 40–49, 50–59, 60–69, 70–79 and so on. The average score for each age group then gives a measure of Intelligence at that age. By comparing the different groups we can look at the effects of ageing. This sort of approach is called 'cross-sectional' because it compares a cross-section of different ages.

The problem is that the subjects in the study were all tested at about the same time. They were of different ages but also could differ in lots of other ways. Consider as an example the staff and residents of an old people's home. On the whole the staff are younger than the residents. This is because they were born later! But because they were born later the staff also have had a different background from the residents. If you have spent time talking to older people such differences are often a source of great interest. Hearing what it was like as a child 60 years ago or what working life was like can be fascinating. Some of these differences might also affect people's ability to do the intelligence test: the amount and type of education for example.

Thus the differences that we see in intelligence tests will be a mixture of the effects of ageing and these other variables. If we want to predict how the young groups will perform when they grow old we may find this very difficult.

Such changes in successive generations have been going on for a very long time. Over hundreds of years the changes can be striking as we marvel at how small were the suits of armour of mediaeval knights or other such things. In this century there has been a steady trend towards earlier sexual maturity and each generation has been on average taller than the one before. No doubt there are lots of other changes like this which are less obvious. Some will make people better at doing tests, some may make them worse. What can be done?

If you want to study rats or pigeons the answer is relatively straightforward. You simply take a group of your chosen species and test them regularly over their life span. With any luck you can get a full picture of the ageing process in rats in 3 to 4 years. Study ageing in fruit flies and you can be home in time for lunch. Sadly not all of us are very interested in the effects of ageing in other species. Such study may tell us very useful things about changes in physiology but is unlikely to shed much light on memory for words. I find it hard to apply findings about how old rats find their way round mazes to counselling older people.

The approach of following individuals across time to determine the effects of ageing is known as the 'longitudinal' approach. Regular assessment of the same individual comes much nearer to our own experience of ageing. The major problem with this method is that it takes quite literally a lifetime. The implications for carrying out such work are very considerable. In addition some major event might occur which affected performance of lots of people but which would not be ageing as we usually think of it. War or revolution could ruin this careful design.

Moreover not everybody tested at the beginning will survive to the end of the study. This is particularly relevant to the study of intelligence. A number of studies have shown that even in apparently healthy people, expectation of life in old age is related to intellectual function. When you attempt to trace your subjects for follow-up a few years after the original assessment those of lower initial IQ score are less likely to have survived. Conversely, those of above average function are more likely to be available for the second test. The longer the period of study, the more this is a problem. In the case of intelligence, longitudinal studies tend to be over-optimistic about lack of decline.

The answer to understanding the rather complex picture is that both types of study have something useful to tell us. The more common and somewhat simpler cross-sectional method can tell us about how today's older people compare with today's younger people. If we are designing a car or planning an adult education programme these are differences which will be important. What we want is to be sure that the product or service we provide suits the customers of today be they young or old. For this sort of task we are unlikely to be very concerned as to whether, for example, the course we want to put on next year for 70 year old people will be suitable for those who will be 70 in another 30 years.

In contrast, think of trying to understand the problems faced by an older person going to live in a residential home or how we should advise those coming up to retirement. Here we are more interested in how each individual deals with changes and adjusts over time. How much of this is due to ageing and how much is due to other causes such as emotional distress or illness? The implication is that if it is 'ageing' then there is an inevitable change, albeit at different rates for different people. Adjustment to this probably involves a realistic assessment of limitations and making appropriate changes in lifestyle.

On the other hand, if the changes are not due to 'age', then resigned acceptance is the wrong solution. Active help or change may be more what is needed. Unless we know the effects of ageing in a longitudinal way then we cannot hope to give the right help to those who need this.

Obviously there is some overlap between these two approaches. However as a general rule we can say that cross-sectional methods tend to exaggerate differences between ages and that longitudinal methods tend to minimise the effects of age. As we have already seen this is especially so for mental changes where performance is related to survival.

Not surprisingly both methods have been used extensively to study how mental function changes with age. The results indicate that all sorts of different changes are found, including little or no change at all!

Types of intellectual change

The most natural division of intellectual skill appears to be between abilities
to do with words and language (verbal skills) and those concerned with visual
and spatial aptitude (non-verbal or performance skills). This is more than
just a difference found between types of intelligence tests. It seems to reflect,
among other things, the way the brain is organised.

Verbal skills include understanding and using words, mental arithmetic
and certain sorts of memory. Performance skills include visual imagery,
solving picture problems and skills like hand–eye coordination. Two overall
patterns emerge, although as we shall see the detailed picture is a complex
one. First, verbal skills seem to decline less with age than performance skills.
Second, skills where speed is involved show most decline with age.

Examples of this include the following. If we look at verbal reasoning or
vocabulary (abilities to do with thinking and using long words!) these show
very little change with age until people are aged 70 or over. Thus the 'elder
statesman' is not at any real disadvantage in writing or delivering a complex
speech compared with his or her younger colleague. Indeed the advantage of
wisdom gained over many years is much more likely to be apparent. Other
verbal skills such as using numbers and some non-verbal ones including
spatial imagery also appear to show little change until well into old age.

In contrast many performance and certain verbal skills show decline even
in those over 40. For example verbal fluency, producing words quickly,
seems to show this pattern. Speed at copying symbols or in completing
visual puzzles also shows definite decline with age. Even so, the decline
for most people is relatively slight and would not be apparent in normal
circumstances. However this does not mean that you can only detect the
difference when someone is doing a special test. The effects of slowing have
been shown to be important in more everyday situations such as learning to
do a new job or working on a production line.

In general the situations most likely to show a decline in ability with age
are ones where someone is required to think or act fast. If the situation is an
unfamiliar one then the effect will be more marked. This has implications
not just for advising elderly people to think twice about taking up Grand
Prix racing. Much more commonly it may show up in a greater time being
taken to adjust to a new situation as might happen in learning to walk again
after a stroke.

Not only do the various types of skill decline at different rates, there are
also differences in the way they change across the generations. We have already seen that we can gain some idea of generational differences by comparing cross-sectional and longitudinal studies. For abilities such as reasoning,
number skills and spatial thinking, the pattern is for longitudinal studies to
show less decline than cross-sectional ones. This means that although there
is some tendency for each individual to show slight decrease in these abilities with advancing age, the more striking difference is between generations.

Someone aged 40 now will be a little less good at verbal reasoning, for example, when he or she is 70 but may still be better then than today's 70 year old is now.

In contrast, word fluency shows the opposite trend. This may mean that later generations are slightly less able in this regard but the main effect is for this ability to decline in middle age and beyond.

Just as there are differences in the way various skills decline with age, so different individuals show differing amounts of decline. The trends to which I have referred are the average for all people. Some individuals fare relatively badly and show a lot of decline. In many cases poor health may be the reason for this and improving health may be important in minimizing decline. A few individuals show very little change so that overall there is a wide range of abilities. This leaves unanswered why there should be such differences but suggests that at least some of the decline could be prevented in some people. Ensuring that all have the best possible old age is a desirable aim.

Learning ability

Part of the definition of intelligence which I used earlier referred to learning ability. Since this is a very important function it has received particular study. Such sayings as 'you can't teach an old dog new tricks' lend weight to a negative view of ageing. It suggests that there may be no point in including elderly people in such things as programmes of education or rehabilitation. This of course may easily become self-fulfilling as those excluded fail to make progress. It may become so pervasive that elderly people themselves refuse to take part on the grounds that they are too old. It will always be possible to find someone who has done badly and to accept this as proof of the assumption.

In fact simple measures of learning ability show little or no decline into old age. More complex learning does show decline but the important factors in this are the same as those I have mentioned for intelligence, namely speed and novelty. A decrease in response speed is one of the most consistent findings of the effects of ageing. We often make predictions about likely achievement based on how quickly someone makes progress early on. Thus when someone makes only slow progress we might conclude that they are incapable of getting very far. The lesson for work with older people is that we must not be too hasty to reach this conclusion.

The advantage of experience

I have already mentioned how studies of speeded tasks such as working on a production line indicate that performance on real-life tasks can be affected by ageing. Such effects are less evident for familiar tasks. This has been shown to be due in part to the way that older people can make use of their experience to develop more efficient ways of doing a job. Wisdom can offset ageing. In the studies to which I referred it was found that older workers would develop their own ways of altering the job to keep up the pace. In some cases such strategies are genuine increases in efficiency but in others they might mean missing out something which the worker decided was unnecessary. If this is wrong then the result is breakdown rather than efficiency!

In recent years the balance of wisdom and ability has shifted somewhat towards wisdom. There has been careful consideration about retirement policies for some jobs such as airline pilots', the upper age limit for jury service and the risks of older car drivers. The insurance companies have recognized that ageing may be a quite positive influence on driving skill.

The best summary of age and learning ability is that training on a complex task is best carried out relatively young. Once learnt the skill may be relied on for many years.

So far I have referred to 'abilities' or 'skills' as if these are easily measured by people's performance on tests. Whilst the performance is readily measured we are always having to estimate the underlying ability, often by looking at performance on several tests. In doing this we may have make various assumptions. One of these can be that everybody is doing the task in the same way. If one person does better than another then it is because they are in some way 'more able'. However age changes strategies as well as abilities. This is seen in the next area I want to consider, memory.

Memory

An apparently straightforward experiment to look at age and memory involved giving young and old subjects a short story to read. The subjects were then asked to recount as much of the story as they could remember. The younger subjects could remember many more facts from the story than the older. Apparently age has a clear effect on memory. (By now you may already be saying 'Ah yes, but this was a cross-sectional study.' If so, give yourself a big pat on the back!)

What makes this experiment particularly interesting is what the experimenters did next. They first of all looked at not only how many things subjects remembered but what kinds of things they remembered. Younger subjects remembered facts. This was a good strategy because this was the way that memory was tested. The older subjects tended to remember themes or principles, what we might roughly call the moral of the story.

The investigators then tried the same experiment on different sets of young and old subjects. However this time they varied the instructions. Some subjects were now told that they should concentrate on remembering facts rather than principles. Others were given no special instructions. The special instructions made little difference to the younger subjects: they did well anyway. But for the older group they improved their score considerably. Their 'memory' was still not quite as good as the younger group's but the difference was much reduced. Evidently strategy is important in remembering things.

Style of thinking has also been shown to change with age. Older people are often said to be more 'rigid' or set in their ways. There is some experimental evidence to support this. In tests of problem solving older subjects have been found to be less quick to change a strategy that is not working. This is likely to be a problem when learning to do something new. Older people tend in such situations to draw on approaches that have been useful in the past in similar situations. This is quite a good way of using the wisdom learned over many years. However if these tried and tested procedures do not work then the older person is less likely to abandon these in favour of something new than would a younger person. In this case there is a conflict between wisdom and new learning.

Sometimes this sort of effect is described as older people showing more caution. Insurance companies who give discounts to older drivers know that caution is a good thing for safe driving. It has been suggested that older people may show a similar tendency in using their memory. They may be more reluctant than younger people to have a guess. Whatever the reason, as was mentioned earlier, most people reckon that memory itself changes as we grow older, not just the strategies we use.

Although we may think of memory as being one thing, it is in some ways as complicated as intelligence. Just as there are different abilities in intelligence, so there are different kinds of memory. We use different types of memory according to the type of material we are trying to remember, the length of time for which we are to remember it, and even perhaps the way in which we make use of our memories. It is easy to imagine human memory as a kind of magnificent biological video recorder, faithfully taking down everything that is received by our senses. To retrieve the memory, you simply put in the cassette, push the right button and sit back to enjoy the show. Every time you play back the memory it comes back the same.

Of course there is no doubt that our memories do not work like that. The whole system is much more sophisticated. To take one example, we can go straight to any part of our memories: to remember leaving school you don't have to run through all the way from the beginning! Similarly we do not have total recall of what happened, of all that our senses receive. Moreover when we remember something several times we may recall slightly different details on each occasion. We may even 'remember' things that did not actually happen.

Many different things may remind us of the same event. For example I can think back to my school days when someone asks me if I remember the headmaster, what was the school uniform or the Latin for 'I am'. But I can also find myself transported back there by a particular hymn or the smell of a certain polish.

There is an important difference between remembering facts (such as how to spell cheese or the capital of France) and remembering personal events (such as where I bought a particular piece of cheese or the holiday I had in Paris). It has been suggested by psychologists for some time that this distinction is important and there is evidence from the study of people with certain types of brain damage that different parts of the brain perform these different types of memory.

The example of 'memory for facts' may be seen as a part of memory for various kinds of 'rules'. This applies not only to obvious rules like spelling but also to things like the names of objects or colours. For these sorts of things we can remember the rule without having any idea of when or where we learned it. Usually when we talk about people learning things, this is what we mean.

When we refer to someone having a good memory we usually mean that they remember incidents that have happened in the past. Thus if somebody recalls when and where they met us, or better still our name, we think of them as having a good memory. Someone who forgets an appointment or does not complete the shopping has a poor memory. This sort of memory is very much to do with ourselves rather than other people. It is the sort of thing we would record in a diary or on a shopping list: not much use to anybody else. Perhaps because it is the sort of memory that we use daily and the sort which most often lets us down, this is the kind of memory that has been studied most. It is also easier to test!

When we talk about memory we often distinguish between recent and remote memory. Recent memory, sometimes called short-term memory, is concerned with remembering what happened this morning or 5 minutes ago. Remote memory covers much longer time spans. We usually think there is a difference between remembering what we had for breakfast and the house where we lived when we started school. I have already mentioned that the length of time for which we have to remember things is important in determining the type of memory which we use. However it turns out that the important time difference is between more than a minute and less than a minute rather than minutes compared with years. It seems that the way we remember things for minutes or years is essentially the same.

Because this is not quite as we might think from 'common sense', terms like short- and long-term memory can be a bit confusing. Psychologists studying memory have therefore introduced special names to make clear exactly what is meant. *Primary memory*, so called because things seem to go there first, is the memory we use to remember things over a few seconds or up to a minute. It is very useful for immediate use and we can think of it as being a bit like a small blackboard on which we can jot things down. It is not a very big blackboard, in fact it only has room for about seven things. Things tend to fade quickly as well so if we want to keep things there for more than a few seconds we have to keep going back and rewriting it. One example of this would be if someone asked us to ring the telephone number 739824. If the telephone is right next to us then we can just pick up the receiver and dial the number. If we have to go to another room to make the call then we need either to write it down or repeat it over to ourselves. If as we go along muttering '739824...739824...' someone stops to talk to us then we may have to go back and ask for the number again.

Secondary memory is a much more permanent store but it takes more mental processing to put things there. Once in this store things can last for years. This is the way in which we remember our own telephone number. We have to put in a lot more effort at first to 'commit it to memory' but then we can recall it at any time later. Indeed as we know it can be stored so well that if our number changes we can go on giving the old one by mistake for quite some time. Whilst the content of what we remember for 5 years is not the same as what we remember for 5 minutes, the mechanism seems to be the same.

The results of some fairly simple experiments used to test memory give us a good idea of how memory changes as we grow old. Primary memory,for example, has received a good deal of attention. This has usually been tested as memory span, the ability to recall a small number of items in the correct order. The illustration of telephone numbers we looked at earlier is a good example. This can be tested quite simply by reading out a list of numbers or letters to someone and then afterwards asking them to repeat them back to you. Most people manage to be correct on lists up to seven or eight items and there is very little change in this until after the age of 60 or so. Even in their sixties and seventies people can still remember five or six items so the decline is quite small. These results are found if you ask someone to repeat the list straight away and without giving any special training or instruction. By using special techniques a few people can achieve remarkable performance, being able to repeat back strings of 50 or more digits. Incidentally this phenomenon also illustrates how memory is not like a muscle. Such special ability doesn't make memory in general much better. People who have learned these techniques have a quite ordinary memory in other ways.

It makes a difference how the material to be remembered is presented. Spoken material is generally better remembered than written. This advantage for spoken material does not change with age. Both young and old people do best when material is both spoken and written.

More often in everyday life we are interested in trying to remember something for more than a minute. Of course one way of testing our secondary memory is simply to use longer lists. If we give someone a list of, for example, 24 words they will only be able to use primary memory for the last 6 or 7. The other items will be remembered by secondary memory (or forgotten!). Studies based on this sort of task have shown that younger subjects are better than older subjects. For example, one study showed that whereas those in their twenties could recall about 14 out of 24 words, people aged over 60 could recall only about 8 (Schonfield and Robertson 1966).

Why might this be? It might be because older people find it more difficult to register the information. Somehow things don't sink in as well as they do for younger people. On the other hand the information may be stored but is less easy to get at when needed. If you put a library book back on the wrong shelf it is as good as missing. Because of the way our memory works it is possible to test which of these is the problem.

One of the basic principles of memory is that recall is the least effective way of showing that we have remembered things. We can also demonstrate that we have learned by recognising something or by learning the same material quicker a second time around. An example of how much better is recognition is the ease with which we can pick out someone's face as one we have seen before even if we cannot describe them. This of course is the origin of the police identity parade.

In the study which I mentioned just now some more subjects were also asked to memorise a list of 24 words. However this time they were asked to pick these words out afterwards from a second, longer list. In this case both young and old subjects did much better as we would expect. Indeed both groups managed to 'remember' about 20 out of 24. Thus age differences depend on how we test memory. On recognition there is little or no difference between young and old.

This is also true over relatively long periods. Another study asked groups of young and old subjects to go through a list of 20 words repeatedly until they could remember at least 16 of them. Four weeks later the older subjects could recall only 75% of the number recalled by the younger group. However their recognition was 90% of the younger.

Both, of these results suggest that there is an increasing problem of getting at stored information as we get older. It is not just that things fail to register. Studies have also shown that older people tend to organise information less well when trying to remember. They are, for example, less likely to group things together into categories and instructions to do this improve their performance. Such instructions have less effect on younger people. Presumably they tend to use such strategies anyway.

Getting material into secondary memory seems to depend a lot on how much we think about that material. For example, if we are shown the word CHAIR we could pay attention to several things. We might notice that it is in capital letters, that it begins with a C, it rhymes with hair or that it is a common piece of furniture. We have to think progressively more about the word as we go from the kind of printing to its meaning. Deciding if it is in capital letters takes only a glance. seeing if it is a piece of furniture takes more thought. Words or other items about which we have thought more are better remembered than those we have treated superficially. So much so that if we make sure that people think a lot about a set of words or other material they will be just as likely to remember them as if we had specially instructed them to do so. Obviously people do respond to instructions such as 'look at this and try to remember it', but it seems to do no more than encourage them to think a lot about the material. For elderly people who may have an expectation that their memory has deteriorated, such instructions can provoke anxiety which hinders rather than helps. In such cases it may be better to get their attention in some other way (Craik 1977).

There are obvious implications here for the way in which elderly people might best be helped to learn new material and to retrieve this.

Exercise

How could you help an older person to
(a) learn to work a new gadget for the kitchen?
(b) remember to take medicines correctly?

Would any of these ideas help *you*?

It is often thought that older people have relatively intact remote memories. Certainly we shall see shortly that one of the most striking things about those suffering from dementia is the contrast between recent and remote memories. A sufferer may have no idea what happened 5 minutes ago, may fail to recognise family members, but have, apparently, no difficulty remembering where they grew up or which school they attended.

This is often seen, wrongly, as an exaggeration of normal ageing. Certainly older people do 'reminisce' a good deal and can provide a fascinating personal account of life 50 or more years ago. However whilst such stories are interesting, and valuable for that reason, there is often no way of checking how accurate they are. Indeed we may even be mistaken as to how 'old' is the memory. After all, the story may have been told many times before and the memory 'refreshed' on each occasion. If the story was told a couple of weeks ago then the 'age' of the memory is more complex than we might at first think.

There have been several attempts to compare younger and older people's memory for events several years ago. There are limits to this in that someone aged 20 cannot remember back for 30 years. However, when comparisons have been made, then the findings suggest that those over 60 show poorer remote as well as recent memory. Even so one study (Schonfield 1972) showed that subjects aged over 70 could correctly recall 45% of their school teachers by name, which is still impressive. Even those in their twenties, that is 50 years nearer the original experience, could recall only 67% correctly. Once again it was found that for recognition there was better performance all round and less difference between younger and older people.

What then are some of the implications for everyday practice? To turn an earlier saying into a question, 'Can you teach old dogs new tricks?' A reasonable conclusion would seem to be 'Yes, but not quite as quickly.' Whilst there is clear evidence for a decline in memory there is still plenty of remaining capacity. There are also things which we can do to ensure that the best use is made of this ability.

1. Information should be presented at a reasonable rate, indeed letting people work at their own pace seems a good idea.
2. It is helpful to use several ways to convey the same information: spoken *and* written for example.
3. We can help by suggesting good strategies for remembering things (e.g. organising items, looking for rules).
4. Finally we must not expect that older people will learn at the same rate as younger people. A few exceptional ones may do so but most will take longer. We must beware of assuming that 'slower' means 'not at all': persistence pays off.

Abnormal ageing

Anyone working to help elderly people is in danger of forming a strange idea of what ageing is like for most people. In particular those who work in any kind of staffed care such as a residential home or a hospital could be forgiven for thinking that senility is the norm. In many places like this most of the residents may seem at least a little confused or forgetful and many have clear evidence of more serious decline. This is not because the figures that I quoted at the beginning of this chapter are wrong. It is because decreased memory and other skills make it very difficult to live an ordinary independent life at home, especially if you live alone. Such handicaps also can impose special burdens on those whose live with the sufferer. The result is that those with such conditions are much more likely to be admitted to care than someone who remains fully mentally alert. This poses special problems for other residents and staff and I will say more about this in chapter 8. For now I want to look in more detail at the difficulties which intellectual impairment presents to the sufferer and at some of the ways that we can help him or her to cope with this.

Confusion

One of the first issues to resolve is what is meant by 'confusion' and the several other terms that are used to describe these problems. Examples include confusion, disorientation, dementia, senility, senile dementia, Alzheimer's Disease, brain failure and chronic brain syndrome. Even this list is by no means complete. There is much confusion about confusion.

I will not try to explain what I think other people mean by these various terms. What I will do is to say what I mean by those terms which I shall be using here and then try to be consistent in this book.

All of the above terms are used to describe conditions where the function of the brain is impaired by physical illness. Some describe the way this is shown in what the sufferer can or cannot do (e.g. confused, disorientated) and others describe the cause, or what is thought to be the cause, of this (e.g. Alzheimer's Disease). So far, so good.

Unfortunately some of the words are used, sometimes even by the same people, to describe *both* the collection of problems or symptoms *and* the presumed cause of these. Thus if someone talks, as I have already done, about 'dementia' you cannot easily tell what I mean. My use of this term will be restricted to a description of the collection of symptoms and problems arising from gradual mental impairment. Such difficulties include forgetfulness, not knowing where you are, what time it is or who other people are (disorientation for time/place/person), difficulties with speaking or understanding, difficulties in actions such as dressing.

These sorts of problems should strike a chord with anyone who has worked with older people suffering from any illness, either physical or mental. This is because not only does dementia as I have described it affect 1 in 5 of those aged over 80 but similar problems may come on suddenly as a symptom of other illness. Thus many old people become forgetful, disorientated and so on when they have an illness such as a chest infection or a heart attack. It can come on as quickly as the illness itself and usually disappears as the person recovers. This is what I shall refer to as 'acute confusion' and it is a symptom just like pain or nausea.

Not surprisingly, because they have symptoms in common, acute confusion and dementia can be mistaken for one another. Usually the important difference is how long the condition takes to develop but even this may not be clear. The thing to note here is that in either case the person is experiencing an abnormal decline in mental function due to illness and proper diagnosis with treatment where possible is vital. In most cases of acute confusion when the underlying illness is treated the sufferer recovers the mental function he or she had before the illness.

Other people are especially important in letting the doctor know that something is wrong with an older person's mental function. By the very nature of the symptoms, namely mental impairment, there is less chance that the person him or herself will say that all is not well. The way things are organised, getting health care depends very much on someone saying all is not well. Usually it is the patient who says 'I don't feel well.' Even in the case of children we rely on parents to report this. But for the mentally frail elderly person there is not necessarily any such person.

Moreover, not only is the person suffering from mental impairment unlikely to go to the doctor saying 'I don't feel well' let alone 'I feel as if I am becoming disoriented', he or she is likely to resent this suggestion from somebody else. The few people who do go to their doctor complaining of their poor memory are more likely to be suffering from depression than dementia. Whichever way you look at it, getting help for the mentally frail is quite a problem.

It is clear that we need to take a positive approach to the problems of diagnosis of these conditions. Attitudes to ageing are very important as it has all too often been assumed that 'senility' is an inevitable consequence of growing old. Even when such attitudes do not prevail there is still a reluctance to seek specialist help on the grounds that nothing can be done. We have already seen that this is not true for acute confusion: what about dementia?

The causes of dementia

In contrast to reversible confusion, dementia does not go away. The problems of continuing mental impairment place great strain on sufferers and carers. The condition is characterised by gradual onset. This is one reason why it has often not been recognised as an illness. The course of the illness over a long period is unremitting decline although the rate may vary according to the cause of the dementia.

The most common cause is a disease of the brain which results in abnormalities of brain chemistry. This disease can appear in middle-aged people but is much more common in elderly people. It was first described by a German doctor and was named after him: Alzheimer's Disease. Had he been called Smith or Jones it would have made spelling and pronunciation a lot easier! For a long time it was thought that there were two different diseases, one which afflicted middle-aged people and one which afflicted elderly people. Because we now know more about the way the brain is affected by these conditions they are now generally thought of as the same illness. There are important differences in the way patients are affected: younger patients deteriorate faster than older patients with this disease. (Interestingly this same difference also happens in other diseases.) Nowadays we therefore refer to Alzheimer's Disease in younger people and to senile dementia, Alzheimer's type (SDAT) for the disease afflicting older people. The age at which this distinction has been made has tended to be 65 years. More recent evidence suggests that the difference in the course of the illness depends on age of onset being above 70 or even 75 years. It is yet another example of our having to revise our notion of 'elderly' upwards.

This type of dementia (SDAT) accounts for about 75–80% of all cases in old age. The other main cause is brain deterioration brought on by having lots of little 'strokes'. Each stroke is a disruption in the blood supply to a small part of the brain. It is just a small version of the major stroke which often results in paralysis of one side of the body. Each little stroke does not result in a big drop in brain function but the result in the end is increasing mental impairment. An interruption to the blood supply is known medically as an infarct and so the dementia which results is called multi-infarct dementia (MID). It is very loosely related to what has often been given as the cause of dementia, hardening of the arteries. However the latter is an almost universal effect of ageing whereas this type of dementia is not that common. MID accounts for only 15–20% of cases of dementia. The remaining few cases of dementia are due to rare and generally untreatable conditions that need not concern us here.

The detection of dementia

The fact that dementia is for the present untreatable has tended in the past to overshadow the positive things that can be done for the sufferer and those who look after him or her. This has begun to change, probably in part because the increasing number of elderly people means that these conditions are now more common. Certainly a great deal of effort is going into seeking some sort of treatment which might remedy the changes in brain chemistry we now know to occur. If such a treatment is found then we will have to think very much more about accurate and early diagnosis. Even now this must be the starting point for other kinds of help.

Although the cause of dementia is a neurological disease, help and care for sufferers is provided from very many sources. In particular the condition can result in considerable behaviour problems so that the skills of those involved in treating mental illness are often called for. This can present some problems, especially for early diagnosis. If the sufferer is reluctant or unable to perceive that there is a problem then he or she is unlikely to agree to be seen by a psychiatrist. One approach to this problem recently has been the setting up of 'Memory Clinics' in some general hospitals. This offers the chance for a full medical and psychological assessment without the implication of mental illness. It may not tackle the underlying problem of the stigma of mental illness but can get help to more of those who need it.

In those cases where there is evidence of dementia help should focus on two main areas. First, we need to have a detailed understanding of each individual's skills and deficiencies. The process of diagnosis tends to concentrate on what someone cannot do. We also need to know what he or she can do in order to help the person make the best use of remaining abilities.

Second, we must pay careful attention to ways of helping those caring for the sufferer. Dementia is like any long-term illness, it puts a strain on those affected directly and indirectly. However it also imposes extra burdens because of the way it affects the ability of the sufferer to maintain personal relationships. This latter topic we will look at later (see chapter 8). Let us look now at the sorts of problems we observe in those who suffer from dementia and ways of helping with these.

Helping those with dementia

Some examples of the problems are shown in Table 2.1. These are examples which have often been cited when I have been discussing this topic with nurses, care assistants and others. Usually I start with the question 'What do 'confused' elderly people do?'

It is important to distinguish between the difficulties which *all* those with dementia will experience and those which will apply to only a minority. Memory problems, especially for the recent past, affect all those with dementia. Wandering and aggression, for example, are by no means

Table 2.1   Problems in Confusion

Being Forgetful	Wandering
Talking in the Past	Misidentifying People
Unaware of Surroundings	Mixing Night & Day
Conversation Difficult	Not Able to Dress
Being Uncooperative	Incontinence
Shouting/Swearing	Poor Eating Habits
Not Washing Clothes/Self	Mishandling Money

universal. We must be especially concerned with the behaviour problems which can occur. They may only affect a minority of those with dementia but they are the cause of enormous stress and are very often the reason why carers are no longer able to cope.

It is helpful to think of disability as broadly divided into three categories, physical, mental and social. Physical disability covers such things as difficulty bathing, dressing, walking and using the toilet. Mental disability includes forgetfulness, disorientation, impairments of speech or understanding and being unable to recognise familiar people. Social disability includes verbal abuse, aggression, hoarding things, degraded habits and wandering.

Each individual sufferer will show some combination of these kinds of problems. This varies greatly between individuals and the same person may show different problems at different times. Consequently there is an enormous range of need. On the one hand Mrs A. may be quite cooperative, mobile, able to understand instructions yet very forgetful and unable to cope without considerable supervision. In contrast Mrs B. may be equally forgetful but irritable, abusive, unable to use the toilet appropriately and constantly insisting that she must return 'home' to where she used to live 30 years ago. Looking after Mrs A. is very different from caring for Mrs B.

Both of these ladies will share common problems that are related to the underlying illness. The impairment of mental function will include memory, especially secondary memory for recent events. Primary memory is not so affected so that patients with dementia are not too bad at repeating back telephone numbers. What they cannot do is recall the number after 5 minutes or even 2. This leads to considerable problems since so much of daily life involves carrying out an organised plan of action. Preparing a meal, for example, means having to do the shopping, assemble the ingredients, locate the cooking utensils, remember to light the oven and to take things out when they are cooked. One eminent physician working with the elderly reckons that if an elderly person is burning out more than one electric kettle a month then there is cause for concern.

Such problems are much more evident in unfamiliar surroundings. If you live now where you were 30 years ago it matters less if you think it still *is* 30 years ago. This means that taking someone into hospital or into a residential home often makes things very much worse. Sometimes the first sign that something is amiss can be when someone gets lost whilst on holiday or visiting relatives. Moving house is not a good remedy for early dementia.

However, just as with normal memory, recognition is better than recall. Thus someone with dementia may when at home resolutely deny that he or she has ever been to a day centre which he or she attends regularly. Nevertheless this same person may great familiar faces on arrival at the centre and in due course learn the layout of the place albeit with some difficulty. Cues are a real help to memory and so we can help by ensuring that important places are clearly marked and visible. If all the toilet doors are a distinctive colour and clearly marked we stand a much greater chance of teaching a 'forgetful' person where to go.

We have also seen that how much attention is given to information affects how well it is remembered. In addition to signs, colours or other cues we must point these out and not just put them up and assume that that will do the trick (Hanley *et al*. 1981).

In a similar way familiar places may evoke appropriate behaviour which was learned a long time ago. A trip to the pub, for example, may bring out a set of skills which transforms a patient with dementia into a customer enjoying a drink. In the dining room the use of a tablecloth and cutlery not only looks more homely, it maximises the chances of someone using their own eating skills.

Verbal reminders, spoken and written, can also help people to remain in contact with daily life. Reality Orientation (RO) has received much attention in recent years and in many ways has come to symbolise a whole philosophy of care rather than just a set of special techniques. The many activities developed in this approach deserve a book in their own right and examples of such books are listed at the end of this chapter. It would be fair to say that some of the claims which have been made for RO have been rather exaggerated. It has certainly made a big difference to the way in which many staff view the care of mentally frail elderly people. However it was originally described as a 'therapy' and at times people have written as though it has some effect on the underlying process of dementia. Sadly there is no evidence for this and it is best viewed as a valuable aid to the function of patients. Some advocates have also not made clear that it is most beneficial to those of mild to moderate impairment. It may even be that its greatest value is where apparent disorientation is the result of an impoverished institution rather than brain disease (Powell-Procter and Miller 1982).

Of course forgetfulness and disorientation are not the only problems which can arise in dementia. I have already referred to impairment of language (both expression and understanding) and spatial skill (e.g. seeing and doing). It can be quite hard to appreciate what it must be like to suffer from such handicaps. We are more capable of appreciating sensory loss such as deafness or poor sight. We only have to block our ears or close our eyes.

We might even have some empathy with those who are mute. But having a disturbance of language is *not* the same as being deaf or mute. It is more like finding oneself in a foreign land where nobody speaks a word of your language and you speak none of theirs. Your can hear that people are speaking to you but you cannot make sense of the sounds. Whenever you try to speak the wrong words or even jumbled nonsense comes out.

The effect may only be partial so that you can manage only with great difficulty or it may be more or less total. Other ways of communication, for example using gesture, tone of voice or posture, may be intact so some communication is still possible. But this is rarely sufficient and can be very frustrating. It can tell us that someone is happy, cross or upset but not why this should be. Put this together with a memory deficit and all sorts of problems can arise. It is unlikely to do much good getting cross with someone who has done something inappropriate but who suffers from advanced dementia. He or she may grasp that you are cross but is unlikely to appreciate why and is equally unlikely to do better next time. Here is another reason why accurate diagnosis is important in understanding behaviour.

Problems of visual perception or control of movement can be even more difficult to understand. If you know that someone is blind then you can offer the right help so that they can manage a simple activity such as going to the toilet. But it can be very hard to grasp the fact that although someone can see the toilet they do not know what it is or how to use it. Perhaps it is a bit like finding oneself on a TV quiz show, being shown some new piece of scientific equipment and asked to guess how to use it.

Simple actions like getting dressed become very difficult indeed if you lose track of the difference between left and right or cannot make sense of up and down.

It is very important to understand why somebody is having difficulty in doing something. Take as an example someone who is said to have difficulty dressing appropriately. Apart from physical limitations it might be that he or she cannot remember what to wear or cannot work out the right movements to put the clothing on. Each of these requires different sorts of help. You need to know whether someone requires a gentle reminder about what to wear or whether they need help with the individual actions in dressing. This implies a careful assessment of each individual.

The complexity of these problems is nowhere more apparent than in the interpretation put on behaviour problems. It is especially so when often the elderly person with dementia looks quite normal. It can be very hard for carers to tell whether someone is being 'confused' or 'naughty'. The interpretation will depend as much on the emotional state of the carer as on the type of behaviour. If the sufferer has just been taken to the toilet at 3 a.m. but on being put back to bed is immediately incontinent this can understandably be described as 'deliberate'. It may be no good asking 'Why did you do that?' and the cause may be deduced from other signs. These may be quite subtle such as the 'twinkle in the eye' and affected very much by how the person seeing them feels. Those supporting the carer must tread a fine line between taking all that he or she says at face value and being so sceptical as to make the carer feel rejected.

Dementia poses special problems for those who live alone. Memory difficulties lead to great problems paying bills for whilst most of us would like to forget about them actually doing so is not helpful. Handling money may be a problem due both to difficulties in arithmetic and inability to appreciate the need for security over money. Once someone has reached the point where he or she is unable to sign his or her own name even receiving a pension means relying on somebody else.

The increasing number of elderly people suffering from impairment has meant increased work for the agencies that deal with the management of financial affairs for others. Until recently in Britain the only way of taking over the financial affairs of someone suffering from dementia was through an order under the Court of Protection. This ancient body has the job of arranging for the affairs of those judged to be mentally incapable to be managed by somebody else. There are special procedures for this including a requirement for a medical certificate and there are procedures for revoking the order should the person recover. This of course does not happen in dementia.

Many people with physical handicap arrange for someone else, usually a relative or a solicitor, to handle some or all of their affairs under a Power of Attorney. However this has to be set up while somebody is of sound mind. By the time dementia is advanced it is too late. Until very recently such a power also had to lapse if someone became mentally impaired even if the best interests of the person would have been best served by letting the arrangement continue. There is now however a procedure called the Enduring Power of Attorney which can include the provision that it is to continue even after mental decline. It still requires the person to have no such impairment when the power is set up but can continue if mental impairment should occur.

The law in this area still does not provide adequately for the needs of the mentally frail elderly. There are at times both too few ways of managing the affairs of those at risk to themselves or others and too little protection for the rights of these vulnerable people. Until now we have concentrated on the needs of mentally ill younger people, their rights and the risks of treatment. This can be expected to change as the need grows.

In a number of ways things will really come to a head if and when we have a cure for dementia. Early detection will then be a matter of even higher priority. We may find it necessary to screen large numbers of elderly people in the way that we have for a long time been used to doing with young children. However the practical problems of doing this will be immense. With children, getting a good attendance at a clinic is relatively easy. Most children have caring parents who want their offspring to be healthy. Compulsory schooling offers a further opportunity to track down children routinely. Both factors are not the same for older people.

However this is a problem for the future. At present we have no treatment and there is no known way of preventing dementia. Mental exercises, keeping one's brain active, has no effect on the progressive nature of these dreadful diseases. This is not to say that keeping up interests and activities is useless. This is certainly a good idea but it helps how we feel about our lives and ourselves as we grow older rather than the power of our brains. Emotional well-being is the topic of the next chapter.

References

Craik, F. I. M. (1977) Age differences in human memory, *in* J. E. Birren and K. W. Schaie (eds) *Handbook of the Psychology of Aging*, Van Nostrand Reinhold: New York.

Hanley, I. G., McGuire, R. J. and Boyd, W. D. (1981) Reality orientation and dementia: a controlled trial of two approaches. *British Journal of Psychiatry* **138** 10–14.

Powell-Procter, L., and Miller, E. (1982) Reality orientation: a critical appraisal. *British Journal of Psychiatry* **140** 457–463.

Schonfield, D. (1972) Theoretical nuances and practical old questions: the psychology of aging. *Canadian Psychologist* **13** 252–266.

Schonfield, D., and Robertson, B. A. (1966) Memory storage and aging. *Canadian Journal of Psychology* **20** 228–236.

Further reading

Sprott, R. L. (1980) *Age, Learning Ability and Intelligence* Van Nostrand Reinhold: New York

A collection of papers by several authors giving more details of the many studies of ageing and mental function.

Murphy, E. (1987) *Dementia and Mental Illness in the Old* Papermac: London

A lucid practical book aimed at the general public.

Mace, N. L., and Robins, P. V., with Castleton, B., Cloke, C., and McEwen, E. (1984) *The 36-Hour Day: Caring at Home for Confused Elderly People* Hodder & Stoughton/Age Concern England: London

A useful book for relatives and other carers

Holden, U. P., and Woods, R. T. (1982) *Reality Orientation: Psychological Approaches to the 'Confused' Elderly* Churchill Livingstone: Edinburgh.

Covers both the practice and theory of RO.

See also several books published by Winslow Press including a series 'Managing Common Problems with the Elderly Confused'.

Chapter 3

Feeling and Doing

What does it feel like to be old? Like so many experiences it is hard for any of us truly to understand what someone else is feeling. We are in many ways imprisoned in our own selves and can never really 'know' what some other person is experiencing. Nonetheless we often do share common experience and so can sympathise and understand at least to some degree.

Shared experience is often as important as professional training. For example carers may get at least as much from someone who shares a similar role as they can from those paid to help them. But such sharing must always be about the present or the past. We know what it is to be as we are now, we can remember what it used to be like as we were. Can we know what it will be like to be as we will be?

A central part of what sort of person we are is our 'personality'. The word itself is derived from the ancient Greek word for a mask. This is because in Greek theatre the actors would wear special masks to show what sort of character they were portraying. Today we use the word personality to describe the ways in which we relate to the world around us, how we feel and how we act: the kind of mask that we tend to show to others.

Personality is particularly important in psychology as it is an example of finding rules which govern our behaviour. The idea behind personality is that we tend to react in roughly the same way when dealing with a variety of different situations. What is going on around us will of course make a difference, but the sort of person we are also has a big effect. We all differ widely one from another but each of us tends to be consistent in how we feel and act at different times. Thus someone who might be described as a 'worrier' will be upset by lots of different things. He or she will worry not only about money, health or whatever but also about whether he or she has upset somebody, whether it will rain tomorrow and so on.

In just the same way we can describe other characteristics of people's behaviour which show the same kind of consistency. It is possible for us to predict how an individual will react in a given situation from knowing how he or she has reacted to other situations in the past. Psychology is about finding rules of behaviour of just this sort.

35

Because we are all familiar with the idea of personality or character, all this may just seem like common sense. What can psychology tell us that is special? One answer to this is the importance of systematic measurement. Our common sense ideas of personality are based on our own limited observations of other people. As we saw in chapter 1 we use the same sort of process to form our ideas of what a typical 'old person' is like. We also noted that such ideas are very often wrong!

What psychologists have done is to measure the feelings and behaviour of very many people from a wide variety of different backgrounds. Often this has been done by asking people themselves how they usually act and feel. By putting the same questions to a lot of people, for example in the form of a questionnaire, it is possible to see emerging patterns of behaviour. Another way of finding out about personality is to study relatively fewer people but to do so in great depth.

The interesting thing is that in many ways the results of these very different kinds of approaches are remarkably similar. They suggest that there are two major areas in which individuals can vary in their personality.

The first of these is a dimension of personality known often as 'introversion–extraversion'. Roughly speaking this has to do with how easy we find it to get on with lots of other people. Somebody who is very extraverted likes to meet people and likes to be the centre of attention. The introvert on the other hand may prefer his or her own company and find meeting lots of new people unrewarding. Not surprisingly these personality differences are often reflected in types of job that people do. Being a salesman, for example, tends to suit the extravert better than the introvert.

The other major way that people differ in their personality is, as I have already implied, in their tendency to emotionality. The 'worrier' tends to be a more emotional type of person, often being sensitive to both pleasant and unpleasant events. This can be contrasted with the person who is emotionally very stable, who hardly seems to be upset by anything. This sort of characteristic has been shown to be related to such things as how likely people are to experience something like depression and indeed to how sensitive individuals are to painful injury.

Such 'dimensions' of personality do not of course predict exactly what each person will do in every situation but they do give a better guess than if we knew nothing about the person at all. They are important to understanding ageing because the general rule is that personality does not change greatly as we grow older. If you want to know what you will be like when you grow old, take a good look at the sort of person you are now.

This is not of course to say that some older people do not show a very different personality from when they were younger. However this is very much more likely to be due to illness or some other major change than to the effects of ageing. In the previous chapter I noted that personality change is often a feature of senile dementia. This is illness, not old age.

Nevertheless there are slight changes in personality which do seem to be related more directly to ageing. It has often been claimed that people's individual differences become exaggerated as they grow older: they become more like themselves. Certainly studies of the personality dimensions to which I referred before have suggested slight shifts with advancing years (Neugarten 1977). In particular it is a consistent finding that individuals tend slightly to become more emotionally sensitive as they grow older. Similarly there is a shift away from extraversion towards introversion.

It must be emphasised however that such changes are indeed slight. There are much bigger differences between generations. If today's teenagers seem to be more extraverted than were their grandparents, grandparents in future will be similarly extraverted. Again the message is that our best predictor of 'personality when old' is not age but 'personality when young'.

It is even difficult to know whether some of such slight changes as we do find due to age might not in fact be due to other age-related things. For example we may assess how extraverted someone is by how much time they spend in the company of other people. However lots of older people go out less than they used to for practical rather than emotional reasons. They often cannot afford to go out, may be in poor physical health or may suffer from loss of hearing which makes conversation in a crowded place difficult. It would be wrong to attribute all their change in behaviour to changes within their own personality.

Personality is therefore something which we infer from our observations of other people. These 'observations' include not only what we can see directly but also what others have noticed and, especially, what people say about themselves.

When an older person is said by others to be behaving strangely or to have shown a personality change this must be cause for very careful concern. Illness is one obvious possibility. Emotional disturbance is certainly a common problem in older people. As we shall see shortly, depression, not dementia, is the commonest mental disorder in late life. Personality change is nonetheless one of the most distressing effects of dementia as far as relatives are concerned. Usually the problem arises because someone who was always placid and considerate has become awkward, irritable and aggressive. However I have occasionally met the spouse who remarks that the patient used to be bad-tempered and has now become more placid! It is the *change* that betrays 'illness' rather than the resulting personality.

Sometimes however it is not that the personality has changed, rather it is the older person's circumstances. The frail elderly person who has always lived alone but now as a result of physical illness must come into hospital or a home may have particular difficulty. He or she may simply not be of a sociable disposition such that his or her personality now clashes with the surroundings. Eccentricity is not illness nor is it personality change. There are plenty of people who are only as 'odd' as they have always been. It may be a change in circumstances rather than a change in personality that causes problems.

One particular example of this is the effect of increasing frailty and 'physical dependence. If someone has always tended to be bad-tempered and difficult to get along with this probably does not matter much when others can cope with this by keeping out of the way as far as possible. However physical illness, especially the sort of chronic (long-term) disability which is more common as people reach advanced old age, often means having to rely on other people for help with everyday things. The usual image of a cooperative and grateful older person being tenderly cared for in his or her declining years can be very far from the truth. It may be true for the great majority of frail older people but for a small minority it is far from reality.

For those who have never got on well with others whether they be family or acquaintances things can be difficult indeed. The strain on relatives, who may be providing help out of a duty driven by guilt rather than affection and joy, can be immense. Difficult clients are often seen as 'unpopular' by professional carers but at least they have the satisfaction of knowing that they are doing the job for which they get paid. For families the motivation for carrying on can be stretched to the limit.

Fortunately such instances are rare. The great majority of older people can relate harmoniously with those around them. The point to make here is that if things are getting difficult we need to take account of not only a person's personality now but also how they have been throughout their lives.

If we recall that about four out of every five very elderly people show no sign of dementia, the chances that 'senility' is an adequate explanation for difficult social relations are fairly limited. In order to help each individual properly we must take the trouble to understand how they are now and how they used to be.

By now you should have a fairly good idea of how we might do this. However let us pause to consider two things. First, what information do we need to make an assessment of personality? Second, how might we find out this information?

With respect to *what* we need to know it would seem a sensible thing to be guided by what is already known about personality. Two useful areas to focus upon would be the 'dimensions' to which I have already referred. We are likely to find it helpful to know about a person's emotional sensitivity (are they a worrier, do they tend to get upset easily and so on) and their degree of extraversion (how much do they like meeting with other people, how easy do they find it to talk to people and so on). We will obviously need to know both how the person behaves now and how they have tended to be throughout their lives.

With regard to *how* we find these things out the obvious starting point is the person him or herself. I suppose that one could argue that the right method of enquiry would be to give the person a personality test but, at the risk of making myself redundant, I cannot honestly say that this is appropriate. Such tests typically consist of a whole series of questions concerning

'How do you feel if...' and 'What do you do when...'. This has the advantage of being very systematic. It makes sure that each person is asked exactly the same questions. It is also easy to summarise the answers which have to be of a yes/no or often/sometimes/never type. Such systematic methods are very important if we want to know about general 'laws' of personality and how they relate to ageing. However this is meant to be a practical book about helping individual older people so I prefer to focus on practical methods. In this case the obvious answer is to talk to the person. If you want to know something, start by asking.

However beginning with the opening line 'Good morning Mrs Jones. Tell me what sort of a personality do you have?' is not likely to be a huge success. Similarly approaching a person who has just come into hospital and asking 'Do you get upset easily? Do you tend to worry a lot?' will tell one nothing useful.

Not surprisingly the sorts of questions which personality tests ask can give us a few useful hints as to how to start. We may seek information about day to day behaviour particularly as it relates to relationships with other people. Finding out about somebody's personality is a central part of getting to know them as a person. It is something which we all do to some degree in our own personal relationships. What psychological knowledge can help us to do is to do this more efficiently and skilfully. This is not to say that it can turn us all into a cross between a mind-reader and a master interrogator. Contrary to popular belief, psychologists are neither of these. However being skilful does help us to reach a better understanding of the person and so help them more.

Exercise

How would you describe (a) your own personality?
                        (b) the personalities of

the people you identified in the exercise in chapter 1?

Such matters take time to explore. The right approach is one of empathy and warmth which is going be helpful in many more ways than in just gathering information. I will turn to these matters in more detail later in this chapter. For now let us consider other aspects of adjustment in old age. How do older people feel about being old?

Adjustment and ageing

Like all stages in life, some people seem to cope better with the demands of growing older than others. We can all think of examples of those who seem to be happy and contented with their age and others who are distressed, bitter or resentful. Each of the transitions of life reveals both success and failure in terms of adjustment. It is reasonable to suppose that if we are helping older people well one of the results should be that as many of them as possible should feel contented and as few as possible distressed. What makes for successful adjustment to ageing?

The first point to emphasise is that successful ageing is not an illusion. Some stereotypes of older people seem to imply that there is just no way that you can feel good about growing older, at least once you are grown up. Children are only too keen to reach the next birthday milestone and often keep track of the months as well as the years since they were born. Traditionally adults seek to disguise their age. Women are exhorted to buy expensive anti-wrinkle creams, men turn to hair weaving and Grecian 2000 to suppress what are seen as the visible signs of advancing years.

It may be hard therefore to imagine that anyone can feel good about growing old. Indeed to some extent older people often share this expectation. Studies which have looked at how 'old' people feel have confirmed the anecdotal reports of some older people. When feeling fit and well those who are older do not feel any different from when they were much younger. The experience of ageing is one of continuity. The body which contains the 'person' looks older but the person inside feels the same.

It often requires some event or experience to trigger the realisation that one is growing older. The event may be a major and public one, such as retirement, or it may be personal or seemingly trivial. Examples of the latter would be the sudden realisation that the face staring back from the bathroom mirror is no longer youthful or when someone in the bus queue urges you to 'Hurry up Grandad!'

Similarly the experience of illness is often said to bring the feeling of 'growing old'. When 'unwell', for example when troubled by arthritis or some other condition common in old age, one can feel very old indeed. Since some physical limitation, at least in terms of reduced maximum capacity, is a universal fact of ageing, it is quite possible to become preoccupied with the negative aspects of being older. But there are benefits also to being older, for example being freed from the routine imposed by working life or the demands made by a growing family. Adjustment is the appropriate balancing of these plusses and minuses.

Are these just interesting and thought-provoking ideas or is there some way in which we can usefully measure adjustment in older people? This would seem to be desirable since it might help us to distinguish those who might most benefit from help in achieving better adjustment. As part of their systematic study of behaviour psychologists have given considerable attention to this problem.

Life satisfaction

One of the distinguishing features of those who appear to be 'well adjusted' is that they both look forward with interest to the future and look back with satisfaction to what has gone before. They are unlikely to see life as an unbroken success from birth to the present but they do not spend lots of time thinking 'If only things had been different ...'.

One study of older people is often quoted as illustrating the different ways in which people adjust to growing older. The sample studied was not typical in that it included only retired North American men (Reichard *et al*. 1962). However its conclusions do seem to capture the flavour of styles of adjustment for both men and women.

The study involved interviews and other assessments of two groups of older subjects. One group were judged by others to be well-adjusted, the other poorly adjusted. It was found that the measures seemed to go together in such a way as to suggest that there were broadly five styles of adjustment.

The first of these described a 'mature' group who seemed to be well-adjusted. They looked forward to the future with pleasure and back at the past with satisfaction. Their lives in retirement had much in common with their lives during the time that they were working. Their increased leisure time had been devoted to taking up interests which they had previously enjoyed but not been able to pursue sufficiently. Often the process of retirement itself had been a gradual one, moving progressively from full-time work to part-time work and to full-time retirement. These people's attitude to death was similarly positive in that they generally accepted its inevitability without fear or anxiety. Likewise they were realistic about the limitations of ageing.

There was a second group who also appeared content with ageing. However their particular style was more passive. They saw old age as a time for doing less and letting others take the lead. This approach was captured by the title 'rocking chair' ageing. Again there was evidence for continuity. For example these people tended to have more dominant spouses and presumably had in part at least chosen them for just this reason.

The other groups showed various problems in adjustment. For example some people were very defensive or 'armoured'. They coped by pretending that there was no such thing as growing older. They tended to keep very busy and active. In some ways there was no such thing as 'retirement'. They appeared to make great efforts to ensure that they were busier than they had ever been. Doing nothing was seen as a sign of decay and decline in old age was not perceived as intrinsic but because people let themselves go. Illness and death were very threatening and were topics to be avoided.

Another group of people were bitter and resentful about growing older. They looked on their lives as having failed to fulfil their potential. This was seen as due to other people having got in their way or failed to give them a fair chance. They were fearful of the future in general and of dying in particular.

Finally there were some who also viewed their lives as having been failures but who blamed this on themselves. They had many regrets that they had not taken opportunities given to them. They were generally pessimistic about the future but saw death as a merciful release from their present situation.

It cannot be said that such styles describe all the possible ways in which individuals react to the challenge of growing older. Indeed there were many subjects in the original study whose thoughts, feelings and attitudes did not fit neatly into the groups described. Nevertheless I think that the styles which emerged do give us some idea of the wide variety of ways in which people do react and can suggest what to look out for when trying to help older people.

One important area is how people view their own lives. This is of course true of younger as well as older adults. Someone who is very depressed will very likely see his or her life as a failure for which he or she is to blame. However as people grow older looking back becomes especially important. When we are younger we spend most of our time looking forward and think of our age in terms of the time that has gone before. As we grow older the balance shifts. We tend to think of age in relation to 'time remaining' which is often therefore particularly precious. We spend correspondingly more time looking back. How we feel about what we see seems to be closely related to our present well-being. It has therefore been suggested that the extent of this 'life satisfaction' is a good measure of adjustment in older people. There have been a variety of questionnaires designed to measure this (Linn 1979). In pretty well all cases they involve asking the question 'Do you in general feel satisfied with your life?', though not necessarily in so many words. This may sound as if such questionnaires are trivial and irrelevant and this is certainly not the case. As in the case of personality questionnaires it is sometimes easier to build up a picture of the general pattern from specific examples.

If we accept that such a questionnaire can give a useful measure of life satisfaction then there is no shortage of studies which have aimed to find out what is related to this. The results of these emphasise that growing older is a continuous process with the rest of life. The important factors which decide if older people have high life satisfaction are rather what we might suggest for ourselves. Thus the top priority is usually health, followed by income and social relationships. The problem with growing older is that not simply one but often several of these factors change together. If you are afflicted by chronic illness in old age then you are also likely to have low income (most pensioners are not wealthy) and quite likely to be widowed or otherwise lonely (30% of older people live alone). This coincidence of disadvantage can make a real impact on well-being.

In some cases the improvement of people's reported life satisfaction has been used as a measure of the success of some sort of help. For example one study of older people in residential homes looked at whether arranging for volunteers to visit individuals regularly increased the recipient's life satisfaction (Power *et al.* 1983). No such effect could be found though this may just mean that the measure was inadequate rather than the visits made no difference. On the whole it is probably not appropriate to use life satisfaction as a measure in this way. It is rather a global measure of adaptation and might not be expected to change as a result of something as modest as having a regular visitor. More major transitions, such as a bereavement or giving up one's home to move into a residential home, are much more likely to be significant.

One important lesson to learn here is that whilst many problems of 'loss' are common in old age they are not inevitable nor do they necessarily lead to poor adjustment. There are plenty of people who do find meaning in their lives despite suffering a bereavement or some other great change in their life. It simply will not do just to shrug our shoulders and say 'Well what can you expect at that age?' If that is how we feel we are more likely to be a hindrance than a help. There are ways that we can help (we shall look at some of these later in this chapter) but we will not even try to do so if we think that nothing can be done.

To be busy or not to be busy?

One of the questions most often asked of the problems of ageing is 'What can be done to prevent...?' We noted in the previous chapter that activity, especially mental activity, does not ward off dementia. Nonetheless there may be lots of other reasons for keeping mentally and physically active as we grow older and the importance of this has been much debated.

Some years ago it was suggested that there was a natural process of 'disengagement' as people grow older. It was noted that older people tend to become less involved with the world about them and tend to withdraw from positions of activity and responsibility. This disengagement was suggested to be the 'natural' process of ageing and therefore not to follow this path was to risk discontent. This theory, and its counterpart, 'activity theory', have generated a good deal of debate and research. The results can best be summarised by referring back to the principle of variability which we noted in the first chapter. Neither activity nor disengagement necessarily lead to good or bad adjustment. For example, in the groups of older men whom we considered above there were both active happy and active unhappy groups.

From the point of view of 'prevention' the most important factors are those that relate to life satisfaction and each individual's personality. If we remember that those with higher income and education also tend to live longer then it would seem that life becomes more unfair as we all grow older. Those with more education are likely to have better paid jobs and therefore to have better pensions. They are thus likely to live longer and happier lives. Now of course the extent to which older people in general have enough pension is a political one beyond the scope of this book. The point to make here is that it is how society treats older people which largely determines how they feel. There is nothing inevitably miserable about growing older. Nonetheless emotional distress is common in old age and we must therefore consider the origins of this and what can be done to help.

Emotional disturbance

Depression

Although dementia is the most feared mental disorder of old age depression is the most common, at least in the 'young' elderly, that is those aged up to 75. Exactly how common it is depends on how severely you define it, but depression of such severity as would be generally considered to need special help or treatment affects about 5% of those aged over 65. If those with milder depression are included then over 20% of 70 year olds have been found to suffer in this way (Post 1982).

The question of severity is important in a number of ways. First we should draw a distinction between being unhappy and suffering from depression. Everybody who suffers from depression is unhappy but not everyone who is unhappy is suffering from depression. We use the word depression to describe both the mood of unhappiness and the more serious emotional disturbance. This can be confusing but it does emphasise how closely connected these states are.

Secondly the severity or type of depression influences what sort of help is the most appropriate. Very severe depression will require specialist psychiatric help perhaps involving treatment with drugs or other therapy. Less severe states may be better helped by concentrating on the person's thoughts, feelings and ways of coping. What is going on around the person may be important whatever the severity.

Thirdly we must to some extent judge the severity in relation to what has recently happened to the individual. If someone is crying a great deal and we know that he or she recently lost his or her spouse and has had to go into a residential home this looks like grief. If that same person has been widowed for 10 years and been living happily in the same place for 5, we might be wrong to draw the same conclusion. However we must beware of overestimating the 'normality' of depression. At least three-quarters of even the young elderly are not depressed. There is more to good adjustment than simply being appropriately unhappy. Normal unhappiness does not persist for weeks, months and years. Even if it is brief then it is deserving of our attention. If it is prolonged then it deserves active help.

The severity of depression can also often be judged by the presence or otherwise of a number of different signs (what people look like) and symptoms (what people say they feel like). Tearfulness, being slowed down in thought and action, worrying about the future, poor sleep, loss of appetite and loss of interest are all common features. In more severe cases individuals may feel that life is no longer worth living, that they have done something dreadful for which they are being punished or that their body is rotting away or has some other serious medical condition.

Two particular features are noticeable in older people suffering from depression. The first of these is that older people with depression more often feel that they are suffering from a physical illness than do younger people. This is a problem because of course physical ill-health is indeed more common in older people. It is less easy to put the symptoms down to 'hypochondriasis' when it is actually quite likely that someone may be physically unwell. Often it is a matter of degree. The pain or disability experienced by someone with depression will be rather more than we would expect from what is known medically to be wrong. This requires of course that we have a good idea of someone's state of physical health. Good medicine is essential.

Secondly older people who are suffering from depression are quite likely to say that they feel their memory is failing. This is much more likely to happen in depression than in dementia when of course there really is a deterioration in mental function. Again telling the difference between these conditions is very important and may call for specialist skills. As a psychologist one of the most rewarding experiences is to be able to reassure an older person who has been complaining of poor memory that in fact there is no evidence for this. What we then have to do is find out what is really troubling that person but simply the reassurance can relieve much of the burden of distress. Conversely perhaps the most upsetting cases are those where one finds evidence of mental decline of which the sufferer is all too aware. Thankfully such cases are the exception rather than the rule.

Perhaps not surprisingly, many cases of depression in older people are related to what has happened to them or to their personal circumstances. These are usually referred to as 'life events'. One study showed that a number of different factors were related to depression in older people. These included bereavement, having to move house, chronic ill-health and bad news about somebody close to them. Where all these things coincided the likelihood of depression was greatly increased (Murphy 1982).

The other important finding from this study was how common was depression among those who were chosen at random from older people living at home. Depression of a severity the same as that found in those referred for psychiatric help was present in approximately one in six of the 'community' sample. The relationship between depression and life events was especially marked in this group of older people who were not seen, presumably, as needing special help for their depression. What may be happening is that those around them, and indeed the older people themselves, are seeing the depression as 'appropriate' given their many difficulties. Unfortunately this is to deny them the chance of counselling, treatment or other help which might lessen their distress.

Anxiety

If depression is extreme unhappiness, then anxiety is an excess of worry. We all worry about things some of the time but most of us are not worried all of the time. We have all experienced the feelings of anxiety when faced with some stressful event such as taking a driving test or having to stand up and talk to a lot of people. The feelings that we get are pretty well all signs that our body is getting ready for action. Our heart beats faster, we breathe more quickly, our mouth dries up and we start to sweat. If we watch someone taking part in a big sporting event we can often see other evidence of 'anxiety'. The player waiting to receive service in a tennis match will move erratically before crouching down to watch for the ball with muscles taut, ready to pounce.

In the case of the tennis player the need to be ready for physical action is obvious. The usefulness when we are just waiting to go into a job interview is less clear. In that case we need to have a clear head and feelings of panic will do nothing to improve our chances of getting the job. The feelings that we have of getting 'ready for action' are thought to be leftovers from our ancestors. If you are walking through the primaeval forest clutching a spear and you hear a rustle in the undergrowth it is as well to be ready for anything. If it turns out to be a small animal you might be quick enough to catch dinner. If it is a large one you might be quick enough to run away.

These days the sort of 'threat' we encounter is more likely to be going into hospital or having to walk again after a fall. Neither of these is much like being in the jungle. We need to be alert but we do not need to be too wound up. When the feelings of anxiety get too great then we have panic.

So far I have focused on the physical feelings of anxiety. These are not necessarily the most important but they are perhaps a little easier to understand than the thoughts that can be the real problem. Anxious thoughts would include not only the worry that I have already mentioned but other less identifiable feelings that something terrible is going to happen. The 'something' may not even be anything in particular, it is the thought that counts. This can make it rather difficult to be reassured since you do not really know what is the matter.

One other reason why the physical signs of anxiety are important is because, just as with depression, these seem to be especially strong in older people. If you know that you have trouble with your heart, perhaps have suffered a heart attack in the past, then a panic attack may make you think 'heart' rather than 'head'. Perhaps just because physical illness is more common in older people, this confusion is more of a problem. Not only are there problems with the direct effects of anxiety but there are other indirect effects. For example prolonged rapid breathing (hyperventilation) can cause dizziness and chest pain as well as being like the breathlessness which can result from lung or heart disease. There are differences which can be found, for example the feelings of anxiety may come on when someone is sitting still whereas the breathlessness of chronic bronchitis is worse on physical exertion. Nonetheless it takes careful assessment of physical and mental state to be sure which is which.

Not surprisingly feelings of anxiety are very common. One study found that over 40% of a sample of older people suffered from some degree of 'neuroticism' including anxiety and depression. These often go together so that someone may both be anxious and depressed although this is not necessarily so. In about half of these people there was evidence of lifelong 'problems' of this sort. They had always been 'worriers'. In the other half these problems had come on in old age and for them depression and anxiety were the major features. These figures relate to the investigator's definition of 'neuroticism'. When the older people themselves were asked if these feelings bothered them, only 18% said that this was so. An even smaller number (11%) were judged to have problems which had come on in later life and which might benefit from specialist treatment.

Thus just as with depression, these problems no doubt relate in many cases to circumstances. The stresses may be more common as we grow older but neither they nor such prolonged distress are an inevitable consequence of ageing.

Other mental illness

Dementia, depression and anxiety account for the great majority of mental disturbance in later life. Even among the most seriously distressed, those admitted to psychiatric hospitals, only about one in ten of the older people admitted suffer from some other form of mental disturbance. A small number suffer from symptoms such as hallucinations or ideas of persecution which are not part of some other illness. Such conditions respond as well to treatment as do similar illnesses in younger people in whom such conditions are relatively more common. As we have seen with other problems it is important to understand what someone is doing in terms of his or her usual behaviour. Thus if someone has always been a rather solitary person who tends to think that other people are up to no good such behaviour may not concern us at least in terms of 'needing help'. If however that person has always been friendly and sociable then the change to being suspicious and withdrawn may give more cause for concern.

In helping people we must decide first whether anything should be done and second how best to help. This is, as we have seen, a special problem in helping those with dementia since the sufferer does not usually recognise that anything is wrong. It is up to others to notice that something is wrong. In some cases it can be that others are suggesting that help is needed when in fact none is appropriate. There is a difficult balance to be reached between older people's right to care or treatment and their right to independence. We can easily either neglect obvious need or force help on those who do not wish this. No wonder that sometimes it feels as if you just cannot win!

For the present I shall leave the question 'Is help required?' to one side and concentrate on 'How can we help?' Let us therefore turn to consider some of the ways of helping to minimise emotional distress in older people.

Helping with emotions

Listening

Often one of the biggest problems is knowing how to begin. We shall look at the problems of bereavement in detail in chapter 5 but one thing that the bereaved often complain of is that other people tend to avoid them. The same can also happen with those who are emotionally distressed. To see one reason why we need look no further than ourselves and what controls our behaviour. Most people, especially those in the business of caring for others, aim to make people happy. Few of us get a real thrill out of making someone cry, those who do are dangerous people indeed. A smile or a warm greeting are powerful rewards as we know only too well.

Unfortunately when someone is upset, for example if they have been bereaved, they are likely to cry easily so that the first thing that may happen when someone goes up to them and says 'Hello. How are you?' is that they burst into tears. This is not at all rewarding for most people who, whether consciously or otherwise, will be less likely to start a conversation with that person another time. However I know of no way of helping those in emotional distress that does not involve some form of social interaction. Ignoring people just does not seem to work. The first point is therefore that in order to help we must be active.

The next thing we must do is to listen. This may sound passive and so at odds with what I have just suggested, but should not be so. One of the growth areas of psychological study over the past 15 years or so has been the ways in which we interact socially. Although we pay little attention to such a familiar activity as holding a conversation, this is in fact a highly complex process with its own rules and procedures. Knowledge of these can give us insights into how to improve our performance. In the world of commerce this has been accepted for many years. A good insurance salesman will spend a lot of time perfecting his technique so that we are more likely to be persuaded by his sales talk. The skill of a successful market trader may look at first very different but in its own way this too is a polished performance from which we can learn. Now obviously we do not necessarily see ourselves as trying to 'sell' anything as we talk to someone who is distressed. However there are ways in which we can say that we have been more or less successful. If we do the job well then that person is going to feel better at the end than if we do the job badly.

We tend to think of the role of the talker as the important one and the listener as somehow secondary. Perhaps this is all the more so when we have grown up surrounded by broadcasting which is such one way traffic. On the whole we do not get very far trying to talk to the radio or the television. Indeed it makes no difference if we nod off for a while. The programme will still continue. The listening we are talking about here is a much more active process and is the most important first step in starting to help.

Some of the important elements are fairly obvious. We need to remain alert and to pay attention. At the end of a long day this is easier said than done. Listeners spend most of their time looking at the person who is talking. Staring down at your watch gives quite the wrong impression. The way you sit, nod and grunt all tell the person that you are listening to what they are saying. This is backed up by the sort of remarks you make, for example whether they reflect what the person has been saying.

There is not the space here to describe in detail the way to become a good listener. I have suggested some reading at the end of chapter 9 that covers this in more detail. If you can manage to make use of a video camera and recorder then watching yourself listening to someone can be a powerful if initially slightly shocking experience.

All of the things that I have described so far in this section apply to listening to someone of any age. What are the special additional factors that apply to older people?

First of all sensory loss may be a problem. Since being a good listener involves giving feedback obviously someone should be able to hear and see this as well as possible. Even those who have developed hearing problems in late life use lip-reading to help them just as we all do. Of course being able to tell what two spies are telling each other by watching at a distance through binoculars is a very special skill. But we have all seen a film in which we can tell straight away that the soundtrack has been dubbed. Indeed we are so good at this that a cartoon series made recently in Welsh had to be redrawn in parts before it could be produced satisfactorily in English. If your hearing is not as good as it used to be then being able clearly to see someone's mouth really does help.

Secondly there is the question of time. We noted in chapter 2 that a decrease in speed is one of the most universal facts of ageing. Thus although verbal skills are not very much affected by ageing quickfire talking is likely to be a problem. Thus we must set aside enough time. Of course this is especially true for those who are depressed because this itself slows people down. It may be wrong to assume that someone cannot answer at all just because they cannot answer quickly.

Time is also important because older people often describe their present distress in terms of what has happened in their life as a whole. Indeed this process of life review is often a useful one in helping older people. The experience of an older person who readily launches into a lengthy tale of their past life is well known. The appearance of a fresh face is often the cue for this. It may leave the listener wishing they would 'get on with it and come to the point'. However 'the point' may be the story itself. The setting of what has happened recently in the context of 'my life so far' can be a valuable end in itself.

The difficulties of being a good listener are made more obvious when you are not hearing the story for the first time. This can be a particular problem with an older person who has some degree of forgetfulness. He or she is generally better able to remember what happened a long time ago than what happened just recently. 'What happened recently' can include telling this story to you last week, yesterday or even half an hour ago. The skilful listener in this case will direct the conversation on to the next stage, perhaps 'coping with things now', without seeming to reject the person telling the story.

Exercise

Arrange simply to watch one of your colleagues listening to someone else. Watch the listener rather than the talker.

What do they do?

How do they sit?

Where do they look?

Just being a good listener is not going to turn anyone into a skilled psychotherapist but it will help to understand people and, equally important, make them feel understood.

Empathy and understanding

Understanding somebody else's feelings is the core of empathy as distinct from sympathy. If we are sympathetic towards somebody then we share in their feelings. If we empathise with them we understand their feelings yet remain detached from them. Many studies have shown that it is the latter which is an important ingredient in helping with emotions. At first it might seem that empathy is second best. Isn't it better to identify as closely with someone as possible so that you do indeed share their troubles? The answer does seem to be 'no'. Perhaps we do better to look on very troubled emotions as being a bit like a quicksand. The more you struggle the worse things become. If someone comes to help you it is much better for them to stand at the edge of the quicksand and offer you their hand to pull you out. It is little or no use that person leaping into the quicksand to join you. That way all that is likely to happen is that you both go under. In order to help people we must preserve a degree of detachment. It is empathy rather than sympathy that counts.

One example of this is the problem of 'reasonable' depression to which I referred earlier. If someone has suffered many troubles we may be tempted to say 'What a shame. I can really sympathise. If all that had happened to me I would feel depressed too.' But that does not acknowledge that other people have suffered similar misfortunes and have come to terms with these. That is the sort of knowledge which empathy adds to the equation. It suggests the response 'I understand how you are feeling but I can see that things can get better.' That is the hand over the quicksand.

Psychological therapies

There are a number of psychological therapies which can help older people as they can younger. There is not the space to describe them in detail but I have suggested some further reading for each of these.

Anxiety management

As anxiety is such a common problem techniques of anxiety management are often useful. Mostly these involve a combination of relaxation techniques, practice and positive thinking. We noted above that anxiety is closely associated with problems of tension and abnormal breathing. It is possible to teach both progressive relaxation and breathing techniques to older people. Little or no special adaptation of technique may be required though the most common of these is to allow for arthritis or hearing loss. The former affects the mobility of joints which may prove a problem in the 'tense up' part of a 'tense and then relax' exercise. The answer is either to limit carefully the 'tension' and concentrate on relaxing or to omit 'tensing' altogether. Techniques such as meditation are alternative forms of relaxation which may prove beneficial.

The problem of hearing loss is apparent if you have ever tried to say 'Be calm and relaxed' whilst trying to shout. The message and the tone just do not go together. Fortunately technology has been a real help here with the invention of the portable personal cassette recorder. It is possible to provide quite ordinary instructions for the exercises and for these to be played at sufficient volume through the headphones so that all but the totally deaf can have adequate volume. What is more the instructions are entirely private and available whenever the person wants to use them. The problem of older people not being able to cope with the technology is grossly overrated, sometimes by older people themselves. With appropriate instruction and support they can and do successfully employ this method.

The other essential element is for these techniques to be put into practice at the appropriate time. This means identifying what are the situations that provoke anxiety. Sometimes these can be fairly obvious, for example going to hospital or trying to walk again after suffering a bad fall. At other times it may be less clear what is going on, for example if difficulty in family relationships is the problem. Careful enquiry, good listening and good watching can often reveal this however. Finally it can be that the problem is with what someone is thinking rather than what they or other people are doing.

Changing thinking

Often the most distressing things are the thoughts which are inside our heads. What we imagine might happen is far worse than the worst thing that is actually likely to occur. Similarly when we are depressed it can be shown that we find it more difficult to remember happy events and so our mind becomes full of bad memories. It is not then sufficient just to say 'snap out of it'. If this were so many people would find it much easier to be much happier. These problems with thinking can be almost automatic so that the individual may be barely aware what it is that is causing the distress. The thought may be fleeting but the bad feeling lingers on.

There are various ways of helping with this sort of problem, one of the most important of which may simply be identifying it in the first place. Actually 'catching' the thoughts that make you anxious or depressed allows you to look at them objectively and to challenge them. It may be possible to compile a simple list of the evidence for and against a particular thought or feeling and so to evaluate how 'true' or realistic it is.

Similarly it may be important to review with someone his or her past to achieve a balanced recall of good and bad events. This might involve looking at recent events (what happened this week or yesterday) or further back in time (what was it like during the last war/the Depression etc.). Whatever the exact procedure required, an important contribution of the helper is as an objective sounding board who is not influenced so directly by the powerful emotions which so distort the picture. This, as we have already seen, is the essence of empathy.

Talking and doing

The emphasis so far has been on talking and listening rather than doing. Of course most of those who are involved in helping older people are recruited in order to do something rather than as a good listener or counsellor. The intention here should not be that all this 'doing' stops and everybody sits round being wonderful listeners whilst the practical needs are neglected. Rather it is to aim for a balance in which time spent listening and talking is not seen as time wasted.

One of the best illustrations of this problem was described to me by a professor of geriatric medicine. He told me how on his ward rounds he would quite often go into a ward where a nurse was sitting and talking with a patient. Almost invariably the nurse would, on seeing him, look rather uncomfortable, stop talking and start doing some 'nursing' task. He would then have positively to encourage the nurse to resume the previous conversation.

Often the most valuable comments made by older people in distress are made to those helping with a basic practical task such as cleaning the floor or having a bath. In the latter case this may in part be because it is one of the few times when an older person can spend some time in private with one other person. There are many times when it is the emotional rather than the physical help that is required. However it can sometimes be seen as more acceptable to ask for practical rather than emotional support. We have already seen that this means that distressed older people may focus on physical illness rather than emotional distress. Since both are often present this only means a change in emphasis. The physical illness is exaggerated not invented. Just the same sort of thing happens with practical help in the home. If someone is visiting to clean the floor it may be the visit rather than the cleaning that is important. Such duties could not equally well be done by robots.

Even so, not all those who help frail older people need to be trained counsellors, let alone psychotherapists. Indeed there is no suggestion that following the points outlined in this chapter will turn anyone into either of these. It is important however that we recognise that the contribution that all those who do help can make will be greater if these simple principles are employed. In the majority of cases it will simply mean that there is an added benefit to the practical help which is the reason for being there in the first place. In a few cases someone may require special help and it will be more likely that this need is recognised so that such help can be arranged.

Practical help is especially needed by those older people who are suffering from physical handicap. Such handicap is more common among older people and they are very likely to suffer from emotional distress. I shall therefore consider their particular problems next.

References

Linn, M. W. (1979) Assessing community adjustment in the elderly, *in* A. L. Raskin and L. Jarvik (eds) *Psychiatric Symptoms and Cognitive Loss in the Elderly*, Hemisphere: Washington D.C.

Murphy, E. (1982) Social origins of depression in old age, *British Journal of Psychiatry* **141** 135–142.

Neugarten, B. L. (1977) Personality and ageing, *in* J. E. Birren and K. W. Schaie (eds) *Handbook of the Psychology of Ageing*, Van Nostrand Reinhold: New York.

Post, F. (1982) Functional disorders: I Description, incidence and recognition, *in* R. Levy and F. Post (eds) *The Psychiatry of Late Life*, Blackwell Scientific Publications: Oxford

Power, M., Clough, R., Gibson, P., and Kelly, S. (1983) *Helping Lively Minds: Volunteer Support to Residential Homes*, Research Report, Social Care Research Team, University of Bristol.

Reichard, S., Livson, F., and Petersen, P. G. (1962) *Ageing and Personality*, Wiley : New York.

Further reading

Coleman, P. G. (1986) *Ageing and Reminiscence Processes: Social and Clinical Implications* Wiley: Chichester

Describes both the patterns of adjustment to late life and the role of reminiscence. Includes some very interesting case studies.

Open University Course P577 (1987) *Working with Mental Health Problems in Old Age* Open University: Milton Keynes

Covers all types of mental health problems in late life.

Wattis, J. and Church, M. (1986) *Practical Psychiatry of Late Life* Croom Helm: Beckenham

Includes the application of psychological therapies for older people.

Hanley, I. and Hodge, J. (1986) *Psychological Therapies with the Elderly* Croom Helm: Beckenham

A collection of papers covering a wide range of approaches.

Chapter 4

Coping with Handicap

As we saw in the last chapter, one of the many factors leading to depression in later life is poor health, especially over a prolonged period. Because such health problems are relatively more common for older people, it is worth devoting some time to thinking about what can be done to help those who find themselves in such situations. There is some danger that in thinking about their special problems we may become unnecessarily downhearted about the 'normal' effects of ageing. Our first experience of older people may be important in determining how we approach helping them. The reaction of a young student thrown into caring for a group of very frail elderly people may be to resolve never to do such work again. Certainly one study on a special course in Geriatric Nursing which was intended to encourage people to take up work with older people was found to have the opposite effect. Those who took the course were less positive about working with older people.

Hopefully however by now you can still remember that the majority of older people lead contented lives and this includes many of those who have some sort of difficulties. Even in the most 'at risk' group in the study of depression most of those in that group were not depressed. There is therefore every reason to suppose that we can do something at least to help those who find it more difficult to cope.

There are two main variables which we must consider in trying to help each individual. These are the nature of the handicap and the nature of that individual. This may seem obvious but all too often one or both of these is inadequately understood so that the help given is inappropriate and unsuccessful. The fact that some handicaps are 'worse' than others is not hard to appreciate. Disability is even officially graded for the purpose of deciding the level of compensation or benefit to which each individual may be entitled.

It is also not hard to appreciate that some people are better at coping with adversity than others. We know, for example, that there is a relationship between an individual's personality and the likelihood that he or she will

55

suffer from depression. This is as true for the situation when the depression arises because of some physical handicap as it is for any other reason.

Not everybody is equipped bodily to be a first class sprinter or weightlifter. We know that however much we practise few of us would ever achieve Olympic qualifying standard. Often however it seems that we do not appreciate that there are also differences in emotional resilience. It is often implied that because Mrs Jones is coping at home with a severe handicap Mr Thomas ought to be able to manage as he has a lesser degree of the same handicap. This may be true as a general rule but is an assumption when referred to an individual case. The idea that 'people with this sort of disability can live at home on their own' is as much a stereotype as the idea that 'all old people are deaf' and just as likely to be wrong.

Returning to the analogy with sport, we also know that each of us can improve our own performance with training and practice. This has been behind the recent surge of interest in running the marathon. Similarly it is reasonable to expect that with extra support and advice people may improve their ability to cope with a handicap. With such help many more will achieve independence and well-being than would be the case if we left each person to his or her own emotional resources. It really is worth trying to help.

So we must take into account *both* the handicap *and* the person. Moreover we must remember that adjustment, or lack of this, will depend on an *interaction* between the handicap and the individual. Someone with severe arthritis in the knee will respond less well if he or she has always been a keen gardener rather than an avid reader of books. In this case the disturbance in lifestyle depends on both handicap and lifestyle. The keen reader will be more devastated by a stroke which affects language but leaves his or her limbs unaffected. The gardener may cope better with this. It does not matter much whether we think of arthritis as more serious than a stroke. Nor does it help to know whether gardeners cope better than readers. We need to understand both aspects and how they interact in order to appreciate fully the effect on the individual.

Some of the variables which must be considered are set down in Table 4.1.

Table 4.1   Factors Affecting Adjustment to Handicap

The Individual	The Handicap
Personality	Severity
Attitudes	Extent
Social Relationships	History
Interests	Cause
Activities	Prognosis
Expectations	

The individual

I have already referred to the importance of personality as an influence on the adjustment of the individual. This is true not just for obviously 'psychological' problems such as depression but for other symptoms such as pain. With regard to depression, those of a more emotional temperament (e.g. 'worriers') will be more likely to react with extremes of anxiety or depression.

With regard to pain, personality affects both the experience of pain and how much pain is reported. Normally we rely on what other people say spontaneously in order to know what pain they feel. It is possible however to look in more detail, for example by asking people to complete a special rating scale to tell us how much pain they feel. If we do this we find that those who are more emotional tend to experience pain more. How much this is communicated to others depends on the individual's degree of extraversion. Those who are more outgoing are more likely to tell others that they are in pain. Thus someone who is a worrier and an introvert may suffer a good deal of pain but appear to others not to do so. Others who are more outgoing will be less inclined to keep such a stiff upper lip.

Similarly attitudes to illness affect how people react. If being ill is seen as a sign of weakness then it may be very hard to accept the limitations of such illness in oneself. Others may see disability as a challenge which must be overcome and respond accordingly. Each individual's image of him or herself is likewise very important. In the last chapter we saw how a fear of ageing can lead to great efforts to minimise the physical changes such as greying hair and wrinkled skin. If physical appearance is a central part of being 'well' then someone afflicted by a handicap such as a stroke may find it very hard to face meeting other people. Seeing oneself as a 'cripple' may be a powerful reason for avoiding others.

Not surprisingly other people, especially those close to you, are very important in determining how well you cope. Those with the support of someone in whom they can confide are better equipped to cope than those who have no such support. In most cases it is family and friends who provide this but for some it may be necessary for another person to take on this role. We noted before how important it is to be a good listener. It may be that the most useful thing is to provide the opportunity for social contact as many older people have found when they have attended a day centre or club. Sometimes the solution to an emotional need is the provision of something as practical as a place on a mini-bus.

In an example I gave before we saw how the individual's interests and activities prior to the handicap influences adjustment. The relationship between the handicap and the activity is usually fairly obvious as in the case of a needleworker with failing sight. However it is important to recognise that the standard achieved in the activity is very relevant for many people. Even if still able to surpass most people's efforts the contrast with previous ability may be the deciding factor. If you have striven very hard to achieve a very high standard in the past it may be hard to accept less than this as the norm.

Just as our ideas of ageing are in large part formed from those older people whom we meet, so our ideas of what it means to be disabled come from our experience of others. In recent years professional views and indeed general social views of disability have changed greatly. There is less tendency to see those with some form of handicap as being in need of care and protection. They are seen more as needing help in being independent. But if you are in your late eighties then your view of things may be very different from those who are trying to help you. This can lead to problems, for example where attempts to promote independence are seen as being 'harsh' or 'cruel'. This is often complicated by the fact that the disabled elderly person may be paying for the care that he or she is receiving. He or she may then take the view that if I am paying for this then you can do things for me.

When the British Parliament was debating the abolition of the workhouse and the setting up of residential homes for elderly people, much emphasis was given to the relationship between the cared-for and the carers. The old relationship between 'in-mate' and 'master' which pervaded the workhouse was to be replaced by the relationship between 'guest' and 'hotel manager'. In today's atmosphere of rehabilitation this is hard to sustain. Not many of us would choose to stay in a hotel where the staff encourage us to do things for ourselves because it good for us. The 'hotel' model may be somewhat out of date but the average resident of an old people's home was in his or her forties when this was put forward. If you are going to agree with someone how best you might help them, you need to know that you both have the same set of rules and expectations.

Similarly ideas of illness are often based on the prevailing attitudes of a generation or more ago. This is particularly true for some conditions such as heart disease or epilepsy. We now know that moderate exercise at the right time is a valuable part of recovery from a heart attack. Long-term bed rest creates more problems than it solves. It is not always that easy to convince older patients or their relatives that this is the best course.

Epilepsy has the additional problem of being a condition of the brain and is often a source of apprehension and fear. In the past those suffering from this condition were discouraged from taking part in many everyday activities lest these should provoke a fit. Again this expectation, perhaps formed from the experience of contact with some long-departed relative, may affect the way someone responds to learning that they have suffered an epileptic fit in late life. Such fits are quite common after a stroke and it is not hard to see how the idea that 'epilepsy means needing protection' can get in the way of an active programme of post-stroke rehabilitation.

The handicap

Not surprisingly the severity of the handicap is very important in determining how someone is affected emotionally as well as physically. A condition that has been suggested to be particularly associated with depression is stroke. However one study showed that if you look at other conditions with a similar degree of handicap they too often lead to depression (Robins 1976).

One of the major reasons for this is that such disability seriously disrupts our ability to control what happens to us. Experiments have shown that repeated experience of failure, especially failure to solve problems, can lead to feelings of helplessness and depression. One way that this seems to happen is that people's assessment of their own ability to control things changes. The good things that happen are put down to 'luck' and the bad things are attributed to their own failure. Altering these perceptions as well as giving more success is needed to overcome this.

Related to the severity of the handicap is its extent. It matters, for example, whether a stoke affects just one leg, an arm and a leg, or both limbs and the person's ability to speak. As we have previously noted, older people are more likely than younger to suffer from multiple problems. Thus a particular illness may be compounded by poor sight or hearing. A disability affecting one particular faculty, for example hearing, will be more serious for that individual if failing sight has already led that person to rely more heavily on that particular sense. Pain may or may not be a feature of the disorder and the effects of chronic pain can be destructive indeed.

There are also important differences between those conditions which come on gradually, for example most sorts of arthritis, and those which happen suddenly such as a stroke. On the whole the latter give less scope for adjustment and may thus cause particular distress.

The cause of the condition may have both practical and personal implications. Diseases such as dust-related lung disease may be due to a person's occupation and this may result in some sort of compensation being available. It is also likely that such people will know others with the same condition and have more practical experience of its effects on others than if the cause has nothing to do with where they live or what they do.

Finally the course of the underlying disease is important. Some, like stroke, result in the worst handicap at the beginning and things generally improve, at least to some extent, as time goes on. Others, such as arthritis or dementia, are progressive and the patient is left to cope with the fact that there is to be progressive deterioration. The most striking example of this is of course cancer because it is often so immediately life-threatening. The care of the terminally ill raises particular issues and we shall look more closely at these in the next chapter.

For now let us turn to consider some of the particular conditions I have referred to and see what special features each has in terms of psychological tress and adjustment.

Stroke

Several of the examples that I have already given have referred to the problems of stroke. There are two reasons for this. First, stroke has many features which make it especially likely that there will be problems of adjustment. Secondly, stroke is comparatively common. Certainly in the United Kingdom it is the most common cause of long-term severe disability. It is therefore worth careful consideration and approaches to its prevention and rehabilitation have recently been the subject of a good deal of attention.

A stroke occurs when a blood supply to part of the brain becomes suddenly interrupted. This is most often because one of the blood vessels supplying the brain has become blocked though it may also be due to a blood vessel bursting. Obviously this has a devastating effect on the affected part of the brain and leads to the death of at least some brain tissue. It has less catastrophic but more widespread effects on other parts of the brain so that a wide range of functions are affected. Often the main effects are confined to one half of the brain so that most disability is apparent on the side of the body controlled by that side of the brain. Thus a person affected by a stroke will typically have some loss of function in both the arm and the leg on the same side of the body. The opposite limbs are usually unaffected. The two halves of the brain also tend to control different types of mental function. The left half of the brain controls the right half of the body and, in most people, the powers of language. Thus people whose right arm and leg are affected are most likely to have difficulty reading, writing and generally dealing with words. The other side of the brain tends to look after our ability to make sense of things around us so a stroke on this side can leave people unable to do things like work out how to put on a jumper or follow directions.

You may have noticed that I have been using words like 'tend to' and 'may' when describing the effects of a stroke. This is for two reasons. First of all the arrangement of the blood supply to the brain is very complicated and the extent of a stroke may vary greatly depending on exactly which vessel becomes blocked. Secondly the way the brain is organised to cover functions like language and other special skills varies from person to person. There are some people, for example, for whom it seems as though both halves of the brain deal with language and even a few where the functions of the left and right halves of the brain seem to be reversed!

There are even differences between men and women in how the brain is organised. In men the two halves of the brain tend to specialise more than they do in women (McGlone 1978). This means, amongst other things, that for those who have a stroke affecting the right side of the body, men are about three times as likely as women to have problems with reading, writing and other aspects of language. This probably accounts for the fact that if you look at a group of older patients being seen by a speech therapist for therapy following a stroke the majority are men. This is despite the fact that there are many more older women than there are older men and so more older women actually suffer a stroke.

It is clear that a stroke affects many aspects of function controlled by the brain. Indeed about a third of those affected by a stroke die within the first few weeks. About half of those who survive go on to make a complete recovery and the remainder, a third of those suffering a stroke, are left with a significant handicap.

A stroke is so called because it is, in the words of the *Oxford Dictionary*, a 'blow dealt by fate or nature'. It strikes suddenly and is thus as traumatic an event as a sudden accident or other unexpected misfortune. When we remember that it can leave the victim paralysed and unable to communicate it is not perhaps surprising that anything up to 40% of those afflicted have been found to be markedly depressed (Robinson and Price 1982). This can often go unrecognised, especially when the victim is unable to express him or herself. One problem may be that depression is seen as being 'understandable in the circumstances'. It is however important to draw a distinction between a state of 'grief' as we would expect to follow any great loss and a longer lasting and more serious depression. At the start we need to give time and support just as we would to someone who had recently been bereaved. If, however, after some weeks things do not improve then however traumatic is the loss some extra help may be required.

For some people the most effective help may be treatment with drugs though in many cases this may be inappropriate or insufficient to ensure recovery. Support, counselling or psychological therapy may be needed as an addition or as an alternative. From a psychological point of view there is obviously a real problem of 'helplessness' for some people. There may be loss not only of independence in mobility but also loss of control of bladder and perhaps bowel function or, perhaps worse still, an inability to communicate one's distress to others and to get support from them. The loss of control may include difficulty with emotions whereby trivial events may bring tears or laughter. If during an ordinary conversation you suddenly keep bursting into tears this is itself very embarrassing and distressing. That this is not the same as depression is revealed by the fact that the sufferer may actually deny being depressed and can be quite easily distracted so that the crying stops as quickly as it started. It does however make things very complicated for the patient and his or her family and friends.

Not surprisingly the process of overcoming such trauma is often a long and difficult one. It means combining the many practical skills of therapists with the support of the patient and his or her family and friends. Many believe that this is best done in the setting of a specialist unit where the several skills required can be concentrated.

The help and support of others who have themselves suffered a stroke is often very valuable especially in dealing with cases where individuals find it difficult to face the world because they are ashamed of being 'crippled'. This may be a special problem where someone has always been very fit and active prior to the stroke. Such patients may often say 'You don't know what its like', and say so quite forcefully. Empathy here is not enough, the patient must believe that the person with whom he or she is dealing really does understand. It is here that those who themselves have suffered similarly can have much to offer.

As well as the problem of helplessness it may be necessary to deal with a 'fear of failure' before physical therapy can really help. Some people feel that if they can no longer walk the 2 miles into town then there is no point in learning how to walk 50 yards. Others who have learned to accept more limited goals may have much to offer here also.

Not surprisingly one advantage of a specialist unit is that it brings together a number of sufferers and at any one time there will be people at various stages of rehabilitation. To see someone whom you know to have a similar problem improving and getting ready to leave hospital can be a great encouragement. Unfortunately we must also be sensitive to possible problems. In a disorder such as stroke people are often in a rehabilitation setting together for quite some time; certainly for weeks and possibly for months. The very same relationships which build up between people to help and support one another lead to pain of separation which we must at least acknowledge. This is true for both the relationship between fellow patients and that between staff and patients.

Similarly there is the problem that the pattern of recovery from stroke is very variable. Whilst over a large group of patients we can see that most (of the recovery happens in the first few months, some individuals show very different patterns. It may be quite discouraging for one patient to see someone ?who came to the unit later making more rapid progress. Likewise it is very hard to answer the question 'When will I get better?' or, even more so, 'When will I stop getting better?' This variability in rate of change is made more complex by the effects of age. As a general rule older people do take longer to recover or to relearn skills. It is very easy to conclude that the person who is progressing more slowly is not going to make as much progress in the end. This may work as a very rough rule of thumb (a stereotype) but it is not 'a good rule for predicting individual outcome, especially at different ages.

Variability is also a problem in appreciating the way in which a particular individual has been affected by a stroke. I have already referred to the way in which the brain and the functions it controls may be impaired. Because the damage is not visible it may be easy for others, especially those for whom this is unfamiliar, to misunderstand the problems. This is most often a problem when there is little impairment in the use of arms and legs. At least if you are paralysed on one side of the body people can see that something is wrong.

One example is those whose ability to express themselves is affected by a stroke. If they recover they often complain that people used to shout at them as if they were deaf. They do find it difficult to follow conversation but this is a problem of understanding not of hearing. In rather the same way there can be problems in appreciating other difficulties in mental function. Someone whose sense of space has been affected may find it very hard to learn how to put on a jumper even if his or her arm has made a good recovery. Such a person may understand the instructions, can even repeat them back to the therapist but still doesn't seem to make progress. This can all too easily be put down to the patient being 'awkward' or 'uncooperative'. This puts the blame firmly on the patient which may help the therapist but hardly helps otherwise.

Even someone's emotional response to the effects of a stroke seems to vary according to the part of the brain that has been affected. Those who have suffered a stroke on the left side of the brain tend to react with distress and tearfulness to their difficulties. It has even been described as a 'catastrophic' reaction. Those who have suffered a stroke on the right side of the brain tend on the contrary to be apathetic and indifferent to their handicap.

This may be related to the problem of 'neglect' also shown by such patients. Those who have lost the use of their left arm and/or leg often ignore the affected side of the body. In extreme cases they may even deny that the affected limbs belong to them and complain that someone has left an arm in their bed! More usually such patients just do things like only shave one side of the face or comb the hair on one side of the head. Such 'odd' behaviour can be quite alarming to the patient's family who may fear that it marks the onset of some dreadful mental instability.

In fact the outlook for someone who has suffered a stroke can be quite encouraging in that the most severe handicap is at the start, from which point things tend to improve. The extent of the progress can be limited especially in the case of a severe stroke or when someone has suffered several previous strokes. However further strokes are not inevitable. The likelihood of having a stroke is increased if you have had one before, especially if problems like high blood pressure remain. With this caution we can however say that stroke is not a progressive condition.

Arthritis

Osteo-arthritis is perhaps the condition most associated with 'old age'. It is a disease of the joints which degenerate so that they no longer work smoothly and without pain. Stiffness and aching joints are seen as the body 'wearing out' and as one of the disadvantages of growing old. In fact the truth is not quite so pessimistic. Certainly degeneration of the joints is very common in late life though the cause remains something of a mystery. Although the notion of mechanical wear and tear is an attractive one the process seems to be much more complex. Certainly it does not account very well for the fact that one joint, for example one knee, may be much more affected than the other. Both knees are after all just the same age. Fortunately very marked changes with severe disability are the exception rather than the rule.

The major problems from a functional point of view are those of limitation of movement and pain. Both of these are distressing but nonetheless there is some variation between different individuals in coping with these. Those who have been most active will be the most affected by such limitations. This will depend also on the relative involvement of different joints. To the lifelong lacemaker the loss of nimble fingers will have special meaning.

The variation in how people deal with pain means that there is not always a simple relationship between those changes which can be seen in the joints (for example on an X-ray picture) and the symptoms reported by the sufferer. In cases where there is much damage and few symptoms there is little cause for concern. In the reverse case, where there are few signs of joint damage but much in the way of symptoms, there is more of a problem. One reaction to this is for the symptoms to be described by the doctor or nurse as 'psychological'. This has a number of implications for the patient and those trying to help him or her.

Perhaps the most important of these is that somehow the pain is less real than that which is due to more severe pathology. This impression may be heightened if the patient complains of severe pain at home and this gets better when he or she comes into hospital even if no 'treatment' is given. There is consequently the danger that there can build up a barrier between patient and therapist. The patient feels that the therapist is implying that the pain is 'put on' or that the sufferer is somehow malingering. The assumption here seems to be that there is some conscious process going on, that the symptoms are deliberate and under the control of the patient. Even if the therapist thinks otherwise it may be very difficult to convince the patient of this.

This is because for most people, old or young, their model of pain is a mechanical one. Pain is due to illness or injury and the answer is to treat the cause or to eliminate the signals of pain. Again we are back to stereotypes. As a general rule for guiding us as to how we should respond to pain this works jolly well. We feel pain when we are injured or ill and we deal with it appropriately. However it is not correct for all people all of the time. We all recognise in fact that this is the case for extreme situations. We know that there can be situations, notably on the sports or battle field, where individuals do not feel pain until the excitement or crisis is over. Even our own experience tells us that we can sustain a minor injury which we do not notice as long as we remain preoccupied with the task in hand. It should not be a great surprise then that pain and injury are linked a little imprecisely.

In the case of some individulals the situation may be more complex still. For a very few people the meaning of pain may have been altered in a more complex way. If someone has been in a difficult family situation for many years then the reporting of pain may have had other effects. It may, for example, have meant that he or she has been able to avoid emotionally difficult situations. Moreover the pain will indeed actually feel worse if someone is distressed. In the case of older people the problem is often difficult to resolve for several reasons.

First there is the fact that it is usually possible to demonstrate at least some degree of physical deterioration. Some degree of osteo-arthritis is very common so we cannot simply conclude that the symptoms are without any physical cause. Secondly, the older you are the longer you may have been learning, albeit unconsciously, that experiencing pain has effects on those around you. Note that I have said 'experiencing' rather than 'reporting' pain. The pain is all too real however great or small is the 'psychological' component. Thirdly the older you are the more likely it is that you have some other stress, either short or long term, to contend with. We know that the presence or absence of such things as anxiety affects how we feel pain. Emotions are not the cause of the pain but they do affect how it is perceived. The analogy I usually use is that of a radio. The signals from the injury are like the signals sent out by the radio station. Our emotions act like the volume control on the set. The more distressed we are the louder the signal comes through. Curing the illness or injury is like blowing up the radio transmitter but this is not always possible. Painkillers can dampen the signal down but for the very sensitive this may not be enough. It is for them that emotional well-being may be especially important.

It is important to remember the fact that arthritis does not of itself cause direct mental problems. Obviously someone severely affected may have other conditions which do, for example that person might also have suffered a stroke or have senile dementia. However in a continuing care setting such as a hospital or a residential home the person who only suffers from severe arthritis can have problems of adjustment precisely because of this. Such a patient will often stand out as being the most mentally alert client but is very reliant on others for any kind of social contact. Because mental problems are often more difficult to manage in the community those in institutions are likely to be so afflicted. This may mean that those who are fully alert can be relatively isolated and rely on staff and visitors for company. Fortunately this situation is relatively rare since the mentally alert arthritic person can take full advantage of every mechanical and electronic aid to independence so does not need to leave his or her own home unless there are very marked problems. In the rare case however the individual will be all too able to appreciate that he or she cannot manage in his or her own house and problems of relocation (see chapter 7) may be considerable. This is all the more so since the arthritis itself may have little or no direct effect on life expectancy so that the person may have to look forward to many years of high dependency. How this is viewed will depend on how good we are at helping someone adjust to handicap.

Lung disease

Long-term lung disease such as chronic bronchitis is also associated with no major direct influence on mental function. Such conditions are however often the source of considerable handicap and can be compounded by psychological problems. Just as with arthritis we have the problem of judging the balance between physical pathology and behaviour. Even in younger patients this difficulty is not unknown and several of those who are referred to specialist out-patient clinics are found to suffer from 'disproportionate breathlessness'. The term refers, as you might expect, to the situation where the patient's report of breathlessness is not in line with what we would expect from the results of physical examination.

However it has also been found that the type of symptoms as well as their severity seem to distinguish such cases. Thus those with the breathlessness typical of lung disease will report that their symptoms are worse when they try any kind of physical exertion. Breathlessness at rest is not typical (Burns and Howell 1969).

No doubt each medical department looking after older people has a number of patients who are elderly, live alone and who seem to come in regularly with an apparent worsening of their lung condition. The nature of the condition is such that periodic episodes of deterioration are to be expected. However there tend to be a few of these patients whose symptoms settle very quickly when they come into hospital. The comfort and security of hospital seem to be as important for them as any physical treatment. Just as with the patient in pain, the breathlessness is all too real and ideas of 'malingering' are usually entirely inappropriate. Nonetheless we must not be surprised if changes in social circumstances play a part in improving the prognosis of some cases.

In the case of breathlesssness the link with anxiety is even closer than in the case of pain: it is a symptom of anxiety itself. Thus it is a challenge to both patient and physician to distinguish whether this symptom is due to emotional rather than physical problems.

Even in cases where there has been no indication that the breathlessness was disproportionate to the pathology it has been shown that symptomatic relief alone does not necessarily lead to recovery of function in day to day activities. It seems that graded practice, perhaps because it builds up confidence, is a valuable addition to rehabilitation. There is also evidence that a significant proportion of those who have been in hospital for an episode of worsening lung disorder remain anxious or depressed several months after discharge (Peach and Pathy 1981).

Those who have depended on physical activity for work and recreation are naturally the most affected by chronic lung disease. The condition has in the past been associated with certain types of work, notably mining and other jobs where there is a lot of exposure to dust. This is still true for some older men, especially in areas where many used to work in such industries.

However the major cause and, equally important, irritant of poor lungs is of course smoking. Sadly the trend among younger generations (those under 60!) is for women to become more like men in their smoking habits. Thus in the future we may expect to see older men and older women with the disabling effects of this unfortunate addiction.

There are several reasons why it may be especially difficult to change smoking patterns in older people. First there is the problem that people, both old and young, assume that 'you cannot teach an old dog new tricks'. As we have already noted, the only truth in this is that some learning is a little slower. It is the attitude rather than the truth which is the real problem.

Second, many older people do not feel that it is worth the effort. Things are so bad already that stopping now really is not going to make that much difference. In so far as there is irreversible damage to lung tissue this may be so but there is no doubt that stopping smoking would very much help to stop things getting worse.

Third, we have the problem that those who would find it relatively easy to give up smoking will be more likely to have already done so. There is no doubt that people differ in this as they differ in everything else and those who are still smoking in late life include those who find it most difficult to stop. There are very few people who start smoking in late life so the older smoker is likely to have been a smoker for very many years.

Fourth and finally there is the major stumbling block of 'what else is there?'. This is a particular problem for those around the person whose support and encouragement is so important in changing this sort of be-haviour. The argument runs something along the lines: 'Poor old chap. He can hardly get around any more with his chest so bad. It isn't fair to suggest he gives up smoking. After all, he's only got that and his TV.' This really betrays our poverty in imagination if we only think of stopping things and not helping to promote other activities. What kind of environment is so limited that smoking is the main 'interesting activity' available?

There are some complex ethical issues concerned with people's right to do as they please with themselves and the extent smoking impinges on others. The latter may be direct (annoying the other people in the same room) or indirect (imposing an extra burden on those who have to provide the care as the chest complaint gets steadily worse). These are fascinating but there is not the space to discuss them here. They are important to the situation of older people as they are to younger. For the moment it is best simply to note that any method aimed at helping people stop smoking depends first on them wishing to do so. Only then is any kind of strategy able to begin to be effective.

Heart disease

Smoking is also a major cause of heart disease so much the same issues apply. Indeed as breathlessness is often due to heart disease much of what was said above regarding anxiety also applies to those with heart disease. In fact there is perhaps even more overlap between emotional distress and heart disease than lung disease.

Besides breathlessness there is the occurrence of palpitations, giddiness and other symptoms. Moreover the heart is generally seen as being particularly vital. The threat of sudden death looms large. The result is that quite often an anxious person who has had a heart attack in the past may be repeatedly readmitted to hospital with 'chest pain' for which no cause can be found. Again we have the problem that we know there to be a very real 'medical' problem of heart disease so we cannot easily dismiss the symptoms as 'all in the mind'. The sufferer him or herself is all too aware that he or she has 'heart trouble' and may be very worried about having further attacks. The suggestion that some of the symptoms could be due to 'anxiety' can often be interpreted by the patient as implying that they are malingering. They are not malingering and they have the history to prove it!

This fear can be such as to prevent the patient from doing many activities, especially any which are seen as requiring physical activity. Increasingly this is recognised as a significant barrier to recovery and many heart specialists now advocate supervised exercise programmes as a part of the treatment after a heart attack. Age simply adds to the problem of expectation and attitude. Older people are expected, indeed may themselves expect, that the normal thing to do is to take it easy 'at their age'. There is good evidence however that simple counselling about resuming everyday activities has a very beneficial effect. One study showed that the number of readmissions to hospital was reduced without any adverse effect on medical outcome. Those who received counselling, who were all elderly, did much better in terms of recovering their previous level of function than those who turned up to a routine out-patient clinic where only standard medical advice was given.

Trauma

The conditions described thus far have a mixture of sudden and gradual onset. There are some other instances where the sudden onset of the handicap is one of the major features. Such cases include those due to accidents (falls, road traffic accidents etc.) and those due to surgery.

The situations where accident is the feature are little different in terms of emotional impact than for the same injury at a younger age. This may not always be appreciated. For an elderly person with a spinal injury, for example, rehabilitation goals can easily be too limited. People tend to think in terms of getting someone well enough to be cared for in a home rather than back to independent living. Indeed the system of services and of benefits sometimes seems to favour this particular myopia. For example, you are eligible for mobility allowance only if you become disabled under the age of 60. Certainly for the older person the process of rehabilitation is rather longer. But provided there is no problem of intellectual deterioration the eventual outcome may be equally satisfactory.

For some disorders the effects of impaired intellectual function are a relatively common problem since those who suffer the injury are more likely to be both physically and mentally frail. Thus the success or otherwise of recovery from a fractured femur, one of the most common injuries in old age, depends very much on the person's general level of physical health and on their mental function (Baker *et al.* 1978). Those who suffer injury are moreover likely to be more frail than comparable people of that age. Those who try to help with such problems could therefore be forgiven for thinking that recovery from injury in the elderly tends to be very poor. We are back once more with the problem of our general views, our attitudes, being based on our biased experience.

There are other situations which are not usually termed as 'trauma' but which may be similarly traumatic for the older person. I am thinking here of those who have to undergo surgery such as an amputation or a colostomy. The reasons for amputation in older people are usually related to difficulties in circulation of the blood to the limbs. Thus they are not usually carried out as an emergency and there is the opportunity to prepare the person for what is going to happen both physically and emotionally. Even so some people react badly to the loss of a limb and their distress can greatly impede their subsequent recovery and adjustment. Just as in other conditions successful rehabilitation is quite possible, albeit somewhat slower.

On the other hand those who arrive in hospital with a bowel obstruction need emergency surgery. From the patient's point of view he or she comes in with a severe abdominal pain and wakes up to find that he or she has to cope with adjusting to the use of a colostomy bag. This can lead to very real problems of adjustment, including some who cannot even bear to look at themselves let alone learn the techniques of changing the bag. Fortunately this sort of problem is well recognised and the help of the specialist nurses (stoma therapists) is particularly valuable. The only problem may be to ensure that these skills are made available to all the older people who might need them.

For all types of trauma one additional difficulty for the older patient is that there may be implications for where he or she lives as the result of the change in condition. This does apply also to younger patients of course but the range of services, adaptations and benefits tends to allow more of the younger patients to return to their own home. There is an implicit value judgement in deciding that someone is or is not eligible to have major alterations, for example to their house. It would appear at times as if there is the hidden assumption that the older patient will not live long enough to make it worthwhile. This assumption is not I must emphasise in the attitudes of those directly caring for the older patient. It is implied by the system that allows more varied options and greater benefits to the younger disabled than to those who are older. It is here that we see society's ageism. Overcoming this sort of problem is well beyond the scope of most of us. It is of more practical use to consider some of the ways we can apply psychological knowledge to helping those older people who suffer from a handicap.

Exercise

Go through the list of conditions described above and consider how each would affect you. Which of your present activities/interests would be most affected by each?

Compare your list either with that of a colleague or one which you make for someone you know well.

Helping with handicap

As we have seen there are many different problems that can arise and impede someone's adjustment to a chronic illness or disability. We need to remember, however, that most people make quite successful adjustments without the need for special help. It is only for a minority that very great problems arise. Of course if we are supportive and helpful then this will benefit everybody. We must not just leave people to get on with coping and wait to pick up those who are failing to do so.

In terms of using psychological approaches these can be based on both what we know of how 'normal' adjustment takes place and on special techniques designed for those who have major psychological problems. For example if we are trying to help someone who is sad and withdrawn we may both encourage them to talk about what has happened to them (express the 'normal' feelings of anger and so on) and use extra techniques to change the way they think about their present position.

Since we are seeking to change people's behaviour and help them to overcome problems it is convenient to look at the overall approach from a 'problem oriented' perspective. This simply means defining carefully what are the person's current problems and setting targets for overcoming these. This approach has become increasingly widespread in recent years as a complementary approach to that of 'diagnosis and treatment'. It is especially useful for situations where there are many different things going wrong and where some at least of the difficulties are not illnesses for which there is any effective treatment. Both of these factors apply to the older person who is more likely both to have multiple problems and to suffer from 'untreatable' conditions.

If we think only in terms of 'illness' which needs to be correctly diagnosed and treated then the implication of that illness being 'untreatable' is that we sit back and do nothing. Thus somebody suffering from a stroke or from dementia might, on this basis, get very little help since there is no effective 'treatment' for these conditions. However there is much that can be done to help overcome the problems which follow from these conditions.

Similarly if we are faced with someone who has very many different illnesses and problems then it is easy to become overwhelmed by this. There is no one solution to the problems and we do not know what to do for the best. This is avoided if we can identify specific problems which can then be considered with strategies which can help.

In many ways the difficulty which we face in dealing with this is the same as that which challenges the sufferer. There is a real danger of becoming overwhelmed by the situation. Things can look so hopeless that it is too much even to begin. One further difficulty with thinking only of 'illness' is that this usually implies the patient being rather passive. He or she relies on the expert to give the orders (prescribe the treatment) and may expect to do little more than agree to swallow tablets or undergo surgery. Problem solving implies the therapist working with the patient which is a more realistic approach for the majority of cases.

Problem solving

The elements of problem solving may be identified thus:

1. Identifying needs and resources
2. Setting goals
3. Defining strategies
4. Monitoring progress
5. Providing feedback and evaluation

1. Identifying needs and resources

If we are trying to decide how to find our way to a particular place there are at least two things we need to know: where we are now and the directions from here to our destination. The first step is therefore to find out where we are now.

In terms of helping those with handicap we need to know a good deal about the person him or herself and the nature of the handicap. We need to know what that individual's interests have been, what are his or her family circumstances, that individual's personality and attitude to his or her present difficulties. We need to know the history of the problems, whether things have changed suddenly or slowly, what is the extent of the disability and, just as important, what abilities remain intact.

This sort of information may need to be gathered from a wide variety of sources not just the individual him or herself. Family, friends and formal carers all may be able to help build up a picture of this person. This information must be carefully and sensitively gathered. We are looking for things to help not material for a good gossip. It must be confidential whenever appropriate but also available to all those who are cooperating in providing help. It is no good one person collecting lots of very useful information if this is only stored in that person's head. It should be recorded confidentially but in some way that is accessible to others involved in helping that person.

The need for this has been recognised in some of the recent developments in record keeping. The Problem-Oriented Medical Record and the Nursing Process, for example, increasingly reflect an effort to encourage a problem oriented approach and for the routine recording of a wide range of information.

The collection of such information needs to be a collaborative effort with the patient. Asking for such information may not be easy if this is seen simply as being nosey. However self disclosure (telling somebody else about yourself) is an important part of building up relationships. My own experience is that older people in particular also enjoy finding out about other people so that the process of self-disclosure is very much a two-way process. This may be a problem for some professionals who are uncomfortable about giving this much away about themselves. It may also be why many people find it easier to talk to the cleaner rather than the doctor. In fact some studies have even found that people can find it easier to give more honest information on their problems to a computer rather than to a person.

Since relationships are so important in helping people overcome psychological problems, it is as well to get off to a good start. Taking the right interest in the person is a strong foundation.

2. *Setting goals*

Having identified the main needs and strengths with an individual, these must be broken down into specific goals. Again this should be a cooperative effort with the person whom we are trying to help. Indeed any effort is pretty well bound to fail if the person we are trying help wants to achieve something else. For example we know that whatever we may be able to do to help someone give up smoking there is no point in even starting if the person does not want to achieve that goal.

This is especially important in the case of those who are severely disabled. As able-bodied people we are often in a position of very considerable power even if we do not choose to be so. It is all too easy to decide what a goal should be on the basis of what we 'know to be best for the patient'. This can then cause all sorts of problems when that person refuses to cooperate. For vulnerable elderly people there may be the special problem of some degree of forgetfulness or other mental problem. The whole issue of consent is then extremely complex. As we shall see in chapter 5 this is particularly so in the case of terminal care.

The goals then should be agreed with patient, relatives and other carers. They should also be quite specific and in some way measurable. It is very fine to have some goal such as 'improving Mrs Jones' quality of life' but how can we tell if we have achieved this. Something like 'increasing the number of times Mrs Jones can visit her sister' is going to be much easier to evaluate in terms of success or failure.

The goals must strike a balance between the impossible and the trivial. It is no good setting a goal with someone which it is virtually certain cannot be achieved. All that this will do is to ensure that person experiences failure. Similarly it is not much good setting some trivial goal which represents no progress. Praise for this will ring very hollow indeed. Again cooperation helps here because the patient and therapist will often have different views about what it is reasonble to achieve. A suitable goal is likely to be a compromise between these.

3. Defining strategies

So far we have considered 'where we are now' and 'where we want to be'. The next step is to agree on 'how we are going to get there'. The goals that we are now trying to achieve are likely to be quite different from those that we might have originally imagined. For example it may have become clear that the patient we were all set to help learn to walk again is really needing help to see this as a realistic goal. Thinking and feeling as well as doing are all possible targets. The strategies for these might include those of anxiety management and cognitive reappraisal which we considered briefly in chapter 3.

The agreement on the part of the patient will include participating in whatever programme has been suggested. The therapist will have also agreed to his or her part of the bargain. Some of this will be to help directly, for example by giving advice and practice in learning to walk/read/dress or whatever. Some of the help will be less direct, for example contacting a particular agency to organise a volunteer to visit regularly.

Part of the specification of strategy should include the time which it is expected to take to achieve the goal. This will vary greatly but as with the goal itself should be a realistic interval. This again may reveal ways in which the patient and therapist disagree. Over-optimism or over-pessimism may themselves be targets for change.

4. Monitoring progress

If the goals have been carefully specified then it should follow naturally how we are to decide how well things are going. Being able to do this is necessary if we are to provide feedback and praise to encourage progress. As we noted earlier, some skills provide their own feedback. For example it is easy to see how far you have been able to walk across the room. Similarly there may in some cases be little need for positive praise when just being able to see progress is reward enough. However this is by no means always the case and we must be aware of how important is our own reaction. Our attention, praise and encouragement must be appropriate to the needs of each individual. For some the main role of the therapist may be to point out simply that progress is being made, especially when change is only gradual. Very often the patient is preoccupied with how he or she used to be before the stroke/amputation/heart attack or whatever. Attention to this can be at the expense of the progress made in rehabilitation.

Success is also important in overcoming the sense of helplessness which can often overwhelm. The attribution of success and failure is linked to the way we feel. If we are feeling unhappy or otherwise distressed then we tend to see the good things that happen as being due to 'luck' or the achievements of others. The bad things that occur are due to our own failure. If we are feeling content then we tend to think the other way around. In either case the way we think tends to keep our mood the way it is. Something fairly special is needed to change from one state to the other. As we have seen, it is often some major trauma which induces a state of helplessness. It requires a positive move, from within or without, to move in the opposite direction.

5. Evaluation

Finally we must decide whether the agreed goals are being achieved and to revise our plans accordingly. If all is going well then we will be able to set new goals which are more advanced. If things have not gone well then we need to consider why and change goals and/or strategies accordingly. This really means going back to stage 1 and updating the position in the light of whatever changes have taken place. If there has been progress then we can see that some needs have been met. If things have not progressed this will likely be because we have uncovered other needs which must be met before our original goals can be achieved. In either case the goals and strategies are not fixed and unchanging. They are worthwhile only as long as they are useful to that individual. We must beware of deceiving ourselves into paying only lip-service to the problem oriented approach. Such an approach is not just a new way of keeping records. It is part of a philosophy of helping others.

The need to define appropriate goals is especially relevant to the area of terminal care. Dying and bereavement are the topics to which I shall turn next.

References

Baker, B. R., Duckworth, T., and Wilkes, E. (1978) Mental state and other prognostic factors in femoral fractures of the elderly. *Journal of the Royal College of General Practitioners* **28** 557–559.
Burns, B. H., and Howell, J. B. L. (1969) Disproportionately severe breathlessness in chronic bronchitis. *Quarterly Journal of Medicine* **38** 277–294.
McGlone, J. (1978) Sex differences in functional brain assymmmetry. *Cortex* **14** 122–128.

Peach, H., and Pathy. M. S. (1981) A follow-up study of disability among elderly patients discharged from hospital with exacerbations of chronic bronchitis. *Thorax* **36** 585–589.

Robins, A. H. (1976) Are stroke patients more depressed than other disabled subjects? *Journal of Chronic Disease* **29** 479–482.

Robinson, R. G., and Price. T. R. (1982) Post-stroke depressive disorders: a follow-up study of 103 patients. *Stroke* **13** 635–641.

Further reading

Nichols, K. (1984) *Psychological Care in Physical Illness* Croom Helm: London

Describes many of the issues which should be considered in relation to patients of any age. If you think the pendulum has swung too much towards a mechanical model of illness, this gives it a good thump in the opposite direction.

Wade, D. T., Langton-Hewer, R., Skilbeck, C. E., and David, R. M. (1985) *Stroke: A Critical Approach to Diagnosis, Management and Treatment* Chapman & Hall Medical: London

This book is based on a large prospective study of the management of stroke comparing hospital and community care. It deals with all aspects in an authoritative way.

Barrowclough, C., and Fleming, I. (1986) *Goal Planning with Elderly People* Manchester University Press: Manchester

This deals in great detail with setting up goal planning approaches for older people. The whole plans are very detailed and may need adaptation for use in some settings.

Chapter 5

Taking Leave: Dying and Bereavement

Helping the dying and the bereaved is one of the most demanding tasks for those helping older people. Indeed it may at times be more of a problem for the carers than for the older person. It seems to be particularly difficult for us to think ourselves ahead to how we might feel about our own mortality in late life. For this reason it is a topic on which we may learn a great deal from carefully listening to those who are already older.

Death is often a 'taboo' subject, much more so these days than sex, at least for those who have been born since the 1930s. Our attitudes to it are rarely aired but it is a topic which must concern us all if we are helping older people. Whatever our own job it is inevitable that we will before very long face the death of someone whom we have been trying to help. If our job has been to provide physical care then we may have thoughts of failure. If we have been providing psychological help there may be feelings of disappointment or even frustration.

It is rare for many people to be able to feel satisfied about their job when the culmination of that effort was the death of an older person. Yet in one way this should be our aim. To have helped someone to a comfortable and contented death is undoubtedly one of the great achievements of care. To have shared in the strength of that contentment can be one of the greatest rewards.

Death and dying

The first distinction to be drawn is between death and dying. Death as the end of life is something which many people do not find it difficult to accept. This is especially so for older people who often come to value greatly the time that they have left whilst accepting that the end must come. There is often implied some notion of what is our allotted span. Usually this is seen as 'three score years and ten' even though modern life expectancy comfortably exceeds this. Time over and above this is then seen as a bonus so that each fresh day means a little extra time.

In the case of those who are very elderly death can often mean relief from the struggle. This is particularly so for those who suffer from marked long-term health problems. Such people may quite readily admit that they will be quite content to pass away when the time comes. However unless there is particular distress there is usually a strong hint that this time is not here yet. Thus we must be careful to tell the difference between this sort of view of death and the suicidal thoughts which can be a feature of depression. This requires a careful and thorough understanding of the thoughts and feelings of each individual. The depressed person will have many other signs of distress and it is unlikely that he or she will say such things in a simple 'matter of fact' way. The suicidal ideas of depression are cause for positive help and action as we saw in chapter 3.

In contrast the idea that 'enough is enough' is not going to be changed by great efforts at treatment, counselling or whatever. The effort is misplaced and should go into enabling that person to enjoy the rest of the 'time remaining'. On the whole we tend rather to underestimate the power of individuals to decide how long should remain. Anyone with a significant amount of experience working with older people will know that there are occasions when individuals themselves seem to decide that the time has come to depart. This does not mean actively attempting suicide but rather 'turning one's face to the wall' and letting life slip away. It poses quite difficult ethical problems for those providing care. I shall have more to say of this later. For now I just note that some carefully conducted research has shown that 'expressed wish to die' is related to the likelihood that someone will in fact die. This is true even if you exclude those with suicidal intent and ratings of 'risk' based on medical opinion (MacDonald and Dunn 1982).

Whilst death itself may be seen as a threat rather than a release, this is actually more of a problem for the process of dying. This can all too often be seen as a long, painful and lonely experience which is for these reasons to be greatly feared. This may be based on personal observation or on imagined terrors. Whatever is the origin, fear of the process of dying all too often lies behind the fear of 'death' or of an illness such as cancer. As we shall see, the rise of the hospice movement in recent years has done much to remove this image though a great deal still remains to be done.

The fear of dying may be expressed in several ways. It lies behind the taboo on discussing terminal illness and the dread of going into hospital. There is sometimes the folklore among residents of an old people's home, for example, that those who leave to go into hospital do not return. Of course it is always possible to find some example of this in that as those who are ill go into hospital some of them do indeed die. However the fear that this generates may stop others getting timely help for less serious illness. Indeed in extreme cases there may be more pain precisely because the right help cannot be given.

Much of the impact of the hospice movement has been to awaken interest in the need to help people to die with dignity and without pain. Successfully achieving this depends on bringing together good physical and psychological care. It means changes for staff as well as patients. Much of the driving force behind this movement has come from those who, whatever their professional background, work within the setting of a religious organisation. The reasons for this are not hard to see. Religious faith has always been greatly concerned with the unanswerable questions of the nature of life and the meaning of mortality. Religious needs are as important as any other psychological need so it is important to consider how these fit into the complex process of caring for older people.

Religious belief and ageing

It is often thought that older people are in some way 'more religious' than younger people. This is apparently based on a vague notion that they go to church more or in some way have a particular interest in the possibility of life after death. Such evidence as we have from formal study suggests that there is no marked trend for people to attend church more as they grow older. Indeed where there are changes these are in the direction of *decreased* rather than *increased* attendance at formal religious worship. This is not too surprising since there are plenty of reasons why participation in all sorts of activities outside the home tends to decrease as we grow older. This is especially true in very old age when it is much more likely that we might suffer from some kind of physical infirmity which makes getting out and about difficult. This change in behaviour may have very little to do with any change in religious belief. After all, you do not stop feeling hungry just because you can no longer get out to do your shopping.

You will notice that I have referred to the changes in religious belief, nor rather patterns of worship, 'as they grow older'. It may well be that a brief observation of the people attending a particular church, chapel, synagogue or mosque might reveal a disproportionate number of older people in the congregation. This would certainly fit with some 'comic' idea of the brave parish priest preaching his sermon to two old ladies and the church mouse.

If there are large changes over a generation in what people do then this may exaggerate the effects of ageing. We noted this earlier on when considering ageing and thinking (chapter 2). We saw there how important these cohort effects are. There have of course been considerable changes in the patterns of worship in such countries as Great Britain over the course of this century. The number of people attending church regularly has declined steadily although there is now some evidence that this trend is being halted or even reversed. Such effects make a big difference to the apparent effects of ageing which we get from informal 'cross-sectional' observation. In other words it may be that older people today do go to church more than younger people today. But the generation who are now old always did go to church more than today's younger generation. Whatever the explanation, the fellowship of a religious community is of great importance to many people, old and young. Their needs cannot be ignored.

Often however the recognition of this need is confined to an entry such as 'C. of E.' under 'Religious Denomination' in a routine record. Having said this there are many other cases where there is excellent provision for worship both in the place where the person now lives, such as a residential home, or by way of transport to formal worship. It is helpful however to ensure that there is a well-established policy of finding out from each individual patient or resident what he or she would appreciate in the way of spiritual support.

Larger hospitals will be regularly visited by several ministers of different denominations and many will have their own chaplain. Certainly in the area of terminal care and bereavement there is every reason why the chaplain should be an integrated member of the team. There are in fact few places which care for very frail elderly people where this sort of need is not regularly apparent.

The focus here is on *opportunity* for religious worship rather than 'compulsion'. This pattern will be found even in those hospices which are founded on a particular religious denomination. There is no question of the worship being obligatory. Some patients will want to join actively in services, some will wish merely to observe and others will desire to be absent. You cannot force feed spiritual comfort. However such comfort may have very real effects in enabling some people to cope with handicap in general and pain in particular. Pain and suffering raise fundamental question of faith for many: those who suffer, their families and those who care for them. These go well beyond the scope of this book, indeed well beyond the competence of its author. It is sufficient here to note that such issues cannot be ignored in helping the 'whole person'. They are given special consideration by those who are trained in pastoral care and their expertise should not be ignored. Spiritual pain is a real experience for some people.

As with all things the approach to worship must be adapted to the needs of those who are to be involved. There is often some advantage in the case of those with a mild or moderate degree of intellectual loss in that forms of worship are often very overlearned. Many older people who seem extremely 'confused' will show a positive response not just to music in general but to hymns in particular. Regular lifelong practice can be put to good use in this case. In other ways it may be necessary to adapt the form of service. Often formal worship is seen as the 'right' way of doing things. However with careful thought those who are successful in ministering to older people often adapt the detail without altering the central principle. This is not however easy and cannot simply be delegated to the most junior student or other less experienced person.

Of course this is not a problem peculiar to the clergy. The care of older patients is often given to those who do not have a choice. It is often those of the lowest status and the least experience who spend most time in direct contact with the recipients of care. They may therefore be the ones in whom the patient confides very personal troubles including spiritual needs. Support to them, including having approachable senior staff, is crucial if 'confidences' are not to become barriers to communication and burdens too much to bear.

Terminal care

Though such problems are not confined to the care of the dying they do very much come to prominence in this type of care. Issues of ethics are never far from the surface and staff support is as important as ever. The first question that often arises is 'To treat or not to treat?'

It is generally supposed that the advancement of medical science has been such that there are now many more options in deciding the best course of action for any particular patient at any given time. If we have more skills available to us then there are more conditions/problems/illnesses which we may be able to treat. For the great majority of us this means that we have to spend less time being ill and more time being well which is all very desirable. However under some circumstances there are problems in that a particular treatment may not relieve the condition, it may appear rather to prolong the agony. Again this is not a problem peculiar to helping older people. Indeed it seems as though the issue is often more prominent in cases involving younger people. Issues of the use of life-support machines and surgery on severely handicapped children are examples of this. In the case of care at the later stage of the life span the problems are actually more prevalent if only because older people are so much more likely than younger people to suffer from multiple handicapping conditions. The question that taxes the doctor may be more likely to be 'Should I prescribe an antibiotic?' rather than a decision about whether to turn off a life-support machine. However the dilemma remains the same. Taking the decision rests on a careful weighing in the balance of the likely benefits against the possible problems. Let us consider a fictitious but hopefully realistic example.

Mrs Sanders is a patient on a continuing care ward for those suffering from severe senile dementia. She has had the condition for many years and until a couple of years ago was looked after at home by her devoted husband. However he was then no longer able to cope and she therefore came into hospital.

She has until very recently been quite active on the ward, walking up and down and smiling at people she meets. She does not seem to know where she is and at times does not appear to recognise her husband although he visits regularly. Just lately she has developed a cough and is reluctant to get out of bed. The doctor on the ward has examined her and she appears to have a chest infection.

Exercise

Do you think she should be treated with an antibiotic?

Is there any other information you think you should know to help decide this?

I suspect that most people would answer 'Yes' to the first question. However the answer is by no means clear cut although the treatment is fairly easily administered and could restore her quite possibly to her previous level of function on the ward. Moreover it is unlikely that her husband would wish that any other course be taken. Suppose however we add a little more to the story.

It is now two days since Mrs Saunders has been unwell. It is 2 a.m. and the nurse on duty notices that Mrs Saunders' condition seems to have deteriorated. The duty doctor is called and when he examines her he finds that she appears to have suffered a stroke. Shortly afterwards Mrs Saunders suffers a cardiac arrest.
Should she be resuscitated?

Probably now the balance of answers will have shifted and perhaps you will be rather more inclined to say 'No'. The treatment now is unlikely to make any impact on her stroke which might well leave her quite disabled and possibly virtually bedbound. However it is asking a lot of someone who is almost certainly a junior member of the medical staff to take a decision not to intervene. The chances are that he or she will pursue active treatment.

If however we were to change the scene slightly so that Mrs Saunders was to suffer her stroke and cardiac arrest in the afternoon things might be different. In this case the doctor attending her is more likely to know the full details of her case. If things are really working well then he will know her husband and may even have had the chance to talk to him about what would happen if she were to deteriorate. It is in fact more likely that he would not intervene.

Now it may be that you would like to argue with the details which I have given. As it is in any case fictitious this makes very little difference. The point I wish to draw out is that the decision process depends on much more than simply the availability of the medical or other expertise. The decision to act or not cannot just be seen as a matter of skill. It is by no means clear what would be the 'right' decision. Most of us are in general agreement with the stated aim of the British Geriatrics Society which is to put life into years not years onto life.

There is of course a special problem in this example in that the patient herself could not give or withhold her informed consent to treatment. Such mental impairment is often a problem in older people both because of dementia, as here, and because of the likelihood of acute confusion accompanying physical illness. Thus there tends to be particular reliance on the advice and attitudes of relatives even though under the English legal system they have no formal rights to determine the administration of care. To involve them would however seem to me to be desirable although in some respects the tradition has been to ignore rather than pander to relatives.

Nonetheless there are occasions when the judgement of the professionals as to the likely benefits of, for example, surgery is not the same as that of the patient's family and this does lead to problems. Also there are exceptional cases where there may be genuine doubts as to whether the family have the best interests of the patient at heart.

We are all too aware these days that in some sad cases parents do not behave lovingly towards their children. It should not come as a total surprise therefore if we find that there are cases where children do not want to do the best for their parents. In contrast to the situation with young children however there is often no easy way for authorities to protect the interests of a vulnerable elderly person. This concerns wider matters than just treatment however and we shall be looking at this in a little more detail in chapter 9.

Making difficult decisions of this sort is a particular feature of terminal care, although for most cases the wishes of the patient are easier to determine than in the example given.

Pain relief

One of the major concerns of the hospice movement has been to promote high standards of care for the dying, especially in regard to pain relief. As I have already noted it is the prospect of a painful dying rather than death itself which is often the main fear. Thus patients gain greatly by learning to trust those who care for them and their ability to manage pain effectively.

Very few people in western society today would see pain as a good thing and our ability to limit this has long been of great importance. There are a whole range of pharmaceutical agents and other treatments which enable us these days to offer enormous relief from the physical pain of terminal illness, notably cancer. However there are still sometimes problems in changing attitudes to the management of pain, both in patients and in staff. I need not go into detail here since this is already well covered by existing books and I have given some examples of these at the end of this chapter.

One often repeated theme is that often pain relief is too little because of fears of tolerance (getting used to the drug) and addiction (getting hooked on the drug). These are not however real problems for the terminally ill. Other factors play a much more important part in determining patients' survival. This is yet another example of how generalising a very useful rule (e.g. 'morphine is addictive') does not work well for a particular situation.

Of course emotional factors also play a part in pain. Fear of pain creates a vicious circle in actually magnifying pain as do other anxieties. The need for those with terminal illness to talk to others is very great, especially to those who are close to them. Thus opportunities for this or for more formal counselling are an important integral part of any terminal care programme.

Talking with the dying

Although good communication is essential to any kind of high quality care, there is a special case for its place in the care of the dying. The main reason for this is that the very fact of a diagnosis of terminal illness may put up a barrier between the patient and those close to him or her. This usually centres around the question of 'Should we tell...?'

It is very easy to be simplistic and to say that every patient has the right to know what is the illness he or she is suffering from and what the outcome is likely to be. As a counterbalance to the view that 'patients are best left in ignorance' this may have some use but I am not at all sure that it is very helpful as a universal guide to dealing with each individual.

It would seem to be more appropriate to draw a distinction between actually confronting someone with a diagnosis and answering them honestly when the question 'What is wrong with me?' arises. Confrontation is very unlikely to be helpful but telling lies is also likely to make things worse.

The extent to which patients are ignorant of their diagnosis in the case of cancer, for example, is generally overestimated. When someone says that 'Mr Jones doesn't know that he has cancer' what they usually mean is that he has not explicitly discussed the diagnosis with the staff. Few patients are very stupid and many draw their own conclusions from such things as other people's looks, tone of voice or even the fact that they have been going to a particular hospital for a course of radiotherapy.

The problems arise when someone draws the wrong conclusions, particularly if this conclusion is that he or she has cancer when in fact this is not so. The other major barrier to effective care is when someone asks 'Do I have cancer?' and is told 'No' when in fact this is the case. The effort of pretence can prove a major burden to both patient and his or her family at a time when close support is especially needed. Some patients and their families do carry on the most elaborate role play where each pretends that the other does not know what in fact is well known to both of them. It would be wrong to say that this is always a bad thing but it does run the risk of greatly straining the important relationship between the patient and family. Moreover the importance of close relationships is especially great at such a time so any hindrance to communication is a major rather than a minor problem.

Help for both of them may take the form of some independent figure helping them to share what they both already know. Obviously privacy and flexibility of visiting arrangements are very important. Regular visiting over a long period may be quite difficult if it sticks to the traditional model of a bunch of grapes and a chat. It is quite easy for those involved to run out of things to say and yet be under great pressure to keep talking and so avoid the awful question 'What is wrong with me?' Giving the family or other frequent visitor something helpful to do for the patient may be very valuable in sustaining the important visits. It may also be easier for 'difficult' topics to be broached when something else, for example some help with practical care, is going on. Obviously relatives also need support in coping with distressing situations, especially cases where the illness leads to disfigurement or problems in communication. There is also, for older patients, more likely to be some loss of mental faculties due either to a dementia or toxic confusion. Again it can be very difficult to visit someone who seems hardly to recognise you any more.

For this reason the relatives of those stricken with severe dementia often describe the experience as one of 'living grief'. The person whom they knew and loved has, in effect, died. Left behind is their body which seems to be controlled now by quite a different person. This new person may be quite different in personality and quite unable to recognise the family or to hold even a simple conversation. There has been a process of progressive bereavement so that when the final physical death comes it may be hard to react as others might expect. For this sort of situation the experience of other relatives may be very helpful. Some even cope by maintaining links with the ward which they have been visiting for so long. It is not that unusual to find someone continuing to visit a ward some time after their own relative has died. Of course as there are almost always some patients who have no immediate family this is often to the mutual benefit of both patient and visitor.

Such a situation is however not the normal reaction to the death of a loved one. Other kinds of help are more likely to be of benefit to most of those who are bereaved.

Bereavement

Because bereavement is such a universal experience and causes such distress it has been the subject of a great deal of study. It would be wrong here to attempt to provide a full account of all that we know of this important topic. For much fuller accounts I recommend that the reader should consult one of the books listed at the end of this chapter.

What I intend to do here is to summarise what are the essential points of these and what are the special issues for bereavement in older people. Of course the first of these is that older people are much more likely to have been bereaved not just once but several times. There is a frequent complaint among the very elderly that they have outlived their friends and loved ones.

In this respect they are actually more likely to be 'experienced' in handling such loss though in saying that I do not imply that the loss is in any way less deeply felt. However there is a general rule that life events are easier to cope with if they are seen as being 'on time'. Indeed we have already noted that this seems to apply to how older people see their own death. Thus if you are in your late eighties then the death of an older brother or sister is still distressing but there may be some comfort from knowing that he or she had a full life span. The reaction to bereavement may therefore be attenuated and adjustment made easier but the elements remain the same.

Normal reactions to bereavement

It is convenient to group the experiences of bereavement into three categories: disbelief, distress and resolution. The first reaction is often one of numbness and unreality. Although the person 'knows' that the one he or she loved has died there is no real feeling of emotional reaction to go with this. In some ways this is often a good thing in that it allows the bereaved person to cope with some of the practical details like finding the will and making the arrangements for the funeral. Those round about may remark on 'how well he [or she] is taking it'. The person him or herself may actually experience thoughts that 'it isn't really true'—they may feel at times that the dead person is going to walk in at the door any minute and it will all turn out to be a bad dream.

Sooner or later however the reality will dawn and true grief will begin. Often this is described as a feeling of release as the pent-up emotions over-whelm the sufferer. These feelings of grief are episodic and the great sadness is accompanied by tearfulness, anxiety, restlessness and other signs of fear and alarm. This reaction is similar to the reactions to stress which we considered in chapter 3.

These feelings are often accompanied by great longing for the dead person and even a feeling of wanting to search for him or her. We use as one of our most common phrases to describe bereavement the notion of 'losing someone'. This feeling of loss is all too real and may carry with it the desire to search for that which is lost. Threading all through this time however are the pangs of grief which may arise apparently spontaneously from a passing thought or from a familiar sight or sound. The bereaved will often describe how just as they thought they were getting over things someone will say something or some other stimulus will cause them to dissolve into tears.

Mixed up with all the other strong emotions is very often anger and its frequent partner, guilt. Sometimes the anger may be directed at those around the person. It may include those who try to give words of comfort and those who have provided care and attention. 'You *don't* know how it feels so don't try to tell me that you do' might be one expression of this. Anger may also be directed at the dead person: 'How dare he go and leave me with all this to cope with on my own.'

Such thoughts in themselves may lead to feelings of guilt as they are directed against someone to whom the person had been very close. Alternatively there may be feelings of guilt associated with coincidental events surrounding the death. For example there may be feelings that 'If only I had...' covering such things as 'stayed in instead of going to the shops' or 'not had that row with him last night' or any one of many different themes. Here there is either the idea that the death was in some way preventable or that the person died with some doubt over the relationship which has been severed. In either case it is now too late for the person left behind to make amends.

In the great majority of cases these feelings of grief, anger and so on are gradually superseded by some form of adjustment. There are several experiences which help this to happen. One of these is the feeling of presence.

Many people who are bereaved experience some sort of feeling that the person they have lost is still with them. Indeed this may at times be so strong as to appear as an hallucination. Usually these are quite fleeting and take the form of thinking, for example, that the dead person has called one's name or that there is the sound of his or her footsteps coming up the path. Others may describe just a feeling that the person is still around. These feelings are comforting rather than distressing and so contrast with the yearnings to search which I have already mentioned.

Somewhat similar to this is the sense of becoming oneself more like the person who has died. This may mean adopting some mannerism, habit or hobby which characterised the dead person. This may even be noticed by friends or may simply be a feeling of comfort from sitting in a favourite chair or some other familiar spot.

Another process which helps all of us adjust to trauma is that of desensitisation. In states of acute grief every kind of stimulus, thought, sound or sight of something associated with the dead person brings great emotional distress. However with repeated exposure to these things the reaction gradually diminishes. The powerful emotions which are generated may lead to the bereaved person tending to avoid the situations which provoke this. Unfortunately this hinders the process of recovery even though it may make things easier in the short term. This sort of avoidance occurs in other situations also. For example in the last chapter I mentioned how some people faced with a sudden handicap or disfigurement may avoid all contact with this. Thus someone may initially be unable even to look at their colostomy bag following emergency bowel surgery. Obviously there are then problems in terms of that person learning to change the bag and so regain independence. The process of graduallly increasing and repeated exposure accompanied by appropriate support and reassurance is similar to that which is required for the bereaved.

In the case of the bereaved it seems that there is some natural reaction, including the 'searching' which I have already described, which means that this happens without the need for special help. Of course, as we shall see, things can and do go wrong but for most people the grief gradually abates and it is possible to encounter the reminders without being greatly upset.

Indeed for many people the time when they are able to face doing something like sorting out the dead person's clothes or visiting a favourite place is often seen as a landmark in their progress towards readjustment.

It has been suggested that 'selective forgetting' may be one of the strategies which helps people to adjust to bereavement. Certainly this is a very real phenomenon whereby we tend to forget things which are painful or distressing. However there is often in contrast quite vivid recollection of the dead person so the 'selection' must be for parts (e.g. remembering the good times) rather than the whole.

The process of readjustment also often involves rethinking the loss and the implications for one's life. There is a process of gradually making sense of what has happened, of adjusting one's perception of the world and one's own place in it. This often means rethinking 'doing things alone' as now the need for company, for example, may be much more important than it was before. Acceptance of the new situation requires a good deal of hard work, at least hard emotional work. It is often argued that if this work, the grief work, is not done then there can be no very satisfactory outcome. Certainly it is true that there are many instances where people have, for example, not been able to cry or otherwise release their distress. This state of affairs may mean that the person postpones experiencing the distress of grief.

To this extent there is some sense in which things may get stuck so that proper adjustment is inhibited. However there also are cases where the individual seems to remain emotionally over-reactive. In this situation distraction may be more important to reduce a preoccupation with grief. Failure to overcome this is likely to lead to difficulties with social relationships as friends and family tire of continual grief.

Because of this notion of the process of adjustment getting stuck, bereavement is sometimes described as having 'stages'. This implies that there is some sort of orderly progression from one stage to the next. However this is not a very accurate picture because what actually tends to happen is rather less orderly. There is indeed a gradual trend from a state of disbelief to one of adjustment but the change is rarely orderly. Things other people say, the snatch of a familiar song or the occurence of an anniversary can interrupt the calm adjustment with pangs of grief. This does not necessarily mean that someone has failed to adjust, that in some way the process has got stuck before it is properly finished. Problems of adjustment are rather more complicated than this.

Unfortunately many of us seem to think that emotional readjustment ought to follow the same sort of orderly recovery as when we are getting over physical illness. When we get a cold or flu we feel steadily worse over a few days and gradually get better. We 'know' that if we are feeling better today than yesterday, by tomorrow we shall feel better again. The path of recovery is a steady progress.

However in the case of changing feelings then the process is more variable. Because we are all subject to emotional changes from day to day the progress may be 'two steps forward and one back' rather than steadily forwards. This often leads to feelings of dismay when people have a 'bad day' after things have begun to improve. It is easy to see the decline as part of a relapse rather than as a temporary set-back. What is more important is how things are going over a rather longer time. Looking back over, for example, the past month may reveal that there is a steady trend which is apparent beyond the day to day fluctuations. If the steady shift is towards having more good days and fewer bad ones then comparing today with yesterday may not be very helpful.

Abnormal grief

One of the ways that we perceive problems of adjustment is if the grief is excessively prolonged. Of course this rather begs the question 'How long is too long?'

Certainly in bereavement we are concerned with adjustments over weeks and months rather than hours or days. This can make it difficult to tell the difference between a normal process of grieving and a problem of depression. Certainly if I am told that someone lost their spouse a month ago it would not be surprising if that person were to cry easily and feel distressed. If the loss were 18 months ago one might well interpret the situation rather differently.

It is therefore difficult to be exact about when a grief becomes prolonged, though certainly one might as a rule of thumb look for some definite signs of adjustment a few months after the death. Of course we must not forget the importance of anniversaries. If someone is said to be 'depressed' although his or her spouse died a year ago it is very important to find out exactly when he or she was widowed. If it turns out that it was exactly a year ago last Thursday then the anniversary itself may be of importance in determining how that person feels. Similarly it is not uncommon to find that a particular place evokes memories of the dead person. This is especially the case for hospitals where someone may be thinking of their spouse because he or she died in the hospital where they now are.

Both of these examples relate to situations where we might expect things to improve with time or with a return to home. In other cases it may be the home itself which holds more memories and is thus associated with the grief. Being unable to go into certain rooms or an inability to face clearing out a wardrobe may reflect problems in adjustment. In most cases these are basically problems of avoidance and some form of repeated exposure to these situations is likely to be the best way forward. This needs to be done in such a way that the person stays in the situation even if there is a recurrence of grief. The problems usually arise because at the first sign of upset the person leaves the situation. To overcome this it is important that the inclination to flight is resisted. However it is best resisted by a reducing rather than increasing tension. As we saw before, the tension of getting ready to fight can add directly to that of emotional distress. This may mean that the exposure must be quite gradual, initially indeed it may involve no more than talking about the dead person and what he or she used to like to do. It is often very thelpful to make use of photographs or other mementoes to assist in this process. Similarly it may be best initially for there to be someone present so that he or she can provide support and reassurance.

The same principle would apply to helping those who are seeming to avoid social contact. It may be best for someone to go with the bereaved person the first time that they start going to the day centre, bowls club or whatever. Actually the most frequent complaint of the bereaved is not that they cannot face other people but that other people cannot face them. There is a real problem with people not wishing to meet with the bereaved because they do not know what to say. This is very sad because very often they do not need to *say* anything very much. The important thing is to be there and to listen.

My own experience of helping older people suggests that this problem of feeling outcast may be slightly less for them than for younger people. This may just be because by the time you are in your eighties you are much more likely to be experienced in both talking with and being 'the bereaved'. As it is more common and more expected so it is more accepted. Against this however is the fact that the older you are, the more likely it is that you live alone and that you have some infirmity which restricts how easily you can get out to meet people. Thus the best support for some people may be help with transport rather than intensive bereavement counselling.

A few people have problems of absent rather than prolonged grief. This is usually a problem where the person has had long-standing difficulties in expressing emotions. Such a person may have never cried following the death of a loved one and the subsequent events suggest that this lack of grieving is a real problem. Again we can look at this as a problem of avoidance but in this case the difficulties are much more within the individual and it is therefore rather less easy to unlock the problem.

This is not to say that such problems are not amenable to help. They most certainly are. It is simply to make the point that it is often a little more difficult to identify and tackle problems in thoughts and feelings which are not associated with any particular outside event. In the case of older people the difficulty may be compounded by a general reluctance to talk about feelings. This is not some mysterious change that arises as a part of the 'ageing process'. Rather it reflects the different expectations of the various generations. The whole movement towards psychological therapy has been very recent in historical terms. Even words like 'anxiety' have only come into general use in the course of this century. It is hard to say why this might be but in some ways it may be that having to be less preoccupied with basic necessities of life we are now more free to worry!

Whatever the reason there is often a reluctance to discuss emotions and this sort of topic can be very good for illustrating the phenomenon of selective deafness. Anyone with any significant experience of older people will recognise the problem of someone with impaired hearing tending to focus on the things which he or she wants to hear. This need not be a conscious process, nor indeed is it in any way abnormal. We are all, for example, pre-tuned to our own name so that even in a crowded room our ears prick up if someone mentions our name.

This phenomenon is much more common in older people than is the selective forgetting which I referred to earlier. It is an especial problem in trying to use group work with older people as it is all too easy for important messages to be misunderstood. Of course this is something which applies to all sorts of 'talking treatment', not just to helping the bereaved. But having to adapt to meet these needs does not invalidate the underlying aims or indeed the basic methods.

Other problems of grieving can arise when the distress is unexpected, for example even someone you disliked can be the cause of grief. Sadly there are lots of cases where older people do not get on well one with another. Again this has to do with being people rather than with being old. In fact if the divorce rate is anything to go by, older people have some important lessons to teach us on how to make relationships last. However there are nonetheless times when, for example, a older person dies and this marks the end of an unhappy rather than a happy relationship. The one left behind may expect, and so may his or her friends, that this will be in some ways a relief. It comes as quite a surprise when the loss leads to acute grief. In fact because the relationship has been poor there is often less good selectively to remember and readjustment can be really quite a problem. The bereaved person may miss the rows and the aggravation and may even resent that the deceased has had the last word! In such cases it is important to help the person to understand why it is that they are feeling such grief and to encourage the same sort of processes of adjustment as apply to 'normal' grief.

There is also sometimes a problem of paradoxical loss when someone dies after long illness. Although there is the comfort that the person who was so ill is now free from pain and distress, there can be extra losses. This is because the bereaved person may have been the principal carer and this no longer fills their life. Even when someone has been looked after in a hospital or in a home the routine of visiting gives structure and meaning to a life which can seem very empty once this has gone. This may partly explain why sometimes those who are bereaved in this way continue to visit the ward where they have been going for so long. Often this is to visit some other person who they have got to know there so that the sense of useful routine can continue. As I noted earlier, the person they now visit is likely to be someone who would otherwise have no visitors and such a relationship is to their mutual advantage.

Common to the ending of both good and bad relationships can be the loss of the individual's greatest prompt for activity. Cooking for one seems a thankless task and many other activities seem the same. If you have always done things together then it is hard suddenly to be alone. We must also remember that the need for affection does not disappear at 60 so that loss of physical contact leaves a very real gap. In her autobiographical view of ageing which I cited at the end of chapter 1 Mary Stott describes how important grandchildren and pets can be in substituting for the lost partner in terms of affection.

Some of the multiple losses which result from widowhood may account for the fact that the widowed are such a high risk group. Modern medicine does not generally go in for diagnosing people as dying from a broken heart.

This sounds more like Mills & Boone than the *Lancet*. Nonetheless several carefully conducted studies have shown that those who are recently widowed do show increased risk of dying themselves. What is more the effect is most pronounced when we look at death from heart disease. In a study of widowers aged over 54 it was found that the mortality rate during the first 6 months after bereavement was 40% above that which would be expcted for married men of comparable age (Young *et al*. 1963). The mortality rate from heart disease was up by 67%.

A study in a Welsh town found that more than 1 in 25 of the relatives of those who died were themselves dead a year after their bereavement. Less than 1 in 140 of comparable non-bereaved people had died (Rees and Lutkins 1967).

Other studies have shown that the bereaved are more likely to suffer from a variety of physical and, especially, mental problems. Thus there is a very real sense in which helping those who are bereaved can potentially act to prevent other problems. What can be done to help older people who are bereaved?

Exercise

List as many organisations as you can which might be relevant to helping bereaved older people.

Do you know how to contact each of these and exactly what they do?

Check these lists against the sorts of help identified in the rest of this chapter.

Helping older people grieve

Many of the principles of help are the same as those which would apply to helping those with other kinds of emotional distress. Perhaps the first and most obvious of these is the importance of listening. For the bereaved person it is very important for them to have the opportunity to talk about what has happened, the death itself, and about the person they have lost. This is, particularly at first, quite distressing and leads to repeated episodes of acute grief. As I have previously suggested this can be a problem if it inhibits those around the person from simply listening. Mostly people find it distressing to see another person upset and all the more so if they have any feeling that they are the cause of this.It may seem that every time you go next door to talk to Mrs Baker who was widowed recently all she does is burst into tears. You can easily reach the conclusion that you are doing more harm than good. This is in fact very unlikely to be the case but listening to someone grieving is very hard emotional work and not particularly rewarding in the short term. It may be necessary to take a rather longer-term view and look back over several weeks or even months to see how someone is changing for the better.

The complaint that the bereaved make that they are being ignored is mirrored by those around them who complain that they do not know what to say. In fact this usually means that they don't know what to say to make the person feel better, as if in some way such a thing could be said. All too often however there is no such magic phrase, or at least if there is no one has yet let me in on the secret. What is important is to be there as a listener rather than as a talker. This on its own may not be very easy, especially if you are listening to someone being very upset. It may actually be easier to 'do' something so that practical help becomes the explicit reason for being there. This may be a very good thing. There are often very many things that need to be done. In the short term this includes things like making the funeral arrangements or dealing with a will. Later on it may include help with sorting out belongings or redecorating a room.

If this kind of practical help is in addition to listening then the arrangement is obviously an agreeable one. It is important however to avoid the situation where doing something becomes an excuse for avoiding listening. If every time the person approaches the subject of their loved one the visitor is compelled to make a cup of tea or clean the curtains then the really important work, that of grieving, is not going to be helped at all.

Some of the problems that can arise relate to what the person who is grieving may say. Because grief is so disruptive and overwhelming the person may say many things that in another context might be given quite different meaning. For example it will be quite common for someone to say that they can see no future without their husband or wife and that they would hope to die themselves before too long. In fact as we have already seen there is some tendency for this to come true in that widowers do show a higher risk of dying during the first year of their bereavement. However we must be careful to distinguish this from the suicidal thinking and intent of deep depression. This may be precipitated by grief but it will be accompanied by other signs of depression. This can be a difficult distinction to make and where there is some doubt this needs professional advice.

Similarly the person may say quite angry or hurtful things about the one they have lost or indeed about the person who is trying to help them. Again the things said in grief are not necessarily typical of more considered reaction. Feelings of resentment against the loved one because he or she has left them to cope alone may engender feelings of guilt or that one must be going out of one's mind to say such things. Here it is important to provide some reassurance that such thoughts are not uncommon and that they show the strength rather than the weakness of the bond that has been broken.

Indeed the distinction must often be drawn between the emotion which is being expressed and the words used to express this. It is quite possible to accept, for example, the fact that someone is feeling lost and alone without agreeing that the only way out is for them to join their loved one in death as soon as possible. Similarly thoughts of anger and resentment betray the person's distress rather than any very accurate reflection of how they got on with the person who has died. Of course they *may* be an accurate reflection of how the relationship really was but this is not necessarily so.

This sort of reaction to extreme emotion and other aspects of grief can be quite unexpected in both their intensity and nature. Even brief hallucinations, such as thinking you hear the dead person calling your name, which are quite common, may leave a person frightened that they are going mad. They may even be reluctant to admit to these things for fear that other people will think this. Knowledge of what is 'normal' is important in reassuring someone that they are not on the brink of insanity.

Delayed grief

Thus far we have been considering the problems of listening to and helping those who are grieving. The start of this process is not normally a problem. It starts quite naturally and indeed resolves in just the same way. The process may even have a timetable prescribed by religious custom which will, at the appropriate time, encourage the expression of grief as part of mourning. The expression of emotion will also be different in different cultures and a proper understanding of this is essential to interpreting each individual's grief.

However there are times when the bereaved person may avoid all mention of the person who has died to the extent that grieving as such cannot properly take place. Even though this is quite obviously not 'normal' in the sense that most people do not react in this way, it may be tempting to see this as desirable, almost 'super-normal'. Thus it may be that someone will be described by acquaintances as having 'taken it very well' when in fact this means that he or she has not been observed to have shed a tear. There may be many reasons for this. It is likely to be more of a problem for British men than for British women as the expectation of the control of emotions is especially strong for them. It is a 'problem' when the failure to resolve the grief leads to other expressions of distress. For example the distress may be expressed in terms of physical symptoms, such as 'chest pain' so that a bereaved person is repeatedly taken into hospital when no problem of organic heart disease is found.

In the situation where lack of grief appears to be a problem it may be helpful to explore using photographs or other mementoes to stimulate thinking of the person who has died. This must be done with care and compassion, not with confrontation. However simple questions such as 'What did ... like to do?' or 'Is that your wife/husband in that picture?' may be of considerable value. As always the trust in the relationship is very important. This sort of enquiry from someone who is seen as a stranger can just appear downright nosey rather than genuinely concerned. Again the emphasis must be on empathy and sincerity.

Starting again

Beyond the torment of acute grief lies the need to start again. For many older people this means beginning to get used to being on one's own. This may be very unfamiliar since it can well be 50 or 60 years since that person was last alone for any prolonged period. Moreover it is not just the loneliness that is a problem but the taking on of new tasks.

It may not be the intention of twentieth-century feminism but there seems to me little doubt that there is likely to be great benefit to future generations of widows and widowers in the sharing of traditionally separated roles. It is all too common now to find a widower who does not know how to cook or a widow who cannot drive and is bemused by banking. This follows quite naturally from the very strictly defined roles which each sex took in terms of household and other tasks. It is not however a good prescription for coping on you own to have given up all responsibilities in certain areas of your life for at least 40 years.

Taking on new roles, learning to do new things is not as easy when you are in your late seventies or eighties. This is *not* to say that older people cannot learn new things. There is plenty of evidence to indicate that they can learn new skills. However there is evidence that learning to do new things does take rather longer as you grow older. So having to learn to do lots of new things at a time when you are just getting over a major emotional trauma and you are of advanced years is not the best recipe for success. All too often the answer is that others take on the things that the person 'cannot' do and in doing so further undermine skills and self-esteem. It may seem like a good idea to take on the shopping for an elderly man who has always relied on his late wife for this. However if he could be helped to do this, and perhaps some cooking, cleaning etc., he will be much better off in the long term. Unfortunately this 'helping along' takes rather longer than 'taking over' and is often less acceptable to the person needing help. It requires a change in thinking for all those concerned to move from doing for to doing with.

Perhaps we could learn something from the slogans used these days for providing help to developing countries. These often echo the theme 'Give a man a fish and you feed him for a day. Teach him to fish and you feed him for life.' Should we not also be saying 'Give a man meals-on-wheels and you feed him for a day. Help him learn to cook and you feed him all week'?

Of course in this case the benefits are even greater. If that person is also then going out shopping, he is also going to be less isolated, get more exercise and even feel like eating more!

The problems of learning to cope alone are not simply those of doing for yourself. They also include doing by yourself. The pattern of social contact for an elderly couple, for example, may be that they have always done things together. This may especially be the case when they have both lived into their eighties. It is then quite likely that they have been together for 20 or

25 years since the last one of them retired from full-time work. Thus they have become very used to doing everything, going everywhere, together. Being alone, even on a bus never mind at a social gathering, is going to be very strange. We know from studies of learning that if circumstances change behaviour also changes. This is why some people find it helpful to get a new tablecloth to help them stick to a new diet.

The death of a spouse is a much more major change but part of the problem is the same. The cue or prompt for doing things has gone. Thus even if you are quite used to cooking or cleaning it may be difficult to 'feel like' doing it when you are on your own. Again here is an example where the most appropriate sort of help is that which prompts and encourages rather than takes over.

Who helps?

As I have already said, most people rely on their family and friends to help them through the grief and to reach an adjustment to their bereavement. This is the best remedy for the majority and there is no need for us to consider any special help in such cases. We must remember however that many older people, especially those who are very elderly, do not have any immediate family. About one in three of those over the age of 75 have no surviving children. They either never had children or have outlived them. A similar proportion live alone and the most common type of 'pensioner household' is a married couple with only each other for company. Thus we must look carefully at the needs of older people for extra support at times of bereavement. It may be necessary to offer some voluntary or even professional help in order to substitute for the absent friends and family.

I am not suggesting however that we should thrust eager volunteers at every elderly person who has recently been widowed and is living alone. However there is no doubt that we should ensure that there is someone to whom they can turn for help if they so wish. Such people have certainly been identified, for example, as a group who could usefully receive a call from a health visitor specialising in work with older people. Whatever the means we choose, the objective should be to see that each person has at least some kind of social network together with the skills and resources to cope from day to day.

Some will need extra help. Extra emotional help may be explicitly the need but more often it will come 'attached' to some sort of practical help. Thus you may not need a psychotherapist: more likely you will need a home help who is a good listener. What must be done is to ensure that the package given is complete. It is no good pretending that a 'meals-on-wheels' service which relies on spending no more than 2 minutes in each house can provide anything useful by way of emotional support or practice in cookery.

Because bereavement is such a universal experience there may be no special arrangements necessary to meet others who have suffered similar loss.

Those with whom the bereaved person meets day to day may be just the sort of people who can help most. Indeed this is especially the case for older people who are particularly likely to share this experience.

However for younger people and for a minority of older people it can be very helpful to receive support from others who have been through grief. This is the origin of organisations such as CRUSE which are based on mutual self-help for the bereaved. Other schemes have been developed specifically for older people, for example by local Age Concern groups. Certainly any sort of counselling scheme for older people will include helping many who are trying to readjust following bereavenment.

Probably the most obvious source of explicit help for the grieving is the church. As I noted earlier, participation in formal worship tends to decline with advancing years, but interest in spiritual matters may increase (Moberg 1965). Those who have always maintained contact with their particular church will have at least this potential source of support in their bereavement. There will be many others who may resume contact at such a time and benefit in this way. Even those who have not taken part in regular worship may find it very important to attend a funeral service as part of the process of grieving. In almost all circumstances it is most important that the bereaved person attends the funeral of their loved one.

Forgetfulness and grief

There can be particular problems in helping those who are suffering from abnormal memory loss and who have been bereaved. As some 20–25% of those over the age of 80 are afflicted by dementia this combination of problems is by no means uncommon.

The main question that arises is: 'Should we tell?' The forgetful person may at times, indeed sometimes persistently, refer to their loved one, usually a husband or wife, as if he or she were still alive. This can lead quickly to practical problems if the person also feels that they should therefore be leaving, for example, the residential home, because the loved one is waiting for them at home. Is it not unkind to remind that person that they are bereaved and should we not leave them is this happy delusion?

In fact for the majority the delusion is not a happy one. In most cases the person who has died is still perceived as 'lost', even if it is 'missing' rather than 'dead'. It must be a matter of judgement in the individual case but very many of those in this position will fairly easily accept the correct facts. Certainly there is little ground for never telling someone that their spouse has died just because they are 'confused'. If the intellectual impairment is very severe then the impact will be very little. If it is less severe grieving can take place and some adjustment to reality begin. Attending the funeral is an important part in this and even a slight delay can mean that the opportunity is missed. It then becomes progressively more difficult to reveal the truth and any sort of adjustment progressively more unlikely.

We cannot expect the rest of the world to collude with us and the effect of some visiting friend or relative letting slip the truth is unlikely to be minimal. Of course telling the truth will mean having do do more work, will mean having to give more support, but that should not be the reason for any such secrecy.

This kind of secrecy, whether it be about a terminal illness or about a death, can be particularly difficult for families. It can set up very real barriers between older people and their children. Families are at the centre of help for older people and it is to their needs that we now turn.

References

MacDonald, A. J. D., and Dunn, G. (1982) Death and expressed wish to die in the elderly: an outcome study. *Age and Ageing* **11** 189–195.

Moberg, D. O. (1965) Religiosity in old age. *Gerontologist* **5** 78.

Rees, W. D., and Lutkins, S. G. (1967) Mortality of bereavement. *British Medical Journal* **(iv)** 13.

Young, M., Benjamin, B., and Wallice, C. (1963) Mortality of widowers. *Lancet* **(ii)** 454.

Further reading

Parkes, C. M. (1986) *Bereavement: Studies of Grief in Adult Life* (2nd edition) Penguin: Harmondsworth

With good reason this remains the standard British book on this topic.

Bowling, A., and Cartwright, A. (1982) *Life After a Death: A Study of the Elderly Widowed* Tavistock Publications: London

Reports the results of interviews with a group of older people and describes their feelings, thoughts and patterns of adjustment.

Stott, N. C. H., and Finlay, I. G. (1984) *Care of the Dying: A Clinical Handbook* Churchill Livingstone: Edinburgh

Covers mainly the medical aspects but also the emotional needs of the dying.

Kubler–Ross, E. (1974) *Questions and Answers on Death and Dying* Collier-Macmillan: London

Covers many of the questions that both staff and relatives find difficult to ask.

Section II
Getting on with Others

Chapter 6

Family and Friends

One of the most important statistics of ageing is the number of older people who live outside institutions. Among those aged over 65 years, for every one person living in a home or hospital there are 19 living elsewhere. Not surprisingly, many of those 19 are as frail or disabled as the one in a home or hospital. For those at home, rather than in a home, it is family and friends who provide the great bulk of help and support. Without their help the frail older person would be unable to look after him or herself and would quite likely require such intensive care as could only be provided in a home or hospital.

There is much enthusiasm for community care because of the choice it gives people to live independently. However in reality there are very few circumstances where it can be said that prolonged high dependency care can be provided in a person's own home where there are not family or friends to provide the backbone of this care. Like our own backbone, we tend to take this for granted until there are problems. There is often a great deal of fuss made when someone says they can no longer cope with looking after an old person at home. What continually surprises me is that so many people cope for so long without being overwhelmed.

Most older people would indeed prefer to be looked after at home by their family or friends rather than go into an institution. In helping older people we must therefore pay deliberate attention to how we can help those who look after them. This is one of the few cases where compassion and cost coincide. Supporting family and friends in looking after an older person at home is both cheaper and more acceptable to most people. It is usually cheaper than looking after someone in a home or hospital and always cheaper than providing continual paid help in the person's own home.

It is often said that we do not care as much for older people as did previous generations. Through the mists of nostalgia it is somehow perceived that there was a time when the community really did care and old people lived out

101

their days at home. Serious study of the history of caring and British society does not however bear this out. For example sometimes people think that things were better in the time of Queen Victoria when family values formed the foundation of the Empire. However the proportion of older people in institutions then was about the same as now. The increased numbers of old people's homes is because there are a lot more older people not because no one wants to look after older people at home any more. Before the Victorians things were even worse. It required legislation such as the Poor Law to make most parishes do anything for those who were vulnerable because of age or infirmity. Even with this there was every incentive to find reasons why a particular person did not belong in the parish and therefore to insist that they moved on.

Similarly comparisons are often made between different cultures, with western society usually being cast in the role of the heartless materialist. It is assumed that other cultures do much better at caring for their older citizens. This is however a difficult comparison to make since the phenomenon of the ageing society is only now just beginning to overtake developing countries. Indeed the pace of change there is proportionately faster than in the so-called developed countries. It may well be that such countries where there are such greatly increasing numbers of older people will in fact do much better than we have done in terms of integrating their care into traditional family patterns. It is however too early to draw any conclusions.

What we do already know is that there is an enormous amount of caring going on at present in our own society. This care is often unrecognised, especially where the care is successful and no demands are made of any official services. There is no statutory requirement for anybody to visit older people, as there is with children, and see if they are in need of help. Most of the time those who have to provide official help are kept too fully occupied dealing with those whom they know about to worry about those as yet unknown.

However there have been several attempts in recent years to survey systematically the needs of older people for everyday help and how that help is provided. There is general consistency about the findings and I shall therefore use the results of one of these to illustrate how important are family and friends in this regard.

The study to which I shall refer was part of a large scale health survey of over 1,000 people aged 70 years and over living at home (Jones and Vetter 1984). The subjects were chosen from the registers of two General Practices. In one practice every person aged over 70 was included and in the other a random sample was chosen from that age group. All the subjects were interviewed individually in their own home.

Where it was found that the older person needed help with one or more of a number of everyday activities, like shopping or taking a bath, the person was asked to identify if there was someone providing help informally (i.e. not being paid) and that carer was also interviewed. In this way it was possible to obtain information not only on the sort of practical help being provided but also on how the burden of care was affecting the carers (Jones *et al.* 1983).

The first point to note is how relatively little was the contribution of formal services. Out of the original sample of 1,079 people aged over 70, 330 reported needing help at least once a week. Two hundred and seventy nine of them could identify one person as their main carer, 6 were helped equally by more than one person and 37 were in residential accommodation (an old people's home). So less than $3\frac{1}{2}\%$ of those over 70 were in a home. This is only slightly higher than the proportion found for all those over retirement age which is about $2\frac{1}{2}\%$.

Almost nine times as many people were living at home and relying on someone else to provide help at least once a week. In fact using a standard scale of disability nearly half of these were rated as severely disabled so it is not just the fairly fit who remain at home. Of all these people living at home only 28 rely on a statutory helper for their main support: this is less than one in ten of those needing help.

By far and away the biggest group of helpers were the informal carers, the daughters, sons, wives, husbands, neighbours and so on. This group of 1,079 old people had help from no less than 259 relatives and friends. This hardly suggests that people do not care.

What sort of people are carers?

Four out of five carers were women. One carer in four was the husband or wife of the older person and two out of five were the daughter of the old person. Thus, despite the high profile given in recent years to the tendency for women to continue to have paid jobs after marriage, the typical carer may still be thought of either as a spouse, who is likely him or herself to be elderly, or, more commonly, as a daughter caring for an aged parent. Even if we consider only those for whom the main carer actually lives in the same house, for every ten such people, four are looked after by wife or husband and three are looked after by a daughter.

This may well change in the future: it could be a good example of a cohort effect. But if we are concerned with the pattern of care for the late twentieth century then we are right in thinking of this as something mainly done by women.

As to age, about half of the informal carers were aged between 45 and 64 years old. However one in five was aged over 75 so we cannot think of the carer as necessarily being young or middle-aged. Obviously the older carer tends to be someone caring for their husband or wife but this is not necessarily the case. As there are steadily more and more very elderly people, so there are more and more older carers. Thus the lady aged 90 whom I visited recently was telling me of the death recently of her niece who was 'only' 73. This lady is looked after by her daughter who is herself well past retirement age and indeed is herself a grandmother. This means that for many people who are middle-aged or older, just when they might have expected to have been freed from the burden of raising a family this is replaced by that of caring for an older person.

The position of the daughter caring for an ageing parent has been described as the dilemma of the woman in the middle (Brody 1981). Such a woman is in middle age and caught in the middle between an ageing parent and a growing family. This is certainly still true for many but there are also those who are caught between the responsibility of being a caring daughter and that of being a doting grandmother. The changes of an ageing population make a nonsense of very many of our ideas about which role goes with what age. It may even therefore happen that the disabilities which we think go with ageing affect the daughter rather than the mother. Certainly it is quite possible for the carer to have to look after both a parent and a spouse who are in some way limited by such disability as is more commonly found in old age. A daughter may be faced with wanting to provide care for both a mother and a husband who have each suffered a stroke or some other disability. In understanding the needs of carers we must take due note of the *multiple* demands placed upon the carer, not simply on the needs of the particular older person who is the reason for our concern.

Hopes and fears

I have already said that most older people would like to live independently in their own home and be in touch with their family. The element of individual choice is however crucial and it is as wrong to make assumptions about this aspect of ageing as about any other. It is very easy to impose our own ideas of what is 'best' for somebody. We can be wrong in either direction, either assuming that someone needs help they do not want or independence that they would rather do without.

The sort of care that people expect is very much influenced by their background and experience. This may be much more important than the effects of growing older, in other words it may be a cohort effect. I noted in an earlier chapter that how we view the standards of today's average old people's home will depend on what we compare it with. This may or may not also be true of our view of 'community care' but there can certainly be age differences, or at least disability differences, in this also.

For example there is evidence that the balance between the need for independence, freedom and individual choice on the one hand and the need for security and safety shifts as people grow frailer. Many older people thus find that as long as they stay healthy they are determined to stay in their own home and resist the idea of any kind of 'home'. However as they become frailer they are more likely, though by no means inevitably, to be drawn towards the attractions of having less responsibility and someone around to provide help when they need it. Where people have a choice, and that usually means when they can afford it, they are likely to choose to go into some form of 'caring' environment before this is absolutely necessary. This preserves a sense of self-determination which it is much harder to sustain if you become disabled and then find that you are forced to make a similar move.

Although there is now a good deal of talk about how much better it is to be looked after in your own home, the choice of many is not this. Of course there are lots of people in homes or hospitals who wish they could have stayed at home. The message must be that we have to have an adequate supply of many different sorts of care available to those who need or wish this.

The problem for those who have very limited income is that all too often they have only Hobson's choice. There are very few places in any kind of sheltered care. These are therefore given to those who need it now, not to those who might need it in a few years' time. There is an assumption that the providers, not the consumers, know best.

There have been attempts to ask older people what sort of care they would like and whom they would like to provide this. The results simply confirm that it is wrong to think that there is only one answer. Almost every possible form of care is preferred by somebody.

The role of the family is no exception in this. Some older people wish, or in some cases assume, that they will be looked after by their own family 'come what may'. Others wish to remain independent for as long as possible but would definitely not wish to be a burden on their children and would much rather seek some other form of care. Of course it is often quite difficult to find out what exactly someone does want, especially in such a sensitive and important area as this. It may be that a person says one thing which he or she thinks to be the 'right and proper' answer but secretly would dearly like something else entirely. These are often not matters that can be discussed quickly since the factors involved are so complex. One very real danger is that others, be they friends, relatives or professionals, will try to be too clever. It is very easy to think that we can see beyond the veneer of what someone is saying to what they truly feel. However this usually says more about our own vanity than our depth of understanding.

In some circumstances, for example when talking to someone in front of their family, there will of course be great pressures to say the right thing or to hold back for fear of upsetting someone. However there is usually no good reason for not taking things at their face value if such factors are removed. In other words if a person can have the time to talk about their own wishes to someone they trust and in private, finding out the 'truth' is not a great problem. The same skills of good listening apply here as they did to the matters discussed in chapter 3. What people need is a good and wise counsellor. I shall have more to say on how to help people make decisions about care a little later.

The relationship between dependent and carer

Just as we are all unique individuals, so are our relationships. It should not be any great surprise to find that how well somebody copes with caring for a frail elderly person depends on their relationship with that person. It *should* be no surprise, but frequently it seems to be so. Perhaps this is because we have some stereotype of the typical relationship between husband and wife, mother and daughter and so on. This probably owes more to our own family than to any systematic study of the relationships of older people. We can make assumptions based on ourselves when considering things like anatomy and physiology and be right most of the time. Doing the same for social relations is much less certain.

Indeed we know remarkably little about the detailed way in which personal relationships affect the process and outcome of care for older people. We often talk about the details of relationships in trying to help individuals but there is remarkably little systematic study of caring relationships. This is in part because the role of informal carers as a whole has been much neglected, though this is changing. It may also be because the relationships are very complicated and difficult to study, especially when there are ever growing numbers of people needing help.

Nonetheless, even the trends that have already emerged seem to be ignored more than recognised. This is a great pity because the relationship between dependent and carer, or even whether or not there is an informal carer at all, is more closely related to what happens to a frail older person than whether or not they receive help from official bodies such as health or social services. From existing studies of those being looked after at home by an informal carer we can say with some certainty that both the length and type of relationship between carer and dependent are important.

The longest relationships tend to be those of marriage and there is no doubt that having a husband or wife makes a big difference to whether someone can continue to be looked after at home when he or she becomes physically or mentally frail. As far as the process of informal care and support is concerned, marriage is special for at least two reasons. The first of these is time.

It is not uncommon for an elderly couple to have been married for 40 or 50 years and with very few exceptions they have married for longer than they have had children. There are cases of course where older people have remarried, usually where both are elderly widows seeking companionship. This may or may not be recent, for example even a second marriage may have lasted 20 years. On the whole however older people tend to have been married very much longer than younger people.

The second important thing about marriage is the origin of the relationship, namely it generally starts and continues as a mutual voluntary agreement. People do not usually get married until they are adults not only biologically but socially. There can of course be cultural differences here but for the great majority this is therefore a relationship which has been freely entered into and for which there is at least the hope and expectation that it will last 'until death us do part'. During a long marriage there will likely be times when each of the partners has needed some particular help or support from the other. Increasing frailty, especially if it happens gradually, blends into this pattern of long-term mutual support. If things are difficult the carer may be able to look back and think of some particular time in the past when the person who needs care now has been the carer. Having to give support now can therefore be seen as a chance to repay this past support.

Not surprisingly therefore those being looked after by a husband or wife tend to stay at home longer than those being cared for by other relatives or by friends and neighbours. This has been shown to be so for frail older people in general and for the special group of those suffering from dementia and referred for specialist psychiatric help (Gilhooly 1984, Gilleard *et al.* 1984).

This effect seems to outweigh the effect of youth and physical strength which would seem to favour the children or other younger relatives of older people. This may in part be because the children of older people are not, as noted earlier, necessarily themselves young. If you are aged 90 then your children are likely to be pensioners and may themselves not be in perfect health. Moreover it is important to remember that children have not, on the whole, chosen their parents. There are of course strong bonds between children and their parents but this is not the same equal relationship as between husband and wife. Indeed the effects of maturity and independence emphasise an increasing distance between parents and children which may not easily be reversed when this later becomes appropriate or desirable. This may well be one of the reasons why older people themselves differ widely in the expectations of the care they may receive from their families. Some will assume that the family will give them top priority whereas many others hope that they will not become a burden to their children.

There can be important differences between the generations in the expectations of care. There is some evidence that as people grow older those who have been used to the idea of a welfare state see the responsibility of care as shared rather than exclusively that of the family. They also tend to have higher expectations of what help, be it medical or social, should be available. There are also changes in social patterns such as work and leisure which influence the role of carers. The most obvious of these is the great increase in the numbers of married women who continue or return to work after bringing up children. For the generation who are now very elderly it would not be at all unusual for a woman to have given up work as soon as she got married. This, together with a much smaller number of frail older people, meant that there was a much more plentiful supply of women available as informal (i.e. unpaid!) carers. This may make it more difficult for a frail older person to look at the demands of caring from the daughter's point of view. It may be difficult for the parent to appreciate the conflict between the daughter's job or career and the 'duty' to care for an ageing parent.

Whether the relationship is within or between the generations, the quality of that relationship is very important. The description that I have given of marriage as a long-term equal partnership may be far from the reality in some cases. Similarly the bond between parent and child may be weak or based on fear rather than fondness. On the whole it is more difficult to find the motivation to care for someone who has been rotten to you for years.

In the case of today's older people their marriage may have lasted despite such problems, though this is less likely to be the case in later generations. About one marriage in three these days ends in divorce. What will be the effect of this on the pattern of family care in 40 years' time is hard to say. What we know now however is that we should not assume that just because Mr and Mrs Jones have been married for 40 years they necessarily like each other.

It is likewise easy to assume that all parents are good to their children and all children are attached strongly to their parents. Sadly we know that neither of these is universally so. The effects of parental neglect or even abuse may persist through many decades. It may not be readily apparent how much the care of a son or daughter is based on duty rather than joy. Every now and again this is emphasised by a rare case where the behaviour of children reveals a conflict of interest regarding a frail elderly parent. One specific example might be where a relative is pressing for a frail elderly person to stay in hospital, which is free, rather than go to a residential or nursing home which is not. The wish not to see one's parent's capital eaten away by charges for care may not be voiced but the conflict of interests is all too obvious. Nonetheless what seems remarkable to me is not that in a few sad cases the interests of the elderly parent are put second, rather it is surprising that this happens only as rarely as it does.

If we then accept that the nature of the relationship between a frail elderly person and his or her carer is important, how is this affected by disability and by the process of caring?

The onset of disability can affect both partners (Fengler and Goodrich 1979). This is particularly obvious for practical skills such as driving or cooking. If one partner has always taken a particular role then it may be very difficult for the other to adapt to practising an unfamiliar skill. Some skills, like gardening, decorating and changing fuses are, or rather have been, usually done by men. Others, like cooking, washing and sewing, have been done by women. Having to do both sorts of tasks can be quite difficult. Indeed at least one, namely driving, is often not attempted as being too difficult to learn in late life. (I do not suggest that this is necessarily true, just that it is often assumed to be so.) Even something like paying bills may have been the exclusive role of one person rather than shared so that just writing a cheque or balancing income and outgoings can be a real stress.

These sorts of changes may be part of a less obvious but more widespread change in the balance of power. The supporter may now be the supported, the one who took the decisions may now need to be told what to do. This is more apparent in the case of a frail elderly person being cared for by a son or daughter. The roles may be quite obviously reversed compared with previous years. The transition is probably easier if there has been a period of intervening equality. Things may not go so smoothly if mother, now disabled, has always treated her daughter as if she were a little child or if the relationship has in some other way been difficult.

The change in relationship can be emphasised by the need to provide help with certain things such as very personal hygiene, for example bathing and toileting. This can be difficult for both supporter and dependent. Tasks like this may be easier in many ways for a stanger who is 'qualified' rather than for the relative. Certainly when it comes to setting limits to, say, demands for attention this can be very much more difficult for those close to that person.

Sometimes, especially in the case of a very elderly couple, even disability can be shared. Thus one partner may be handicapped by poor mobility, the other by poor sight, but between them they can manage quite well. In some cases even physical and mental infirmity can be complementary. The partner who is physically frail can provide memory and instructions, the mentally frail person the mobility; in these sorts of situations if either can no longer cope, both are affected.

The onset of mental frailty can be said to pose special problems for relationships. This is most vividly seen in cases where the degree of dementia is so marked that the infirm person no longer recognises his or her relative. It may even happen that the sufferer is so convinced that this person is a stranger that he or she is complaining to neighbours or the police. This fortunately happens only in a relatively few cases. Much more commonly the change in personality due to dementia is such that the carer finds it difficult to believe that this person for whom they are caring is really their relative. If the person whom you married was kind, polite and particular in his or her habits it can be very hard to accept the change to an irritable, rude person who refuses to take a bath. The body may look the same but in some way the person inside has already died and a feeling of grief may add further to the burden of care.

Exercise

Suppose you were suddenly to become disabled. Who would look after you?

How would you feel about having help from him/her with
  (a) dressing?
  (b) toileting?

(c) cooking?
(d) feeding?

Are there any other activities you would find it difficult to accept help with?

Stress and strain

Because people differ so much in how they cope with different sorts of problems it can be difficult to predict how much a carer is affected by the stress of coping with a particular sort of problem. This has led many of those who have studied the problems of carers to draw a distinction between the stress and the strain put on carers.

The stress of caring is the number and type of things that the carer has to do and the type and severity of the frail person's disability. For example it is more stressful to have to look after someone who cannot stand alone than someone who can walk without help. Having to attend to someone day and night is more stressful than having to do so only during the day.

The idea of strain is slightly but importantly different. This is used to describe the carer's subjective feelings of burden. This may bear some relation to the objective problems but this is not necessarily so. Thus it might be that the relative frequency of a problem, for example incontinence, is quite low compared with some other difficulty such as needing help with dressing. However the carer may, as many do, find dealing with incontinence much more of a problem. In general problems of behaviour, like wandering or aggression, are associated with higher levels of strain than physical difficulties such as needing help with feeding.

This was illustrated to me on one memorable occasion when I was asked to see a lady who was looking after her severely handicapped mother. The staff on the ward to which the elderly lady had been admitted were struck by how very handicapped she was and were concerned about the burden that this must be placing on her daughter. I was asked to see the daughter to see if this stress was adversely affecting her mental health. The daughter assured me that she was managing fairly well and indeed found it much easier to cope now that her mother was unable to get out of bed on her own. She had suffered from dementia for many years and when she was mobile would wander out of the house at any hour of the day and night. The strain of this was much more than the physical burden now facing the daughter.

Different carers will feel different amounts of strain looking after dependents with the same type and severity of handicap. Just because Mrs Jones can cope with her mother is no reason to assume that Mrs Smith can equally well cope with hers. Even less can we assume that a nephew or niece can cope with an aged uncle even if his problems are just the same as those of others who are being looked after by their children.

If we ask someone 'What problems do you have in looking after...?' we are likely to get a reply that reflects strain rather than stress. It may be much better to ask two separate questions such as 'What sort of help do you have to give to...?' followed by 'How easy or difficult do find it to provide the help that ... needs?' This gives a better picture and may tell us whether someone is struggling with fairly minor problems or is coping well with providing lots of help. These, as we shall see shortly, require different kinds of help. It is rather like the problem of understanding pain which I described in chapter 4. Some people report pain very readily whereas others keep a stiff upper lip and so reports of pain depend on both the person and the nature and severity of their injury.

Styles of coping

One of the many differences between carers is in their style of coping with caring. There have been a number of attempts to look systematically at this. One useful distinction has been between those who cope by being direct care-givers and those who function as managers. Carers who function as care-givers take on the direct work of care themselves and reorganise their own lives accordingly. Those who are care-managers put much of their effort and attention into organising other people to provide extra help. This may involve both agencies like health and social services and more informal networks like family and friends.

Not surprisingly there are differences between the sorts who use these different strategies. Those who have more training in or experience of organising other people more readily adopt the manager style. It is one of the many reasons why practical help from health or social services often seems so unevenly distributed. Someone who has managed to organise one sort of help is quite likely to get other types of help as well. It can make the allocation of outside help look very unfair as it depends on the style of the carer as much as it does on the needs of the frail older person.

It may also be one reason why there can be problems, at least from the scarer's point of view, in the allocation of a benefit like the Attendance Allowance. Although this is meant to be based on an objective assessment of the individual's disability it is very hard to exclude the influence of the carer's feeling of burden especially when the assessment often relies heavily on asking the carer how much help the person needs. It would be impractical to carry out a detailed assessment of need using practical situations as, for example, in an occupational therapy assessment of activities of daily living. However there is little doubt that unless the way questions are phrased is considered carefully the answers depend on the carer as well as the dependent.

Problems in family care

Just as it is hard sometimes to remember that most older people are not in institutions, it is also easy to believe that most families have problems in caring for a dependent older relative. This of course is not so: most people manage quite well most of the time. It is however necessary here to emphasise the problems that can arise since, from a practical point of view, these are the things that lead to people asking for extra help. In looking at the stresses and strains of family care, I have already referred in general terms to some of the problems that can arise. I shall now consider some of these in a little more detail, the psychological factors that can contribute to them and some approaches to overcoming such difficulties.

Guilt

This may seem a curious topic with which to open but I take it first because of what families have so often said to me. I particularly remember one of the first adult education 'courses for carers' with which I was involved. I had just completed the first half of a session on the causes of and problems in dealing with dementia. I thought it had gone quite well and the lively discussion that ensued seemed to confirm that the audience, mostly people looking after an elderly relative at home, had found it interesting. We were just about to take a break for coffee when one carer said 'Well that's all very fine but when are we going to talk about "Guilt"?' The response from the rest of the audience was immediate and positive. To say that this question had struck a chord would be putting it mildly and much of the coffee break and the rest of the session were spent talking about this. Nowadays I include some reference to this problem early on in a session and generally get a similar response.

The guilt about which that carer was talking comes from a number of different conflicts. There may be tension between such obvious clashes in responsibility as family, work and the dependent parent. The frustrations of caring for someone, especially someone who is less than entirely cooperative and grateful, can easily lead to resentment and anger. But feeling angry about your mother or father who is severely handicapped by arthritis or a stroke is hardly acceptable. After all it isn't really their fault that they had a stroke and that you cannot now enjoy the freedom of being retired or spend time with your children or grandchildren whenever you feel like it.

If a kindly friend or neighbour asks 'How is your mother? It must be very difficult for her being so disabled', whatever he or she feels, the carer is unlikely to reply 'Difficult for her! How do think I feel being stuck at home day and night and having to see to her every need.'

In a few cases such feelings may become so strong that they spill over, either into some form of neglect or abuse or, more commonly, into depression on the part of the carer. Both guilt and depression have been aptly described as anger turned inwards onto oneself. The feeling of anger may be very close to that which arises for some other reason, in this case the stress of caring for a dependent person. However because it is difficult to express the anger to the person who causes this directly it becomes bottled up and distorted in these other ways.

One of the reasons this problem is so common is precisely because it is difficult to share. Even though, as the group of carers in the example I gave illustrate, some sort of feeling of guilt is quite common, each individual person is usually convinced that only he or she can feel this way. Because everybody is putting on a brave front nobody wants to admit that there is ever any sort of anger or frustration. Just like the fairy tale of the king's new clothes no one wants to be the first to admit that things are going badly.

Accordingly simply sharing the problem and receiving reassurance that feeling this way is not in some way unusual or wicked helps a good deal. It is one of the many ways that carers, whether in groups or through some informal network, can do so much to help one another. The advantage of a formal setting is that it may provide the reason for taking the first step. Thus devoted carers may find it quite possible to go along to a meeting that is set up to help them in some way be a better carer rather than to do something which is obviously pure recreation. I sometimes wonder whether many of the carers attending an evening course for carers would not get just as much benefit from attending a class in knitting, woodwork or conversational Spanish. However for many of them to attend one of these other sessions would be very difficult to justify, though perhaps after they have met with other carers they may go on to do just that. Whatever the reason despite the fact that an evening class is hardly the easiest thing to get to if you are looking after a frail older person, attendance is always substantial and regular.

Problems in behaviour

'Difficult behaviour' can cover a wide variety of problems. Some, like wandering or shouting, involve someone doing things too much. Others, like loss of interest or lack of personal hygiene, are problems of someone failing to do things. Whichever type of problem is involved, such difficulties can cause particular distress such that we tend to see a very selected sample of even those with dementia referred for psychiatric care.

Only a small minority of those older people suffering from dementia are actually looked after in any kind of hospital dealing with mental illness. Several studies have shown that those who do come into such specialist hospitals are a selected group, namely those with particularly marked behavioural disturbance. Similarly when those caring at home for someone who has been disabled by a stroke have been asked what problems bother them most, behaviour problems feature at least as much as those of physical handicap. What can be done to help in such cases?

The first step should be accurately to describe the problem and to understand what is going on. This might seem a bit trivial since surely the carer knows exactly what is going on. He or she must be only too aware of what the problem is and how often it happens. This is not however usually the case and for at least two reasons.

The first is that all of us in our everyday interaction with other people do not simply observe, we interpret. Even at the level of looking at things we make assumptions about what is going on. Usually these are correct but sometimes we get it wrong as for example in certain visual illusions.

We do just the same in our understanding of what other people are doing. In order to make sense of the world we have to presume that people are doing things for a reason. Thus if we meet someone and they look or talk in a particular way we will say that 'Fred was happy/angry/today' even though Fred did not actually say so to us. In terms of problem behaviour people often use shorthand such as 'He is aggressive sometimes' which does not really tell us whether that person shouts at people every now and then or goes around hitting anyone he meets who has red hair. More difficult still are descriptions of someone being, for example, 'uncooperative' or 'awkward'. This probably means that he or she does not do what he or she has been asked but it implies that this is in some way deliberate. This may or may not be so but we must be very sure of this before coming to such a conclusion.

The second problem is that those who are emotionally attached to a person see that person through their own emotion-tinted glasses. It is therefore very different looking after someone who is a relative from someone who is a patient or client. It may, for example, be much easier to be firm, to remain calm under pressure and so on if you are not yourself emotionally involved. If this were not so then people like psychologists would presumably never have rows with their spouse and have perfectly behaved children. I do not find this to be the case.

One way round these problems is to help people to observe behaviour in a systematic way. This involves first of all defining what you mean by terms such as 'difficult' in a way which allows the behaviour to be counted or in some other way measured. This can then enable the carer to keep a careful record or diary of what has been going on. It is also helpful to record what else was going on just before the problem arose and what happened afterwards.

This sort of record can have a number of benefits. First it help the carer to be objective and to perceive more accurately what is going on. This in itself may relieve some of the strain as the problem may be actually rather less than the person at first thought. Indeed it may be that it shows some other problem to be much more pressing and therefore redirects attention more appropriately.

Second it helps to identify any pattern to the behaviour. The behaviour may happen more on certain days or at particular times of the day. It may happen more when something else has happened, for example after visitors have called or when a regular trip out has been cancelled.

Third such observation may show up ways in which the behaviour is dealt with better at some times than at others. This may be because different people respond in different ways and from their several 'hit and miss' attempts we can focus on the 'hits' for future use.

Finally such measurement gives a baseline against which to judge whether things are changing, either for the worse or for the better. One of the quirks of changing behaviour is that it rarely changes in a steady way, let alone suddenly from 'problem' to 'no problem'. The change tends to be more gradual and take the form of 'one step forwards and half a step back'. It may be very difficult to see such change unless one can take a view over several days or even weeks. It can be very easy to be discouraged if after a good day things do not go so well. It can feel as if all the effort to date has been wasted and things are back to square one. This may be because we often have, albeit unconsciously, an illness versus recovery model of problems. (See chapter 5 p.87.)

Applying this sort of model to changing behaviour leads to gloom and despondency as I have indicated. Keeping a record helps to avoid this. It also tells us when things really are not getting better or are even getting worse. If this is the case then we know that it is time to give up the strategy and try something else. Because a carer, especially a carer under strain, is grateful for any support, he or she may not like to say 'The advice you gave me was a load of rubbish. Nothing has changed at all.' The person who gives the advice is also human and may look harder for evidence of success than for signs of failure. Records help everybody.

The gap between observation and description may itself provide the means to help carers. For example the behaviour of someone suffering from dementia may be described as deliberate when in fact it is not likely to be so. Thus a distraught carer may describe how the dependent person 'won't do as he [or she] is told' whereas a careful examination may reveal that person to have such an impairment of language that he or she cannot understand anything other than very simple instructions. Conversely those who have suffered a stroke which affects their ability to speak but not to understand often complain when they recover that people around them kept shouting at them as if they were deaf or treated them as if they were mentally defective. It is possible to err in either direction.

From what I have been saying so far it may sound as though most carers make a lot of fuss about nothing. This is certainly not so. What is remarkable, as I noted earlier, is how tolerant of difficulty most are. There are relatively few instances when carers' reports of problems are without foundation. It is important to remember this when comparing observations of the same person in different settings. Someone who is causing havoc at home can be no trouble at all in the day hospital or in a residential home. Comparing notes with relatives must be done with care since the relative can easily come away feeling that the professionals think that he or she is at best exaggerating and at worst lying. Remarks like 'Well we haven't seen any of that behaviour here' may be meant to be factual but are unlikely to be received as such, especially by a carer under strain.

People can and do behave very differently with different people and in different places. Familiarity makes a big difference. Whilst a strange environment can add to confusion it can also inhibit some problems. It may not be until someone has been in, say, a residential home for 2 weeks that some of the problems emerge. Likewise there is a big difference between caring as a job where you have regular hours and some time off each day and caring round the clock every day.

It can therefore help to reassure relatives if the possible reasons for such differences are emphasised, unless of course there really is good reason to think that someone is exaggerating the problems. It may encourage the carer to feel that what he or she says is being taken seriously. Helping carers of older people should be a partnership not an inquisition.

Changing relationships

I have already described some of the many ways that dependency in one person can change the nature of a relationship. In some cases the change may be almost as marked as if the dependent partner had died although the change to outsiders will be much less obvious. Naturally the extent of the change will depend on the previous relationship and which partner is now taking care of the other. If you have always given support to someone then looking after them more may not make a big difference. If you always relied on them to take the difficult decisions then things may be very different. If you always went your separate ways then the forced intimacy may be very stressful.

People cope with these changes in different ways. Some do so by emotionally distancing themselves from the dependent person, for example by thinking of the problems of dementia as being like a second childhood or even babyhood. Alternatively the mentally impaired person may be seen as not really any longer the same person so that the task of caring becomes more like that of the detached professional. For many the task becomes an end in itself with the carer taking particular pride in doing everything possible for that person's comfort and well-being. Any of these strategies can work well and it it would be wrong to suggest that they are necessarily bad or maladaptive. Nonetheless problems can arise especially if the strategy only solves part of the problem.

One example of this would be Mrs Brown who was caring for her husband who had suffered a stroke. Besides his physical handicaps the stroke had left him rather slow and apathetic so that he relied on his wife for dressing, bathing and help with the toilet among many other things. One of things she found most distressing was that he still wished to maintain a sexual relationship. This was extremely difficult for her because in order to cope with his need for help with personal hygiene she now viewed him as a child. This conflicted directly with having any kind of sexual intimacy which left her feeling distraught and her husband feeling rejected.

Sexual problems

Problems of sexual behaviour are rather more common than the usual stereotype of ageing would suggest. Old people do not necessarily lose all interest in sexual activity with the passing years. This in itself can be a problem if those around them assume this is the case. It is most noticeable where there is a difference in expectations between a husband and wife. One partner may complain that sexual interest has not diminished saying something like 'I thought we were past all that.' It is less usual, but not unheard of, for older people to complain of loss of interest. In fact sudden loss of interest in sex is just as much a sign of disturbance in older people as it is in younger. The fact that it is not more often a cause for complaint probably reflects a very strong expectation that this is just an inevitable part of growing older.

Of course the likelihood of there being some form of illness or disability which interferes with sexual activity increases with age as does the possibilty of other causes such as the side effects of medication. Where both partners are well there is usually no particular problem except for those who move to a residential home where the owners may not have thought to provide any rooms with a double bed. There are however other times when sexual activity is seen as being inappropriate which does cause very real difficulties.

This is typically for one of two reasons. Most commonly inappropriate sexual behaviour happens because at least one, and usually both, of the people involved is suffering from some form of dementia or acute confusion. Thus a gentleman who is confused may mistake a lady in the home or on the ward for his wife/girlfriend. If that lady is mentally alert then she may be very upset by his advances. If she is herself confused then this is less likely but others, especially relatives, can be very distressed. This is another good example of how important it is to describe behaviour accurately. I know of at least one case where a relative was contacted at short notice to take her father away from a residential home. She was told this was because he had 'tried to have sex' with one of the ladies there. Such a description can easily evoke ideas of rape or other sexual crime. So it was that this man's daughter was left thinking that her father had been branded as a sex maniac and would never be allowed to have another short stay in a residential home. In fact the episode in question had happened while he was acutely confused due to a chest infection and involved a lady who suffered from marked senile dementia. Sensitive handling could have avoided a lot of distress. Of course the results of such incidents in older people are not as serious as for younger people at least in terms of possible unwanted pregnancy.

The problem is rather how distressing they can be for relatives and for the vulnerable elderly people.

In general the answer to this sort of problem behaviour is the same as for any other of the several problems associated with mental impairment. The first priority must be to establish whether there is some treatable cause for the confusion. Where no such cause can be found then consideration must be given to the staffing and physical resources which are appropriate for helping the sufferer. For example the problem may simply not happen when that person is looked after at home or where there is adequate supervision. Because of the legacy we have from those who built many of our hospitals and homes there can be difficulties in catering for both men and women in the same place. This usually means that there are at least some single sex words or homes available. There will probably always be a place for some of these but as yet few patients or residents get much of a choice. They should not be considered a substitute for adequate accommodation and numbers of staff.

The other main type of sexual problem arises when an older person, typically a male patient at home or in hospital, is not confused but shows unacceptable sexual behaviour which may include making explicit or implicit sexual advances to female staff. The unacceptable behaviour may take the form of obvious sexual behaviour, such as masturbation, or less obvious things such as asking the community nurses to give extra blanket baths with special attention to the genitalia. These sorts of problems can be very difficult for young and inexperienced staff who are upset and quite unsure how to react. The problem may however respond to a combination of traditional authority (e.g. Sister telling the patient that this is not acceptable) and counselling about what might be appropriate behaviour. Staff attitudes, expectations and confidence are all very important in ensuring that such problems are resolved.

Old age abuse

Recognition of the sad fact of old age abuse, or granny battering, has lagged behind that for the equally tragic abuse of children. Both are unfortunately more common than is generally recognised (Eastman 1982). In the case of children there is no doubt that the victim is vulnerable and requires the protection of others. The same is not so obviously the case for adults who are the victim of abuse. However we know from the experiences of many battered wives that to say that someone could just walk out if they wished to is far too simplistic. Furthermore some older people are every bit as vulnerable, whether due to physical or mental infirmity, as are children. If an elderly lady who suffers from severe dementia is being assaulted by her husband the prospects for her resolving this on her own are very meagre.

As with other groups the abuse may not be physical. There may be problems of physical and emotional neglect also. It is not enough just to be on the look out for bruises but we must also be alert for signs that other aspects of care are unsatisfactory.

The origins of abuse lie in the history of the individuals involved and in the stress of the current caring situation. It has even been suggested that those who are likely to commit abuse of older people are more likely themselves to have suffered from some such abuse as children. This may or may not be very easy to find out. It is usually a little easier to find out however if there has been any previous history of violence or similar problems. It is important also to look at the needs of the dependent elderly person and how far these can be met by the carer. What can be quite easily dealt with by trained, or even untrained, staff on a hospital ward or in an old people's home may be very different for a lone carer coping 24 hours a day.

What should be done? It should already be apparent that the first thing is to be aware that abuse can happen. Like dementia, it is not a normal part of ageing but it can happen and the worst thing is for it to be ignored. Any organised system of care should have a procedure for dealing with suspected cases of abuse or neglect. Do you know what this is for the organisation in which you work?

The second question to ask is 'Are you sure?' This may seem odd given what I have just said but it is possible for things not to be as they seem. One example which I can recall was a case of a very handicapped elderly lady who was admitted to hospital covered in what looked like stripes from being hit. It in fact turned out that these were due to her having lain for a long time on wet sheets. Her husband was not coping but he needed help with nursing his wife, not advice on controlling his anger.

It is not easy to judge the extent of stress at home from the carers willingness to carry on caring. Often the fact of abuse happens within a relationship where both the partners are dependent on one another. Many carers who are devoted to their relative say that they can understand how abuse can occur even though that in no way excuses it. Anger and frustrations are common components of care. There is often great conflict between wanting to care and yet being unable to cope. Someone may find it impossible to cope when their relative is at home but is equally distraught when that person goes into a home or hospital to give them a break. The loneliness then outweighs the relief.

This can sometimes look to others as if the carer cannot make up their mind. When the person is at home they are asking for admission, when that person is admitted they are asking to have them home again. This sort of approach–avoidance conflict is not peculiar to the carers of older people. We all find it difficult at times to see a balanced view of some situation. This is because we tend to 'forget' the nasty things quicker than the nice. The farther, whether in time or distance, we are from an event or situation, the more likely it is that we will view its positive aspects rather than the negative. As we draw closer the bad things loom larger more quickly so that the balance shifts the other way. Thus we swing back and forth until we can settle at some point where the good and bad balance out. Unfortunately in the case of carers there may be no such point in practice. After all, someone is either at home or not at home, there is no obvious middle way.

The nearest we might get to creating this is some form of shared care in which the dependent person is looked after some of the time at home and some of the time elsewhere. This might be on a daily basis, for example with the person attending a day centre or hospital, or less frequently with the person being admitted for a week or more on a regular basis. Both of these schemes have something to commend them though this may be more so from the carer's point of view than from the dependent's. There are some disadvantages to moving constantly to and fro.

Legal powers

For cases where it might be necessary to think of removing someone to a place of safety the question of whether the person suffering abuse is intellectually unimpaired is crucial. If someone is in full control of their faculties, knows what has happened and appreciates the risks of doing nothing but still is happy to do this there is little that can be done. Such people need to know who to call if they change their mind but it is not our place to stop people doing things which harm no one else however foolish they may seem. If on the other hand the person is not able to appreciate the risks of their situation then some active intervention by others may be necessary. The commonest cause of such disability in later life will be dementia so that a procedure under the Mental Health Act would be appropriate.

Because such situations happen only every now and again the procedures which might help are not familiar. Sometimes this leads to a sense of despondency with people thinking that nothing can be done. This is rarely the case. It may be that nothing should be done, but if something needs to be done and this is appropriate then more often than not the means exist. Bringing this about may prove rather more difficult and the need for greater flexibility, including a change in the law, has been recognised. The range of present legal powers and some of the options for the future are excellently summarised in the report by Age Concern England cited at the end of this chapter.

Helping the carers of older people

In looking at some of the particular problems facing carers I have made passing mention of ways of helping them. Any programme of care for older people should have a structured approach to supporting relatives and I now wish to consider ways of providing this. The elements that this should include are:

1. Contact with other carers
2. Information and advice
3. Access to services

Often these elements can be combined into some form of group support. This may be set up just to provide mutual support or may have some other purpose. For example a group of relatives of stroke patients may come together to hear information about stroke and its effects from a group of professionals. The information and advice are the main aim and it may be thought that using a group is just a more efficient way of doing this. Information can of course be given in other ways, this book is one example. The advantage of a talk or lecture is that the audience can ask questions.

Relatives' groups are not however lectures. They offer the chance not only to ask questions of the speaker but to meet people facing the same problems. The fact that these people have something important in common is itself enough to ensure that they can begin to support one another. The job of professionals here is to help this to happen not to insist that a rigid programme must be followed to the letter. Nonetheless useful information is always valuable and my own experience is that those in a carers' group warm to one another just as well if not better when there is some structured introduction such as a short talk.

Such groups can also be opportunities for people to find out what others get in the way of help be it practical (e.g. a stair-rail), financial (e.g. Attendance Allowance) or social (e.g. a stroke club). It is possible for those who are more experienced or assertive to encourage others to get help to which they may be entitled. Indeed relatives can also act together as a pressure group to influenced the allocation of resources in a way which is often not open to professional staff. Thus a good programme of carer support should be able to provide either the services themselves or advice on how to set about getting these.

How such a programme is organised can vary greatly. It may centre around a particular illness or disability (stroke, Alzheimer's Disease etc.) or around a particular facility such as a day centre. It may, as I have already mentioned, be part of general adult education. It can be linked directly with the use of a resource, such as a group of relatives sharing the intermittent use by their dependents of a place in a residential home. The relatives agree between themselves exactly how the regular rota is to be allocated so that they each receive support at the times they most need it as well as being able to offer mutual support and advice.

A group such as this will meet for as long as the members are using that particular service. Others such as an evening class will meet for a set number of sessions though sometimes there is demand for more.

For some years one successful course has been run regularly at local adult education centres in South Wales. A typical programme is as follows:

TRAINING COURSE FOR CARERS

LOOKING AFTER ELDERLY PEOPLE AT HOME

Venue: Adult Education Centre
Time: Wednesdays 7.00 to 9.00 p.m.

	Topic	Speaker
Session 1	Basic Home Care	Community Nurse
Session 2	Aids and Adaptations	Occupational Therapist
Session 3	Coping with Confusion	Clinical Psychologist
Session 4	Problems of the Deaf	Hearing Therapist
Session 5	Medical Problems	Geriatrician
Session 6	Foot Care	Chiropodist
	+ Benefits & Allowances	Age Concern Worker
Session 7	Lifting Techniques	Physiotherapist
Session 8	Dental Care	Dentist
Session 9	Communicating	Speech Therapist
Session 10	The Role of the G.P.	General Practitioner
	+ course feedback	

Each session consists of a talk, film or practical demonstration and discussion as appropriate. Having a coffee break in the middle helps to break up the sessions and encourages informality. Attendance at such courses has varied between 20 and 50. The great majority of those who register attend every week and in this respect the courses compare favourably with more conventional evening classes such as knitting and conversational Spanish. The courses have been changed in response to the feedback from participants, including the arrangement of additional sessions where these have been requested. The steadily rising number of registrations over the years suggests that they may reasonably be thought to be a success.

Some individual carers may of course require special help. Not everybody is ready to join straight in with a group of others. For example if one is working to help families where there is particular conflict the help may have to be on an individual basis, at least in the first instance. In such cases the course is a resource to which they may be directed at a later date.

There can be a particular problem for carers in that they may not be able to attend the course because they cannot leave their elderly relative at home alone. The ideal is to be able to offer some form of back-up 'sitting service' though in the past some have solved the problem by bringing the older person with them.

Exercise

Collect as many different information leaflets as you can, suitable for giving to carers of older people. How easy was it to get hold of each of the leaflets?

Read them and list the things you learned from doing so.

Relatives and others often complain about finding it difficult to get information, advice or understanding from professional staff. Staff can sometimes be heard complaining about problem relatives so the relationship between formal and informal carers is not always an easy one.

We saw at the beginning of this chapter how informal carers provide most of the care for frail older people. If we are serious about helping as many people as possible it is most important to ensure that all of us work in partnership to help older people.

References

Brody, E. M.(1981) Women in the middle. *The Gerontologist* **21** 471–481.

Eastman, M. (1982) Granny battering: a hidden problem. *Community Care* **27th May 1982** 12–13.

Fengler, A. P., and Goodrich, N. (1979) Wives of elderly disabled men: the hidden patients. *The Gerontologist* **19** 175–183.

Gilhooly, M. L. M. (1984) The impact of care-giving on care-givers: factors associated with the psychological well-being of people supporting a dementing relative in the community. *British Journal of Medical Psychology* **57** 35–48.

Gilleard, C. J., Bedford, H., Gilleard, E., Whittick, J. E., and Gledhill, K. (1984) Emotional distress amongst the supporters of the elderly mentally infirm. *British Journal of Psychiatry* **145** 172–177.

Jones, D. A., and Vetter, N. J. (1984) A survey of those who care for the elderly at home: their problems and their needs. *Social Science and Medicine* **19** 511–514.

Jones, D. A., Victor, C. R., and Vetter, N. J. (1983) Carers of the elderly in the community. *Journal of the Royal College of General Practitioners* **33** 707–710.

Further reading

Age Concern England (1986) *The Law and Vulnerable Elderly People* Age Concern England: London

This report reviews the existing legislation regarding the care of older people. It describes the need to balance the rights and responsibilities of all those concerned and suggests how changes might be made.

Gray, J. A. M., and McKenzie, H. (1980) *Take Care of Your Elderly Relative* Allen & Unwin: London

This book has much the same aim as the course described on p.122: to help those looking after an older person at home. A useful sourcebook.

Gilleard, C. J. (1984) *Living With Dementia: Community Care of the Elderly Mentally Infirm* Croom Helm: Beckenham

Although this book looks at the problems facing those looking after a dementia sufferer, much of what it tells us about carer strain applies more widely.

Chapter 7

Social Ageing

Growing older is, as we have all noticed, much more than merely a physical process. How old we feel depends very much on social and personal events as well as on our physical state. When we are younger we look forward to each successive birthday or to other events which mark our passage towards being 'grown up'. Sometimes these coincide so that reaching a certain chronological age means that one is allowed to do certain things. For example in Great Britain you have to be 18 years old to vote or to buy alcoholic drink.

Other events also mark milestones in our development but are less tied to a specific birthday, for example having a job, getting married or becoming a parent. As we grow older various events continue to mark the passage of time. These may also be birthdays. Dave was 40 last week and my wife and I went to his party. The cards that he received had a lot to say about the way we think about ageing. Because Dave has lost quite a lot of hair there were several references to wigs and cures for baldness. In fact he has been going bald for a long time but the special date made everybody focus on the effects of ageing.

Similarly there are other events which can bring home the idea of ageing but which do not relate directly to one's own birthday. The day your child passes his or her driving test or the thought of becoming a grandparent may be like this. Often people experiencing such events say either that they 'feel old' or cannot believe that they are that old.

On the whole the events that are seen as signs of 'ageing' are ones which mean doing less rather than doing more. Retirement is the most obvious example but there can be lots of others such as no longer being eligible for jury service or being too old to be a blood donor.

Still others are simply examples of realising how other people see you or how you see them. Thus the policemen and doctors seem to get younger every year or you may be taken aback as the bus driver calls 'Hang on, Grandad' and you know he means you.

It may be indicative of the way that we tend to look at ageing but there are few instances where there is a high minimum age for some group or activity. There are not many things, for example, where you have to be 70 before you can join. Groups which are exclusively for 'the elderly' tend to be things like pensioners' clubs which are seen by other people, however wrongly, as being for the frail and lonely. The only obvious exception are the holidays which are designed for those over 55. Even these tend to try and minimise the association with ageing by having titles like 'Young at Heart'. Nonetheless this type of holiday has proved a successful marketing ploy for several holiday companies.

In other cultures positive images of ageing are sometimes easier to find than in our own. In particular the idea of the wisdom of old age has been much more prominent in eastern culture than in our own. The importance of the 'elder' perhaps is more when the acquired knowledge of a society is passed down through spoken rather than written tradition. Western society has made enormous progress in refining, storing and teaching information so that our children can quickly become wiser, in some ways at least, than ourselves.

In those areas where we do still have to rely more on human memory, as for example in the practice of skills, then the importance of wisdom is more apparent. Thus those with particular artistic skill are often very actively employed until well into late life and much in demand as teachers of those who are to succeed them. Those who were sportsmen or women may no longer be 'young' and thus able to compete at the top of their sport but can contribute as coach, tutor and, more recently, commentator.

Unfortunately not very many of us are exceptionally gifted in any of these ways. It can therefore all too easily seem to us that ageing is about giving things up rather than opening up new opportunities. This image is often confirmed by the majority of what we see and hear around us. This is especially true for advertising. Those who are able and willing to spend many millions on promoting the sale of products do not do so without careful thought and planning. They know from careful research who the likely customers will be and what works best in persuading those people to part with their money. On the whole they tend to choose positive images and aim those images at people who have money to spend. This does not often include older people simply because as a group they have not tended to have much money to spend. What is more, promoting something as being for 'older people' runs a real risk of putting people off by association. If being 'old' conjures up images of being frail, lonely and forgetful then not many people will flock to buy a product which makes you one of this group.

Thus the aperitif advertisement features a leggy blonde on roller-skates not an elderly couple enjoying a quiet drink. Milk chocolates are delivered by a daredevil parachutist on skis not by a devoted husband driving a family saloon. The list is almost endless.

There are some exceptions. Savings advertisements do sometimes feature older people, the image here being one of security and providing for one's dependents. Interestingly it is of course just here that older people do figure as consumers. Although as a whole those over retirement age are poor, many older people do have money to invest. They are the investors, the young are the borrowers. Banks and building societies need both.

Some products even rely on fears of ageing for increased sales. Cures for baldness and creams to eliminate the wrinkles of old age are prime examples of this. In recent years there has been a considerable increase in the number and indeed type of preparations available. There is obviously no shortage of those able and willing to spend several pounds on a small jar of ointment which it is claimed will restore youthful appearance. The irony here is particularly strong since the advertisements for such elixirs are often close to those for creams to help you get a tan from lying in the sun. The one sure long-term effect of exposure of skin to sunlight is wrinkles. So you can sell a sun-tan lotion today which will help you to create the customer for your anti-wrinkle cream tomorrow.

Perhaps some of these images do not matter too much. I dare say that not too many older people are seriously disadvantaged or upset by not seeing people like themselves in television advertisements. Indeed, if asked, a good many of them might prefer looking at just the sort of images that are already portrayed. But some images have a more practical implication. What you think it is like to be on a 'geriatric' ward or in a 'home for the elderly' may actually decide whether you seek early help for some practical problem. The idea of a 'geriatric' anything carries with it the image of dependency and frailty. This is despite the fact that the word itself only means 'to do with the medicine of old age' just as paediatric does for children. If your grandchild is taken ill and has to go into hospital you would probably feel it was very wrong for him or her just to go onto an ordinary medical ward. There would not be the right facilities and the staff would not be specially sensitive to the needs of children. A children's ward would be much better.

Unfortunately we know that many older people and indeed their relatives do not have the same view of a geriatric ward as the place of choice in a general hospital. The image is all too negative. Being on a geriatric ward means being old and that is unacceptable. The paradox is that if this sort of fear of being old and frail stops someone seeking help until it is absolutely necessary, it is actually more likely that the person will become more frail. All too often things have gone too far by the time help is available so that the prospect of a full recovery is much diminished. Bad images do not encourage prevention.

Activity and disengagement

Back in chapter 3 we looked briefly at the idea of disengagement and how this related to adjustment in later life. We saw how there are many different styles of adjustment, some successful, some less so. The processes of activity and disengagement are largely marked by social phenomena. Whether or not you are still willing to carry on as an official of the golf club or social centre may have as much to do with attitude as it has to do with ageing. In most cases the sort of person who has always been active in such ways will quite likely take on more, at least in the early stages of retirement. It would not be until well into late life that such people feel that it is time to give up altogether. Indeed it is likely to be some sort of physical frailty rather than age as such that forces such a decision.

Ageing and driving

One practical example of this is the decision to give up driving. Anyone who has a driving licence has, by law, to tell the licensing authority if they develop any disability which might be relevant to their capacity to drive safely. Those who are aged over 70 have to renew their driving licence every 3 years and at that time declare that they are fit to drive. There is no absolute age limit above which one is not allowed to drive but the older one is, the more likely that one will suffer from some difficulty which makes driving no longer safe.

The change from driving to not driving has all sorts of implications. It means being dependent on others whether it be friends, relatives or public transport. For those who are frail or who are not well served by buses etc. the loss of freedom can be considerable. Not surprisingly the tendency is for older people to try and continue to drive for as long as possible, even when the argument of cost favours using taxis for the occasional trip. Being able to go out when *you* decide to can be very important.

Whatever one's age, it is the responsibility of you the licence holder to declare any disability and many older people do in any case curtail their driving. Usually this is a gradual process, for example driving less often or only during daylight hours. It is easier to adapt in this way than suddenly have to face giving up because one has suffered a stroke or has otherwise become too frail.

Ageing and activity

The issue of control, of things happening when you decide they should, is somewhat similar to the idea of events being 'on time'. We noted in the context of bereavement that although age does not remove the pain of grief it may influence how easily this is resolved. Similarly it may be easier to give up some particular activity, for example driving a car, because you are in your nineties rather than because you are 65. Even for an important change such as retirement which may happen because you are at an arbitrary age rather than through choice, it does at least help to know that most other people have to obey the same rules. It is more difficult to adjust to early retirement if this takes the form of redundancy or is due to sickness.

The same principles apply to many other changes which may happen as we grow older. The reality of ageing is that some limitations are inevitable. We have seen before that for intense physical activity like competitive swimming it happens so early that we do not usually think of the change as being due to 'old age'. For most other things deciding to do less is a matter of personal reference. Right back at the beginning of this book I pointed out that it makes very little sense to talk about 'older people' as if they were any kind of homogeneous group. All they share is having completed a minimum number, usually 60 or 65, of trips around the sun. Apart from that they have little in common. Indeed it has even been suggested that the more times you have been round the sun, the more individual you become.

Within such a varied group it is possible to find at least some people who fit almost any description you care to find. Thus perhaps neither activity nor disengagement is the key to successful ageing for everybody. As we shall see in relation to those who live in residential homes it can be very wrong to see a low level of activity as being the same as being miserable and depressed. There are many types of thinking, not least reminiscing about the past, which can be a source of great enjoyment to older people.

Nonetheless it is useful to look carefully at how most older people spend their time. It is possible simply to chart what a group of people do during a set period, for example a day or a week. Indeed this is something which you can do for yourself.

Exercise

Keep an hour by hour diary of what you do for a day or two.

What is the most frequent activity besides sleep?

Common activities will include things like shopping, washing, cleaning, doing one's job, watching TV, reading, visiting friends and so on. Studies of age differences in these very simple sort of data show that, not surprisingly, older people tend to spend more time on the necessities rather than the luxuries in terms of time (Lawton 1977). Sleeping remains top of the list. In fact because of the way sleep patterns change as we grow older it tends to figure more in the day as well as during the night. 'Napping' is quite a frequent activity for older people. The sorts of things that we might like to think of ourselves as doing a lot of as we grow older, for example visiting friends or going out to different places, actually take up relatively little of older people's time.

Most of the time is devoted to fairly mundane activities and adjusting expectations of what to do with one's time is often an important part of preparing people for the most predictable major life event of all in old age: retirement.

Retirement

Of all the events which might be thought of as characteristic of ageing, the most obvious is surely retirement. More often than not the retirement pension is referred to as the 'old age pension' and old people are often classed together as 'pensioners'.

In fact the transition from being a worker to being a pensioner is a relatively recent phenomenon. It has only been in the course of this century that people could rely on having some form of pension to provide at least some minimal income even if they stopped work after a certain age. Previously people had to go on working for as long as they were able. If they became too frail to do so they had to rely on the generosity of others whether family or those who had set up some benevolent trust such as an almshouse. It may well be that much of our fear of old age has its roots in the very real misery that could afflict the few who actually manged to survive into old age.

Thankfully today things are very different. Even though older people are still among the poorest of our society few if any of them are reduced to begging or to starvation. Reduced income may be a severe problem but zero income is not.

In thinking about what retirement means to people it is useful to consider some examples of relevant changes which this brings to the individual and to his or her family. Some of these are as follows:

Being at home more
Having no fixed timetable
Having a fixed regular income
Seeing more of your family
Doing things 'off-peak':
    shopping
    travelling
    sports
    using library
Going on holidays
More leisure time
Change in social status

Exercise

Can you think of things to add to this list?

Go through all the items above and any of your own and decide if you think that each of them is a benefit or if it is a disadvantage. Are there some things which could be either or even both?

Let us now look at some of the things that I included and how these might work out in practice.

Being at home more

At first sight this might seem very attractive. During our working life we tend to look forward to weekends, days off and annual holidays. They are the more precious times which we see as part of the reward for doing whatever is our usual job. When a trade union is negotiating for better pay and conditions for its workforce it will often include a demand for longer holidays and/or a shorter working week.

But it may be that for some people there is a factor of supply and demand. If there are few days when you are not working then those that you do have are valuable. If you have only days when you are not working they are not so attractive.

How you feel about this may depend on the sort of job that you had and the ways in which you got your rewards. Those who have held jobs which they find interesting and not just a way of making money tend to cope better with giving this up. In contrast, and perhaps quite against common sense, those who have had what they saw as boring jobs that really only were worth doing because you were paid for it tend to have more problems. Feeling good about your job does not necessarily make it more difficult to retire.

Of course at the other extreme will be someone who has lived for his or her work, the real 'workaholic'. This sort of person will probably have always resented days off as an intrusion into the important central theme of life, work. For this person having to retire will be very difficult unless he or she can find some other activity to replace this.

Similarly there may be mixed effects of retirement on family relationships. There is the old idea that once he has retired the husband gets under his wife's feet. She finds it difficult to get used to having him around all the time and he disrupts her routine which has evolved over many years. This is probably much exaggerated but can be all too true. Being together for most of the time can put quite a strain on any relationship. If that relationship has relied on distance then there can be real problems.

I remember once being asked to see a boy who had been having severe behaviour problems and had been referred to a psychiatric clinic. Before doing so I took a look at his notes to find out what we already knew. In there was a report on the family. Under 'Marital Relationship' it said 'There are no problems in the marriage. Father works days and mother works nights'. I wonder what will happen when they retire?

For many older couples retirement can be a time of great fulfilment. The extra time together may be a real boost. The point that I want to emphasise here is that the outcome depends very much on what things were like before.

The freedom of having no fixed timetable

Surely it is bound to be a good thing to be able to do what you like when you like to. Again this may be true for some people but is probably limited for most of us. In fact there can be something quite disconcerting about uncertainty and we often strive for routine. In fact one of the things that is often said by younger people about their elders is that they are too rigid in their habits. Very many people build up their own structure which replaces that which disciplined their working lives. The need to do this is not confined to those who are retired; those who are unemployed can find it difficult to keep a regular routine. One of the 'dangers' of being unemployed is said to be that you can all too easily slip out of the habit of getting up at a certain time each morning, or even get out of the habit of getting up at all.

This too can happen to those who retire. One man I once saw had taken to his bed for so long that his legs became bent and wasted. It was only when he became unable to get out of bed to go to the toilet that his wife felt it unecessary to ask for help. Otherwise she seemed quite happy to have him upstairs in bed while she lived her own life just as she had done before he retired. Fortunately this is exceptional.

A fixed regular income

Change in income is probably one of the most important aspects of retirement. We know that in the things which determine 'life satisfaction' there are no great differences due to age. We all feel better about the way things are if we are in good health and have an adequate income. Ensuring these in retirement is something which really needs to begin early in life.

The level of our pension is very important to us when we retire. However the size of our pension is decided often by decisions which we took, or did not take, many years previously. The pensions industry including life insurance companies spend a lot of money trying to persuade younger people to think about their pension. This is often not very successful. When you are aged 25 the idea of retiring seems far too far off to worry about. Making financial plans for retirement is a topic which figures pretty well universally in pre-retirement courses. For those who have built up a reasonable occupational pension the problem may be the relatively pleasant one of how to invest a substantial sum of money. For most, however, the question is more how to survive on a relatively low fixed income. This has implications for all sorts of other aspects of retirement such as one's ability to take advantage of the extra freedom and leisure time, or even to eat the sort of diet that will keep you healthy.

Helping to keep up one's income may be one important reason for some people carrying on with at least part-time work after they have retired. It can also help to ease the transition from the world of work to that of leisure. This sort of arrangement may be easier to make for those who have been self-employed rather than those who have worked for a large employer. It has been suggested that the option of gradually reducing one's working hours should be open to more people and the trend towards part-time work in recent years may help this.

Off-peak facilities

One of the few things often cited as being a 'plus' for retirement is the opportunity to benefit from special reductions in the cost of various items. These include particularly travel by bus or train, services like chairdressing and dry cleaning and admissions to the theatre, cinemas and museums. These reductions in costs can be viewed in two ways. On the one hand many people would argue that they are concessions which have to be given because the basic minimum pension is not high enough. In this way they can be seen as reinforcing the idea that not only are older people poor but they can reasonably be expected to be this way. The retirement pensioner is seen in the same light as the unemployed person or the person who is disabled. They are all people who need special help and consideration. Certainly among the disabled as well as among older people there are many who resent this image and of being dependent on concessions for the necessities of life. Moreover as only some things are available more cheaply there are considerable restrictions on what older people can afford. If you do not happen to like going to museums you cannot benefit from the saving.

On the other hand some of the reductions which are available are there for sound commercial reasons rather than any sense of trying to protect the disadvantaged. Thus cheap travel on the trains may be designed to encourage older people to take up seats which would otherwise be empty. The discount helps to sell seats and thus contributes to the profitability of the operation. The same is also largely true of the discounts given by shops and other services. The dry cleaning firm may want to encourage trade at off-peak times when older people are free to do their shopping. This is good marketing rather than charity. After all, even though older people are not the wealthiest of our nation there are a great many of them and not many businesses can afford to ignore one in six of the population.

There is of course the assumption here that older people wish to avoid the times when shops or other places are busy. This may be true for the majority but there are also some older people who deliberately go out when things are busy just to enjoy the sense of activity. Certainly many, especially those who live alone, will prefer to shop for a little something every day rather than buy a large amount once a week or once a fortnight. Quite apart from the fact that it may be difficult for a frail person to carry a large amount of shopping, there is at least a small amount of human contact in going out to the shops and being with other people.

Increased leisure

The extent to which this is a bonus rather depends on how you have used your leisure time before retirement. Those who have lots of interests may find that even with the extra time available to them there are still not enough hours in the day. There are so many skills that can still be practised and developed. For society as a whole retirement is of course important as a way of providing jobs for younger people. The fact that older workers have to retire at a set age regardless of whether they are still capable of doing the job creates vacancies for others. Where the job involves particular skills, the older person will quite likely be involved in teaching these to those just beginning that trade. When, as often happens now, the skills required are changing rapidly the value of the older worker's wisdom is diminished.

The value of sharing skills and experience is a central idea behind the U3A. U3A is not a food additive but a mutual education organisation for older people. The title is short for the University of the Third Age. The Third Age refers to retirement, the first two being childhood and working life. The idea is that older people can meet with one another and both share their wisdom and support one another in developing their particular skills and interests. It is not a 'university' in the sense of being somewhere where people go to hear lectures and to study. It is rather a loose framework which enables retired people to come together and develop schemes of mutual interest.

Mutual interest is also important in determining how families react to retirement. I have already hinted at the fact that spending more time with your family may be a mixed blessing. Different family members may have quite different expectations of how things will be after retirement. Often this may not be discussed in any detail, perhaps under the assumption that things will work out quite smoothly. It is much better if all those involved, typically husband and wife, think through what are the implications of the change in lifestyle and what each expects to happen.

Changing social status

Like most major changes in life, the precise day of retirement is often marked by some sort of ritual. Traditionally the person retiring will be presented with some gift to mark the occasion. Perhaps the clock or watch which has been associated with this acts as a symbol of all the time that he or she will have to spend.

Because of the problems of reduced income and, for some at least, increased frailty, older people have not in the past tended to have a very strong voice in society. When others have championed their cause it has tended to be in an attempt to speak for a disadvantaged group who cannot speak for themselves.

More recently however there has been an increasing tendency for older people to assert themselves as a group whether as consumers or as voters. The various pensioners' organisations are particularly active in this regard and in some countries there are active political lobbies. In the USA this has been termed the 'Grey Panthers', a reference by analogy to the black activist organisation of the 1960s and 1970s. At an international congress of gerontology in West Germany a few years ago the proceedings were interrupted one afternoon by a demonstration. This was by a group of older people complaining that with all these international scientists talking about ageing the views of older people themselves were nowhere to be heard. Perhaps as the balance of population shifts we will see politicians moving away from kissing babies to shaking hands with older people. After all there are 10 million voters in Britain who are over retirement age.

These sorts of changes will happen more and more as different cohorts grow older. There is already some evidence in Scandinavia that those who are moving into late life now are becoming more demanding in their expectations of services. They do not expect to have to share a room in a residential home or to struggle on at home with only the bare minimum of support. This sort of change could quite easily outpace even the increases in numbers of very elderly people which we have already anticipated.

Pre-retirement courses

One way that this might happen is if more people have thought about their retirement and what they expect from this. This sort of preparation is the aim of pre-retirement courses. At present they are attended by only a minority of those who retire. The courses are put on by large employers, like the National Health Service, by the Pre-retirement Association and by local education authorities. Not surprisingly they are much better attended when the employer gives time off for this purpose. I even know of one commercial organisation which holds its pre-retirement courses in hotels in the Mediterranean. They have a particularly high take-up rate.

Such courses cover things like financial matters (e.g. how much can you earn before your pension is reduced), how to stay healthy in retirement, the pros and cons of moving house, the options for coping with increasing frailty, entitlements to benefits, leisure activities and so on. Many of the principles, for example how to plan a healthier lifestyle, would benefit us at any age and it is well worth looking at one of the several examples of materials available (see reading list at the end of this chapter).

Adequate preparation makes excellent sense. Start today, it is never too early!

Relocation

This rather impersonal term describes another common major life event in the lives of older people, changing the place where you live. This is of course by no means restricted to older people, lots of people move house at some time. However a change in type of accommodation is common in old age as the range of need is so much greater. Thus not only do older people move house but many of them move from an ordinary house into a hospital or into a residential home. A few may move through a succession of different places within a relatively short space of time. Moves of any sort are disruptive whatever your age. The attractions of a new house, a different job and making new friends may be considerable but the actual process of moving is rarely a pleasure. Moreover many of the moves which happen to older people are forced upon them by circumstances or involve giving up being in a place which they have known for many years. If your social network has been built up over several decades it is particularly difficult to settle in somewhere else.

Because of these special features and the fact that older people are seen as more at risk of all sorts of problems, some years ago people began to look at what happened when older people were moved from one place to another. This study was given considerable importance by the fact that quite early on it was found that there appeared to be a very bad effect on some old people. It was found in some studies that the old people who had moved were more likely to suffer physical illness, emotional distress and even in some cases showed a higher mortality (Borup and Gallego 1981). This raised the possibility that for some people the process of moving was actually life-threatening.

This could have lots of important implications for all sorts of services aimed at helping older people. For example in many cases we rely on moving people from one place to another in order to meet their changing needs. If we think of a person who suffers a stroke, he or she is likely to be taken into an acute medical ward for initial treatment, may then go on to another ward or hospital for rehabilitation and could quite likely end up being placed from hospital in a residential home. If he or she should later become more dependent there may be a further move into a continuing care hospital bed.

In many cases this sort of succession of moves may on balance be the best thing. If you are acutely ill and need the benefits of intensive medical technology it is best to go to the right hospital as quickly as possible. If however you are just gradually becoming more frail there may be more adverse effects in suddenly moving, especially if that move is seen as being a one-way ticket. Giving up your home is rarely if ever easy. In the latter case preparation for the move can be very important. It may be much better to give somebody the extra help they need at home rather than simply move them to where it is more convenient for others.

As usually happens in studying people, the more we know about the process of relocation the more complicated the picture becomes. More recent study has shown the balance between the good and bad effects of moving (Ferraro 1982). There are, as we would expect, plenty of times when the beneficial effects outweigh the upheaval. It is worth looking at the sorts of factors that make a difference and what guidelines have emerged for ensuring that moves have a positive effect on those who move.

Bricks and mortar

Perhaps the most obvious change resulting from a move is likely to be the change in physical surroundings. It would seem certain that a move from a cold and damp house to a place that is warm and dry would be beneficial. After all we know that much of the improvement in life expectancy that has led to the growth in ageing is due to better sewerage, housing and heating. Often however things can look very different to the old person who has lived there for a long time. If you have never had a fixed bath and an inside toilet you may be less convinced of the importance of these. We know very well that older people are often reluctant to leave what seem to us very poor surroundings. They are not easily persuaded that they would be much better off giving up their cold damp house for a smart new flat where it is warm and there is a friendly warden to pop in each day and see if you are all right.

On the other hand those who can afford to do so often choose to make this kind of move. If the house is getting too big and the garden threatens to overwhelm you there is a lot to be said for finding somewhere more suitable. This is easier to contemplate if you are thinking ahead and thus able to choose carefully where you go and when. This is a situation where having the capital to move where you choose offers the chance to exercise quite a bit more control over your own destiny.

One common move at the time of retirement is to seek a more congenial climate. This may be in the same country, for example moving to the south coast, or even elsewhere, for example the Mediterranean. Again the amount of choice you have depends very much on how well-off you are financially. Not that making this sort of move is necessarily all for the best. The move may be right away from familiar people and what looked like a nice place for a holiday in August looks much less attractive on a wet Tuesday in November. Once again, thinking it through properly makes all the difference.

Friends and relations

How you feel about where you live also depends on the access which it gives you to the people you like to see. If your children and grandchildren live over the other side of the city, or even the other side of the country, you may be happy to move to be nearer to them. The closest possible move is of course to move into the same house as them but this may not be as simple as it seems. For those whom it suits it can be the ideal solution but this is by no means always the case. It is often said that older people can relate better to their grandchildren than to their children. Sharing a house with several active teenagers can be very different from seeing them once a week for tea.

The growth of the 'granny flat' is one answer to compromise in this regard. It offers a combination of independence and supervision which can indeed work very well. Again, however, it is not very often an option for those who rely on public housing. I do not know of any public housing programmes in Britain which include houses built with a flat attached and specially allocated to a family wishing to take care of an elderly relative.

Accessibility applies to more than friends and relations, it applies to all the range of facilities and services which people use: shops, libraries, hairdressers and all manner of other things. It even applies simply to seeing other people going about their business. We tend to look at a home or hospital for older people set well back amidst beautiful gardens and think 'How lovely and peaceful'. If you actually have to spend the rest of your life there perhaps you would rather be a bit nearer the road, the shops or the school. At least then you see a bit more going on. A colleague of mine was recently involved in interviewing a group of older people who were so disabled that they had to be looked after permanently in hospital. Because of the need to upgrade some of the hospital wards these people had been moved from the geriatric hospital in town to a small cottage hospital nestling among the trees and flowers a few miles away. It looked much prettier but the older people themselves complained that as they were so far out of town they did not receive anything like as many visitors. It is not always easy to see things from another point of view.

Group size

Another important difference between various settings is the number of other people who share that accommodation with you. The biggest difference is obviously between your own home and a hospital or residential home. It is a very big change to move from having at least one room for each person to living as part of a large group. Where you eat becomes more of a canteen than a dining room and where you sleep may be a dormitory rather than a bedroom.

On the whole we tend to assume that for most people the smaller the group the better. Accordingly the 'best' size for both continuing care hospital wards and residential homes has tended to fall steadily in recent years. For the last 10 to 15 years people have been designing and building smaller rather than bigger units. There are some things such as kitchen and laundry facilities which are cheaper to build larger but, even so, many facilities can be designed so that small units share a common core of these kinds of facilities.

Once again, however, we must not assume that everybody likes being either alone or in a very small group. Even families can find it difficult to get along at times. Anyone who has had to share a flat or a house with others will know how difficult this can be if you do not happen to get on with the people who also live there. Generally speaking when people go into a home or a hospital they are not able to choose the group with whom they are living. It may actually be a little easier to find someone with whom you get along well if there are more people to choose from. Alternatively, for a few people it is actually easier to cope by remaining relatively anonymous in a large group rather than having to relate closely to a few people. Whether the move from one setting to another is seen as positive depends very much on the person who is moving.

New horizons

One of the real benefits of moving can of course be the new opportunities which are available in the new environment. If you have been feeling very lonely and isolated as you are living alone and no longer able to get about very well the chance of joining in the activities going on in a sheltered housing unit or in a residential home may be just what you need. If you move to a place where there are several other retired people you may find that there are more people who can share your interests be they bingo, bridge or basketwork.

Similarly if the level of care that you need has changed you may be much better off moving to somewhere where you can more easily receive what is appropriate to you. If you have beeen living alone and worried about being ill and unable to summon help then having others around may be a great comfort. Certainly older people's views of a residential home or hospital seem to change as they become more frail. The balance tips from independence to security.

To move or stay?

The effects of relocation seem to depend very much on this question of balance. If you are going somewhere better (as *you* see it), if you have made the choice to go and if you have been able adequately to prepare for the move it is likely to do you good. If you are made to go somewhere unsuitable and this happens all of a sudden the effects are likely to be quite the reverse.

Exercise

List all the things you like about where you live.

List all the things you do not like.

If you had to move into one room in a residential home tonight what would you take with you? Which of your neighbours would you miss most?

It should be fairly obvious that you might find it very difficult to adjust to such a traumatic move.

These sorts of considerations should be borne in mind when making preparation for any older person to move from one place to another. There are a number of things which we can do to help things go as smoothly as possible. These include

1. Talk about the move as soon as possible.
2. Help the person weigh up the pros and cons.
3. Help the person take as much of his or her personal belongings as possible.

4. Make the move gradual: visit(s) beforehand to get to know people.
5. Make the move reversible if possible: don't give up the flat the day you move into the home, wait a bit.
6. Arrange for someone familiar to go with the person when he or she moves.
7. Make sure it really is the right move.

These are just a few ideas. No doubt you could come up with others. They apply whether, as usually happens, we are helping one person move or whether, as sometimes happens, a whole group has to move. Thus if we are moving a whole group of people we may need to try and move a group of staff with them. This can work very well and adequate preparation pays off both in terms of customer welfare and staff morale.

There are some cases where implementing these sorts of approaches may need to be modified. For example I can think of a few cases of older people with a mild degree of dementia who tended to worry excessively if they were told well in advance about a short stay in a home. For these people it seemed to be much better to leave things until the day of the move and then let things proceed straight away. The important thing is that the approach adopted is the best for that individual. If you are trying to discuss a move into an old people's home, the older person may well become quite upset initially. This in itself is no reason for avoiding the issue. Giving up your home is a reasonable cause of grief. The longer-term outcome is what matters.

The right to stay put

Just before concluding this section it is appropriate to consider briefly under what circumstances it is possible for someone to be made to move against his or her wishes. If someone is having major problems in managing at home there is sometimes the call for 'something to be done'. Enforced removal is however only possible under certain specified conditions.

There are often very strong attachments to the house, the neighbourhood and the memories that go with these. At times the decision to stay can seem to us rather foolish but, thankfully, there is very little we can do about this. We cannot uproot somebody against their will just because we think they are being unwise.

It is only in dire circumstances that we can overrule a person's wishes to stay in their own home. Those who are mentally ill can be forcibly removed under the Mental Health Act if they are a danger to themselves or to others. This may be into hospital for assessment or treatment or as a requirement that someone live in a specified place under a Guardianship Order. These only apply to those who are mentally disordered which of course includes those suffering from dementia.

Those who are creating a public health hazard can be removed under the Public Health Acts, at least until the threat to public health is removed.

Things do of course have to get pretty bad before this is appropriate but it could apply to anyone whether or not they are mentally ill.

Finally those who are elderly and frail and who are not receiving care and attention can be be removed under a section of the National Assistance Act to a place of safety. Again this is only a course of last resort and it involves an application to a magistrates' court.

Much more commonly used are the several ways of helping older people to stay in their own homes by providing or supplementing a network of support. These include practical home care services such as home helps and meals-on-wheels, the development of community networks such as Good Neighbour schemes and other ways of using volunteers and the use of benefits such as Attendance Allowance and Invalid Care Allowance. As we saw in the last chapter, these often depend on strengthening the support already given by relatives and other informal carers. The approach to each individual should be to try and solve his or her particular problems.

Exercise

List all the possible services you can think of which might help a frail elderly person to stay in their own home.

Ask an experienced colleague to look over your list and add any others that he or she can think of.

Whilst this list will be quite long there are often individual circumstances which require something just a bit different. This can be a little difficult if we have only a limited range of relatively inflexible services. What we should be aiming to do is to provide the right sort of support to each individual. One way of approaching this is to use the same sort of goal setting that we might apply to any other type of problem. This would include:

1. Identifying needs
2. Identifying assets
3. Setting targets
4. Deciding on methods
5. Seeing if it works

If this looks vaguely familiar then that is because you have been paying attention. We looked at taking a problem-solving approach back in chapter 4. This applies to social support as well as to the individual's ability to cope with handicap.

The growth in the number of very elderly people has put particular pressure on community services. More and better use of resources is necessary if this type of care is to keep pace with demand (Grundy 1987).

It is only in those cases where such networks of support are no longer appropriate that older people have to move from home into a home or hospital. There are only about 5% of older people who live in this sort of setting. However they are among the frailest and, since many older people spend at least some time in such settings, it is worth looking at these in more detail. They are therefore the subject of the next chapter.

References

Borup, J. H., and Gallego, D. T. (1981) Mortality as affected by inter-institutional relocation: update and assessment. *The Gerontologist* **21** 8–16.

Ferraro, K. F. (1982) The health consequences of relocation among the aged in the community. *Journal of Gerontology* **38** 90–96.

Grundy, E. (1987) Community care for the elderly 1976–1984. *British Medical Journal* **294** 626–629.

Lawton, M. P. (1977) The impact of the environment on aging and behavior *in* J. E. Birren and K. W. Schaie (eds) *Handbook of the Psychology of Aging* Van Nostrand Reinhold: New York

Further reading

Open University (1984) *Health and Retirement: Community Education Package P599* Open University: Milton Keynes

A short course aimed at older people but with a great deal of information of use to carers.

Help the Aged (1979) *The Time of Your Life: A Handbook for Retirement* Help the Aged: London

Goldberg, E. M., and Connelly, N. (1982) *The Effectiveness of Social Care for the Elderly* Heinemann Educational Books: London

Covers several types of intervention including the use of volunteers.

Chapter 8

Living with Others

We all spend some of our time as one of a group of people. This may be in a clearly defined formal group like a choir or a football team or it may be as one of a less formal group such as a church congregation or the spectators at a football match. However not many of us live as part of a large group all the time. Many will have memories of being in the armed forces or at school, particularly boarding school. This is generally viewed as a phase in our life rather than as a natural way to live all the time. We may reminisce about the good old days when we were at school but not many of us actually choose that sort of a life as a long-term lifestyle.

However, for a significant minority of older people much of their time is spent in large groups of just this sort. There are at any one time about 6% of older people living in residential homes or in hospital. The proportion is higher for the very elderly (around 15%) and many more older people spend at least some of their last years in one type of institution or another. Even more will have passing contact with other group settings such as a day centre or a day hospital.

For this reason it is important to consider in some detail the special issues concerning life in a large group. It may not be how most older people live most of the time but is often the only choice for a very frail minority.

Whose choice?

We tend to have quite strong views about how we would like to spend our last years and, indeed, where we would like to die. One popular hope is to die peacefully in one's own bed. Not many of us look forward to spending months or even years in a hospital or a residential home. These are generally speaking seen as options of last resort.

There is no reason to suppose that older people are very different in this regard. In fact recent studies of their attitudes to different sorts of care would seem to confirm this. Most older people would much prefer to be looked

142

after in their own home, although there are some individual exceptions to this. There may be several reasons why being at home rather than in a home is so much more attractive. Most are in some way to do with wanting to be an individual, to be in familiar surroundings and to have the choice to do things one's own way. There are some which are especially applicable to older people.

Those who are very old will often have quite clear memories of a time when institutions were very much places to fear and to avoid at all costs. The workhouse was not a place you went to because you could get the best sort of care there. You went there because you could not look after yourself and there was no one else to support you. The link between these unhappy institutions of previous years and today's care for older people is more than just a matter of misperception. Many of the workhouses of 50 years ago are the buildings which today house geriatric hospitals and residential homes.

Moreover the bad image of such places is not confined to the events of the past. Examples of poor care or actual maltreatment are fortunately rare but do, sadly, occur. They are much more likely to hit the headlines than are the examples of good care which greatly outnumber them. The headlines are especially large when the malpractice occurs in a residential home or hospital so these places can get a very bad stereotype. In short, few of us would feel a sense of overwhelming relief in finally getting a bed in a long-stay hospital ward or a place in a residential home. Even if we are a relative or other informal carer, the relief at having the burden of daily care lifted from us is very likely to be tinged with guilt.

To overcome this requires that standards of such care should be of the highest. It is particularly important that we do all that we can to help those who do need such care to make the most of their remaining years.

The spectrum of care

There is a wide range of different types of institutions provided by various statutory, voluntary and private organizations. Statutory organizations means the Health Authorities, who provide hospitals and in some cases nursing homes, and the local authority social services departments who provide residential homes. Voluntary bodies are charitable organisations who can provide both hospitals and homes. They exist to provide support and care and would not seek to make a profit. Finally there are both individuals and companies who provide either hospital or residential care on a commercial basis.

All of these are non-domestic, that is they are places where you go to live with other dependent people. There is also an increasing number of 'sheltered care' developments, including sheltered housing. In this case you have your own dwelling, usually a flat, and some level of help or supervision is available. Typically this means there is a 'warden' whom you can contact if you need to do so but it can include home help or more intensive support.

The different authorities and the facilities for non-domestic residential and day care are summarised in Table 8.1. These various facilities differ in many ways. For example they aim to provide different levels of care, will have different kinds of skills among their staff, different numbers of staff available and will cost differing amounts both to the client and to the taxpayer. All these factors play a part in determining who goes where though the relationship between an individual's income, disability and the care that he or she receives is by no means straightforward.

Table 8.1   The provision of long-term care

OWNER	SERVICE	LIVE IN	LIVE OUT
Health Services	Geriatric	Hospital	Day Hospital
	Psychogeriatric	Hospital	Day Hospital
Social Services	'Ordinary'	Residential Home	Day Centre
	Specialist e.g. Elderly Mentally Infirm (EMI)	Residential Home	Day Centre
Private/Vol.	Private Residential	Residential Home	Day Centre
	Private Nursing	Nursing Home	

Most hospitals in Britain are owned and run by the National Health Service. The great majority of these are concerned with acute illness and treatment. However all authorities provide some places for continuing care and it is mostly older people who live in such places. Whether the care being provided by the NHS is in an acute hospital or in a continuing care unit it is free to the patient. Thus no matter how rich or poor you are you can be looked after at no charge. The only 'charge' is that after you have been in hospital for some time your state old age pension is reduced and you will not be eligible for some benefits. The reduction in pension happens in two stages, after you have been in hospital for 8 weeks it drops a little and after a year it drops quite a bit further. So after a year in hospital you will receive only a small amount (currently about £8 a week) as an allowance for 'extras' like sweets, toiletries or newspapers which you may wish to buy for yourself. The rest of the pension does not go to the hospital or Health Authority but is kept by the central government department.

In a local authority home, things are financially quite different. Each resident is assessed according to his or her means and charged up to a maximum, currently well over £100 a week. The charge is calculated taking into account both your income (such as state and occupational pensions) and your savings if these exceed a certain limit (around £3,000). If you have no more than the basic state pension you pay the minimum charge which leaves you with the same sort of amount you would get from your reduced pension if you lived in hospital for more than a year. The charge goes to the local authority running the home.

This system can seem quite unfair to some residents. If you have saved carefully all your life you are charged more. If you have spent all your money and not thought of your old age you pay less. Such a system does not seem to favour thrift. The care that residents receive is identical no mattter what the charge they are paying.

Similarly if you own your own house and there is no one living there after you go into the home the capital value of this is taken into account. The extra charges that this means may be built up until the house is sold. The local authority will have first claim on the proceeds of the sale even if you have died in the meantime.

Not surprisingly some residents and some relatives feel aggrieved as they see their inheritance being eroded by the charges for a residential home. It can even lead to some reluctance for an older person to be transferred from a hospital (free) to a residential home (expensive). It does not always help to ensure that the best interests, in terms of the most appropriate form of care for the older person, are put first.

The situation becomes even more complicated when we compare what happens in respect of private homes. The traditional image is that these are for those who are able and willing to pay. If you have lots of money you can choose to go into a home that you like and whose fees you are able to pay. This simple picture however now applies to only a limited number of the many private homes which exist and often only to a minority of the residents in a home.

The current situation is that those on a low income and with less than a certain amount of savings are entitled to claim a board and lodging allowance as part of income supplement. This means that if you go into a home and you are eligible for this benefit your income will be topped up to a certain level. This level varies according to the type of home and the type of disability or illness which you may have. It is higher for nursing homes than for residential homes, for example. Those eligible for day and night-time Attendance Allowance can also claim up to a higher limit for residential care.

This system of payment means that many older people who in the past could not have considered private care are now able to do so. In fact because of the rather odd way in which benefits are calculated some people are actually better off in a private than in a local authority home.

The result has been that in recent years there has been a very big expansion in the number of private residential homes. It has been estimated recently that about 40% of those in private homes are being supported in whole or in part by these payments from the public purse. Again, if you have been too thrifty you do not qualify and you may face the prospect of having to spend most of your savings until you are poor enough to qualify. Just as with local authority homes this introduces pressures quite outside the need for care.

Indeed there is no system for ensuring that those who go into a home actually need the level of care provided by a home. For those requiring admission to residential homes run by a local authority the demand generally outstrips supply so that there is careful consideration as to whether admission is the correct course. No such systematic procedures apply to private homes. This is not to say that homes are therefore full of people who do not need to be there. The simple truth is that we do not know.

As I have already indicated those who can afford to pay for a home themselves sometimes take this step by way of preventive action. It is better to go in when you see that you are becoming more frail rather than have to do so in a crisis later. The situation for those going into a home under the supplement income regulations is even less clear.

Such a picture is indeed by no means a simple one. If you feel confused by all this then you are by no means alone. Moreover in reality the regulations are of course a good deal more complicated than the short description which I have given can indicate. Working out what is best for each individual can be very tricky. It certainly does not just depend on what you want or even on how much money you have.

Maintaining standards

Whatever the type of care that is to be provided by an institution, it is obviously important to ensure that this is of a high standard. In the case of private nursing and residential homes in Great Britain this is done as part of a process of registration. All the details of this are far too complex to set down here but the principles which govern this are worth noting as is the code of practice. The details of this code can help any of us to look at institutions for older people even if we do not have any direct contact with the process of registration and inspection. It can most importantly give us some structure for looking at the care we provide and to see how it measures up.

Private residential homes are registered with the local authority social services department. Private hospitals and nursing homes are registered with the local health authority. Both types of registration are governed by legislation so that, for example, it is illegal to run an unregistered home with more than three residents and you cannot describe a home as a nursing home unless it is registered as such. It is the codes of practice and guidelines for such homes that can provide an outline of what we might look for in a good home.

Exercise

Imagine you are looking for a home for an elderly relative who is no longer able to manage at home. List six things that you would look for.

Read one of the guidelines on good practice in homes such as *Home Life: A Code of Practice for Residential Care* (see reading list at the end of this chapter for details of this).

How does the list contained in this compare with what you have listed?

There are a number of different kinds of criteria which we can use to assess how 'good' is a particular home. Some of these are fairly easy to measure and to define. Physical space and temperature for example can be clearly laid down. All you have to do to check this is to go round with a tape measure or a thermometer.

Some other things are a bit more difficult. For example the quality of the food or the state of decoration. If these sorts of things are very bad then there is not too much of a problem in recognising this. However there may be some room for individuals to disagree about what is 'adequate' or 'satisfactory'.

It is more difficult still to assess the 'atmosphere' of a home. Is it a happy place? Would your relative like living here? This may depend on things like staff attitudes, the other residents and the types of disabilities which afflict them. These may however be the really important things when it comes to deciding whether a place is 'right' for somebody. In some ways the physical features such as size of rooms, adequate heating, lighting and so on are a minimum starting point. Beyond this are the things which decide how much somewhere is an institution and how much it is a home. These often depend on human behaviour rather than on the environment although of course there is some interplay between these. It is more difficult to give high quality care in a place where there is not enough space and some buildings are much easier to make 'homely' than others.

It is in the interactions between the people in the home that we can often see the greatest difference between the good and the bad institutions. Those interactions depend on both the residents and the staff. It is the residents whom we shall consider next.

Residents

I shall use the term residents to refer to those in homes and hospitals even though the latter are usually referred to as patients. All those in any kind of long-term care are residents but those in homes are not necessarily patients in that they may not be suffering from any particular illness.

If we take a look at things from the residents' point of view it seems reasonable to start by asking 'Why do people come into homes or hospitals to live?' This might seem a bit silly in that it is presumably because they need that sort of care. But we have already seen when we looked at the role of families in caring for elderly frail people that the majority of old people, irrespective of disability, stay out of institutions. It is those who live alone or who have other care problems that tend to go into homes and hospitals. Moreover the different types of institutions tend to take different sorts of people, or rather people with different sorts of needs. It may not even be the level of dependency alone which determines the type of home or hospital. It may depend on the previous care that person has received and what particular episode, which in itself might be quite minor, has tipped the balance in favour of care outside rather than within the home.

Hospital care

We tend to think of hospitals as being places where people go when they are ill. This is as true of older people as it is of younger. However there is also often some other factor that has led to the particular admission to long-term care. If we think of the example of an older person who has had a stroke, the idea of illness leading to going to hospital works quite well. If however we think of someone who has been suffering from gradually worsening arthritis for many years it may be a fall or some other illness which finally breaks the fragile web of community survival. It may be that a relatively trivial incident leads to the admission but that once this has happened the carer feels that he or she can simply no longer cope. It may even be that someone who was previously unknown to the professionals who normally provide help at home comes into hospital and it is then discovered that he or she has been failing to cope properly at home for quite some time. It can be that poor housing is the real problem and perhaps the chest infection simply means that the difficult situation is revealed for all to see. Once that has happened it can be very difficult to send that person home even once the illness has been resolved although if he or she had never come into hospital no one would have felt it necessary to take that person out of his or her own home.

Often this kind of admission, especially if it is due to a carer being no longer able to cope, is referred to as a 'social admission'. This is often said in such a way as to imply that it should never have happened but somehow it was unavoidable. Sometimes hearing staff talk about such an admission it almost sounds as if it is the patient or, more likely, the carer who is to blame for wasting hospital time. Missionary zeal to rehabilitate older people and to avoid long-term hospital care can sometimes be overdone.

Whatever the actual circumstances under which someone came into hospital, those who no longer have an acute medical problem and who cannot go home will usually be considered for transfer to a residential home. It is only the most disabled who would continue to be looked after in hospital. Deciding which type of setting best suits the needs of particular elderly people requires a good deal of inter-professional cooperation and understanding. Where this is in short supply argument rather than agreement is all too common.

Residential care

Often of course the person may go straight into a residential home. This may be much better in that it avoids a further relocation but there is then the slight risk that some condition which might respond to medical treatment is put down to old age rather than being actively treated. The same sorts of 'social' factors that I mentioned above in relation to hospitals lead to most of the admissions to residential care. The breakdown of carers, the collapse of self-care and poor housing all contribute greatly.

There is often a good deal of similarity between those who are in hospitals long-term and those who are in homes (Gilleard *et al*. 1980) and I shall go into this in a little more detail shortly. As people change in frailty they are not at some fixed level of disability transferred to a 'more appropriate' setting. This is as it should be since to have an inflexible rule would be to treat people as 'examples of disability' rather than human beings. However frail someone may be he or she will usually become attached to the place where he or she lives. Thus the need for more care, for example, must be balanced against the disruption of moving. As we saw in the previous chapter, the effects of 'relocation' are particularly relevant to frail older people.

Relocation and residential care

For those who have to leave home the problem of relocation is considerable and it is not surprising that many find the adjustment difficult to make. The process may show many of the features of grief which we looked at in chapter 5. The person may feel numb for a while and this may be mistaken for good adjustment ('Isn't he [or she] settling in well') He or she may yearn for his or her home, be tearful and depressed and so on. The process of adjustment may be more difficult still if the person had to leave home suddenly, most of all if this was because the carer had died. This means a multiple bereavement.

The process of adjustment can be further complicated by any significant dementia if this means that the person cannot easily learn his or her way around or remember why he or she has come to live there.

The two most important ingredients to the success of adjustment are time and personal support. For many personal crises the period of emotional upheaval is most marked for about 6 weeks. Thus the natural process is such that most people have begun to settle fairly well within a couple of months or so. Those with some degree of memory problems may of course take a different course. I can think of examples both of people who have settled very quickly, perhaps not being very aware of where they are, and those who seem to take for ever, constantly asking to go home or thinking that they only arrived this morning.

Personal support comes both from the person themselves (what sort of a person are they) and from those around them. Those around can probably best help by being a good listener and responding to the person as an individual. Here again is the theme of continuity in ageing. As we grow older we change as people slowly or not at all, quite the opposite of childhood. The change from one place to another can threaten to overwhelm the individual and so emphasising continuity is important. This can be done by encouraging people to bring their personal effects and having adequate space for these. In hospital it is important to remember that it is very comforting to have your own clothing and that interaction with others is much easier if you have things like a hearing aid or glasses if you normally use these. The feeling of being cut off from the world outside can be assuaged both by visitors and by being able to go outside. There are still lots of places, both hospitals and homes, which do not have room to store people's outside coats and many people have nothing to put on their feet besides slippers.

The problem of being short of belongings can be especially noticeable for those who come into hospital. We all know that when you go into hospital you do not need to take very much with you. You probably do not even need a set of outdoor clothes since, of course, people who are ill spend most of the time in bed in their nightwear. In fact this is not even true of most acute hospital wards and should not be true of any continuing care units. The trouble is that it is not always clear when the change from one to another takes place. Indeed if you call long-term care 'slow stream rehabilitation' does it ever take place at all? But if you are to be living somewhere for the rest of your life perhaps it helps to be clear about this and for the things that mean most to you to go with you. This is all part of the adjustment to relocation.

Who should be cared for where?

From what I have said so far it should be fairly clear that there is quite an overlap between the different kinds of institutions for older people. This can sometimes make it difficult for those working in, say, hospital to appreciate what it is like in a residential home. Suppose we consider the cases of two imaginary people, Mrs Blake and Mrs Davey.

Mrs Blake has been living in Greenfield Old People's Home for about 5 years. She suffers from arthritis and very recently had a slight stroke. This means that she now needs someone to help her get about and to help with things like washing and going to the toilet. She has become rather forgetful over the last 2 years and sometimes accuses people of stealing things from her which in fact she has simply misplaced. After she has been on Lewis Ward for a couple of weeks following a chest infection the consultant feels that she is ready to go home. The ward doctor, Dr Beal, contacts the home who arrange for her to go back there on the following Thursday.

Mrs Davey is also on Lewis Ward following a slight stroke. She has been suffering from progressive dementia for some time but has been looked after by her husband. Unfortunately shortly after her admission he himself had to go into hospital following a heart attack and he died 3 weeks ago. Mrs Davey has no family and could not look after herself at home. She is noticeably forgetful and now needs help to get around and with dressing, washing and toileting. The consultant suggests that she might go to a residential home. Dr Beal contacts the social worker to suggest this but is told 'I'm sorry, she is too dependent, she will have to stay in hospital.'

Dr Beal is very puzzled. He thinks that Mrs Blake and Mrs Davey both need the same sort of level of care. How can it be that the home will take one but not the other?

The answer may lie in the fact that although there is an overlap between those in homes and those in hospital the two are not interchangeable. On the whole those who are the most dependent residents in homes have been there a long time. They were not so dependent when first they went there. It is possible to cater for their continuing care despite increased dependency so long as there are only a few in one home at any one time. To keep this sort of balance means that the 'criteria' for *staying* in a home must be different from those for *going there* for the first time. Thus it is not enough simply to look at a home and conclude that as one resident is very disabled, any new resident could be that frail. This may be true of hospitals but not of homes, where there tends to be a much wider distribution of disability.

Measuring disability

Even if we are not deliberately doing so, we all make comparisons between people. We judge whether we like them or not, whether they are more or less helpful, good or bad tennis players and so on. If we are working with those who are ill or disabled we also do this and use this kind of comparison to help us decide how much help each person needs. For our own everyday purposes our own ideas are quite good enough. But if we are trying to help people in a professional way then such vague individual assessments of how ''disabled' someone is cannot be enough. We need better and more systematic ways to measure disability.

There are almost as many ways of measuring disability as there are homes caring for older people. Certainly when people have tried to look systematically at how much help people need they have very often devised their own scale for doing so. This may mean that this scale has been very useful to them but it does make it difficult to compare one set of results with another. One of the basic principles of measurement is that you try to keep to the same scale or at least use one that compares directly with what other people use.

If I wish to buy a piece of carpet I begin by measuring the size of the room. I will probably use a standard measure which tells me the size in feet and inches. I might then go to the shop and find that they sell everything by the metre. This just means that I have to convert my measurements into metres and all is well. Imagine what it would be like if I did not use a tape measure but any old piece of string that came to hand. I then go into the shop and tell them I want a piece of carpet 27 string lengths long. This only works if I have taken the piece of string with me and the shopkeeper can measure it with his tape measure. Without the piece of string there is no way I am going to get a carpet the right size.

Constructing your own scale can be a bit like choosing your own piece of string. It works fine for comparing one room with another but not your house with one further up the street.

Indeed the situation can be even worse than this. If you use a bad measuring instrument it may be more like trying to measure things with a piece of elastic. Each time you use it you pull more or less hard so the scale itself changes. Someone else using it will also get quite different results; the measure is unreliable.

Likewise it is quite important to make sure that you are measuring what you think you are. If you want to measure how much fruit your apple tree has produced the best thing to do is to weigh all the apples from the tree. If you were not able to do this you might try to count them all. This would be not quite as good but might be better than nothing. It might be quite useful for comparing this year's crop with those from previous years off the same tree.

However counting them would not be a very good way of comparing different trees since one might produce bigger apples than another. The problem here is of 'validity'; counting is not a true or 'valid' measure of the total amount of fruit. In the case of disability we must therefore ensure that the measures that we use are reliable and as valid as possible.

Fortunately there are some standard instruments that are available which enable us to measure disability with at least some precision: enough precision to draw general conclusions about how one group of people compares with another. Two examples which have been quite widely used for measuring disability in homes and hospitals for older people are the Crichton Royal Behaviour Rating Scale (CRBRS) and the Clifton Assessment Procedures for the Elderly (CAPE).

The CRBRS is a short rating scale which asks questions about how much help people need with things like bathing and dressing, whether they are confused about their surroundings and so on. It has been used to compare homes and hospitals as well as to look at how the levels of disability in these settings change over time.

The CAPE also consists of a rating scale for measuring behaviour but the scale can also be subdivided so as to give separate measures of, for example, physical dependency and disturbed behaviour. Moreover the CAPE also includes some brief tests of thinking and remembering. It has been widely used to compare many different groups of older people.

Both of these scales ask specific questions about different areas of behaviour which helps to ensure that different people use it in the same way. It is very easy to ask 'How confused is this person?' but the definition of 'Confused' can depend very much on the person filling in scale. Asking questions like 'Does this person have trouble finding his or her way around the home?' is less prone to disagreement.

Using this sort of scale it is possible to get some idea of the range and type of disability typical of residents in different sorts of homes as well as those in their own homes or somewhere like sheltered housing. The answers for each question are assigned a score which can be added up at the end to give what looks very much as if it might be a 'measure' of disability.

It can be very tempting to use the scales therefore to define the sort of criteria that so baffled Dr Beal in the example above. Could we not say that anyone up to a certain level of disability can go into this home, anyone over this level cannot. Sadly this is not the case. There are at least two reasons for this.

First the scales are made up of several different sorts of items. It is a bit like trying to assess how good is a motor car. Many different things such as fuel economy, speed, looks, comfort and so on must be taken into account. How you put all these together depends very much on what you as a customer are looking for.

Similarly, if we are looking at how to provide the best care for an older person we have to look at many different criteria. It is unrealistic, indeed downright wrong, to expect this to be summarised by a single score.

Secondly there is the problem that although the scales are widely used they are still somewhat unreliable. This means that someone else filling it in might get a slightly different score. It would therefore be quite unjustified to make major decisions affecting where someone lives on just one score for that individual.

These things do not matter quite so much if we are looking at groups of people as over the group as a whole the errors will tend to balance out. However this is not so for individual scores. Such ratings can be used for individuals but they should be used to ask rather than answer questions. By this I mean that it is possible, for example, to use the scale to see whether someone is very unusual for a particular setting. If someone on a long stay hospital ward gets a score which is typical of the sort of person who is in sheltered housing it may alert people to ask the question 'Is this ward the best place for this person?' The answer may be 'yes' for special reasons peculiar to that person but at least the question can be asked.

For groups of people the use of such ratings is particularly appropriate. It may help to answer questions such as 'Are the people in this home now more frail than those who were here a year ago?' It may help to identify reasons why things seem to have changed or to estimate what is going to happen in the future.

Disability in homes

The results of studies of disability in homes and hospitals reveal many things of interest. They generally support the notion that residents have become a good deal more frail in recent years. This is of course quite consistent with the trend towards active treatment of illness and disability in old age and the tendency to try to keep people in their own homes for as long as possible. The former has had a particular impact on hospitals, the latter on residential homes.

Part of this trend has been reflected in the tendency for the proportion of those in residential homes suffering from mental frailty to rise. Most surveys find that these days even in 'ordinary' residential homes about 30 to 40%, about one in three, of the residents have some significant degree of mental infirmity, typically dementia. This can cause considerable problems and may require special solutions.

One reason for the problems is usually the mixture of mentally alert and mentally frail residents (Masterton *et al*. 1979). It is not simply that the latter are more dependent and difficult. I know at least one person in charge of a home who finds that it is the mentally alert residents who give her the most problems. It is the mix of residents and the reactions of both.

For many years there has been heated debate about the desirability or otherwise of having special homes or units for those who suffer from marked dementia, the Elderly Mentally Infirm (EMI). On the one hand there are those who believe they deserve special care, on the other there are those who feel that they should not be kept apart but integrated into the ordinary home. In practice the best policy is one which provides a range of facilities.

We have seen previously that the sort of care required for someone suffering for dementia depends not only on the level of mental impairment but ton their physical capabilities and, especially, on the level of behaviour disturbance. This is particularly true for those who are cared for in residential homes.

Those who are 'pleasantly muddled' may be quite happily integrated into an ordinary home, especially if there are only a few such residents. The mentally alert can be helpful and supportive to that person and assist them in living as normal a life as possible. However if the person is more difficult, perhaps wandering off with other people's belongings or keeping others awake at night, support can all too easily turn to resentment. Then the mentally unimpaired will bring about their own segregation, keeping to one lounge and turning away a confused resident unfortunate enough to wander in. This is not integration, it is victimisation. For this situation a special unit may be much better for all concerned.

We can be certain that the proportion of mentally frail residents will continue to rise as community care succeeds in keeping more of those who are alert at home. A recent report by the Centre for Policy on Ageing (see reading list: *Severe Dementia: The Provision of Long Stay Care*) emphasises that long-term residential care should, for some mentally frail older people, be the best option, not something that is kept as a last resort. For this group we need not be ashamed to aim for high quality residential care.

The problem which arises between the mentally alert and the mentally impaired is but one example of the power of residents. Although individual residents have very limited power in many ways, the influence of the residents as a group is nonetheless a significant force. It will affect not only how the residents interact but may defy the best efforts of staff to introduce some change which they may be convinced would be for the better. For example it is a common sight to see all the chairs in a day room in a home or hospital lined up round the wall. This is usually put down to insensitive staff who find it easier to clean that way. In fact if you try to change this it is often the residents who most resist this and shift the chairs back to their original position. This can then be put down to their being 'institutionalised'. But is this really the case? Perhaps some of these things are not as abnormal as we think or may have to do with the design of the home rather than the attitude of the staff. Of course what staff do matters a lot and how their attitudes affect the lives of residents is the next topic.

Staff

The most expensive part of running any home or hospital is the cost of the staff who work there. Not only do they cost more than heating, lighting and food but their behaviour can determine more than anything else what happens in that home. What are they there to do?

If, as here, we are concerned with the various types of long-term care, then the job of staff can be seen as very similar whatever the setting. However this may not be everybody's assumption since hospitals and homes are different sorts of places. If we look for example at the requirements for registration of homes there would seem to be big differences between residential homes and nursing homes. In practice the distinction can be more apparent than real except for some activities which are obviously 'nursing' duties (like giving injections) and which staff in a residential home would not be allowed to carry out. Most of the time of those who work in homes and hospitals is spent in much the same way, in providing care for residents. The intensity of care required will differ but the basic tasks of help with dressing, walking and so on are common to both.

We should pause to ask here if this is really how things should be. Is the job of staff to care for people and if so what does this mean? Well it is certainly the job of staff to provide care in a general sense. The people who are looked after in such homes are generally unable to look after themselves at least to some degree. However the idea of providing 'care' may also imply that the person who receives care has something done to or for him or herself. This is even more apparent if we think of a long-term hospital. A hospital is a place where people go to be looked after. The very word 'patient' means someone who suffers and is related to the word passive. If you are a patient you have something wrong with you and you may go into hospital to have other people look after you. This is most obviously true of something like appendicitis where as a patient one is even unconscious for the central part of the treatment, the surgery.

But if someone is in a home, a place where they are going to live for many years, being this passive is not such a good idea. In this case it may be much better if the staff help them to do things rather than doing them for them. This will help the people in need of assistance to remain as independent as possible and thus have as much control as they can about what happens to them.

This idea is not just 'common sense'. As we noted previously, when local authority homes were set up by the National Assistance Act in 1948, much emphasis was laid on the move away from the workhouse. The workhouse was at one extreme where if you were able to do so you did work for other people, usually for some sort of public body as if in some way to pay for being kept by the public purse from starvation. It was suggested that with the setting up of residential homes the move should be away from the relationship between the inmate and master and towards that of guest and hotel manager.

Of course this was certainly a good way for things to move, but perhaps the guest/manager relationship itself does not quite capture the best possible image. After all if I go and stay in a hotel I do not expect the person who cleans the room to give me a duster and ask if I would like to lend a hand. Nor do I expect to find myself drafted into the kitchen or being asked to go for some shopping. I might go shopping but it would be because I choose to do so.

But often these are just the sorts of activities which it may be best to encourage people in homes to develop. After all if we look at how older people in their own homes spend their time it is mostly either asleep or in some form of 'obligated' time, that is doing just these sorts of things. If we then take away all the daily activities like cooking, cleaning and so on by 'looking after' someone in a home then we should not be too surprised if they spend rather a lot of time sitting around, sleeping or doing nothing.

Activity and stimulation

The low level of activity is one of the most striking things about all too many places caring for frail older people. It provides an image which drives many younger people to think or say 'I hope I never end up like that'. Is this something that we should try to overcome and if so, what can be done about it?

Part of this dreadful image of 'nothing happening' comes from the considerable silence. The most common solution to this is simply to turn on the radio or the television. Unfortunately this is usually done with total lack of regard for content except when the radio is tuned to the pop music station favoured by the staff. The radio or television is then carefully positioned so that it is as loud as possible and yet just outside the patients' reach. I am sure that there must be something in international law or the Geneva Convention which forbids acoustic torture of this sort. Certainly when I ask a group of older people in a day room if they would mind if I turned the radio off so that I can talk to a resident the reaction is almost always 'Please do, it's giving me a headache.' Perhaps a better response to the silence would be to use it to talk to people and finds out what they would like to do, if anything.

The assumption that doing nothing is wrong runs very deep in us. We cherish the idea that it is better to be busy and that 'The devil makes work for idle hands'. Certainly enforced idleness, such as being confined by a broken leg or some sort of illness, can be very frustrating. We even use locking people up so that they have to do nothing as a form of punishment.

However we must not necessarily assume that everybody who is doing nothing is unhappy. It is true that people who are depressed tend to sit around doing nothing. However the reverse is not true as at least one study found in an old people's home (Simpson *et al*. 1981). This showed that some of those who appeared to be doing very little were spending a lot of time thinking, especially thinking about the past. Some of those who were quite busy were also quite unhappy so that activity was pretty well unrelated to mood.

It is the *opportunity* to do things that is important. There need be no obligation on the residents to join in but if the activity is to their liking then they can do so. Staff are not after all entertainment organisers in a holiday camp. The right sort of activity is crucial. Neither bingo nor bridge suits everybody. Probably one of the worst examples of inappropriate activity was one study where the ideas introduced to the home were taken from work with the mentally handicapped. Polishing coins was but one example of a number of activities little suited to the needs of mentally alert older people.

We come back once again to the principle that older people are individuals. Thus they need activities suited to their individual interests and abilities. Not everybody will be like the 85 year old lady I know who lives in a home but does the quick crossword in the *Daily Telegraph* every morning and who has recently successfully taken up painting and drawing. Some people are like the 'rocking chair' group whom I mentioned towards the beginning of this book. They see old age as a time to sit back and watch the world go by. Some of those who come into a home will likewise expect to be looked after, especially if they are paying. It is helpful if such expectations can be made explicit if only so that due allowance can be made.

There are many examples of what are relevant activities and things like reminiscence have been developed a good deal in recent years. For some idea of the range of activities there are several useful books and articles.

Exercise

Make up your own list of possible activities for residents in a home or hospital.

How does this compare with:
(a) The suggestions in one of the books in the reading list.
(b) The suggestions you get from actually asking residents what they would like to do?

The effect of staff behaviour on residents is of course much more widespread than just through any sort of formal activity. Often the times when staff can get closest to residents are when providing individual personal care such as helping someone to get dressed or to have a bath. Even the way that staff address residents can influence the type of relationship between them. There can be something of a conflict between the need to respect each individual in a professional way (e.g. 'How are you today, Mr Smith?') and the wish to be homely ('Hello Fred. How's things?'). Once again there can be big differences between individual older people in how they like to be addressed and this can only be best determined for each individual. Whatever our own inclination we must resist using any particular form of address, especially one that is 'familiar', until we know what each person likes. Calling everybody 'Luv' as a matter of routine is not good practice.

Similarly staff behaviour may indicate various rules and regulations about what goes on in a home. If staff behave as if they take it for granted that everyone should be in bed by 10 p.m. then that can easily become not just the norm, it can become the rule. How carefully staff listen to complaints says a lot about how much they value the residents' point of view. How rigid or indeed how flexible they are suggests how much confidence they have in what they are doing.

It is often said that older people like routine and like things to be predictable. This is in fact true of all of us. For example, it easy to observe in any home how the residents tend to keep to the same chair in the lounge or the same place in the dining room. This is said to be a sign of their institutionalisation. But this is true of many homes both domestic and institutional.

Exercise

Imagine which chair or chairs you have sat in at home to watch television over the last week.

How many different chairs? Could your family say, if asked, which is your chair?

There is undoubtedly much to be said for things being predictable, but at what point do things become institutional? The answer here would seem to lie in our need to feel some form of control over what happens in our lives. We know from many psychological studies that if we are faced with repeated experiences of being unable to control things by our actions we can become pathetic and depressed. This state is often referred to as 'learned helplessness'. Some people are more prone to this than others but we all need at least some sense that what we do affects what happens to us.

Being able to predict what is going to happen is one way of fulfilling this need but it is only second best. What we need more is to know that we can change things if we wish to. Thus it can be good to know that supper is at 6 o'clock but it is better still to know that you can choose to have supper at 8 o'clock if you want to. It is not so much the basic routine which is a problem. Things are institutionalised when everybody has to conform to that routine.

Of course there may be situations where it is necessary to have a fairly rigid programme just in order to cope. It would be very difficult, for example, to let all the patients in a big district general hospital choose exactly when they have lunch. But this must be less so in a place that is more 'homely'. If 'cleanliness is next to godliness' then 'flexibility is next to homeliness'.

Taking risks

Similar principles apply when it comes to encouraging independence. There is always a balance to be struck between allowing people freedom of choice and independence and the risk which can go with this. As adults all older people are in principle free to choose what they do provided it does not jeopardise the freedom and choice of others. However the presence of both physical and, especially, mental frailty does complicate this simple principle. It is very easy for others to assume that all older people need protection, though protection from what is not always clear. Thus if someone is a little unsteady on their feet it may be tempting to suggest that they only be allowed to walk when there is someone with them. After all, what would happen if they fell and broke a bone?

In very many cases this sort of concern is overemphasised, particularly when staff feel vulnerable and unsupported. The spectre of the coroner's court rises over the scene and it is easy always to be looking to minimise any possible blame to ourselves. This can have the effect of stopping older people from doing almost anything and does not make for good care. Neither downright neglect nor over-protection are the sign of good practice.

Evaluating institutional care

Saying that something is 'good practice' implies that it is better than something that is 'bad practice'. How do we decide which is which and how do we decide how good is the care in a home or hospital? There are two main ways of trying to tell how good the care is in any setting. First, we can look at what goes on in the process of providing care and, second, we can look at what is the outcome of that care.

As with so many things, doing this for continuing care is not as easy as for something like the treatment of acute illness. If we want to know whether one sort of care is better than another in the treatment of, say, appendicitis we can measure how many people having different sorts of care get better and how quickly they get better. The outcome for a nursing or residential home is by no means so obvious.

The process of care

The way most of us start to evaluate care is by thinking in some general way about whether this particular place is the sort of place where we would like to be looked after ourselves or where we would like our loved ones to be cared for. This is quite a useful rule of thumb although it can be a bit difficult since what we might like for ourselves might not be everybody's choice. Similarly it is hard to define this in objective terms that can be measured with some degree of consistency. As we noted earlier, it is easier to measure things about the physical environment ('Is this room warm enough?') than it is to measure psychological factors ('Is this place friendly enough?').

There have been several attempts nonetheless to assess what goes on in homes and to try and decide whether one sort of care is better than another. Most of these are attempts to define what is meant by 'quality of care' or 'quality of life'.

It is generally accepted that for the frail elderly there is more to good care than simply prolonging life for as long as possible. What matters just as much is the quality of life for each individual older person. There is a time when the most intensive use of medical technology is no longer the most urgent priority. It is no good deciding if one home has done better than another simply on how long residents in each home live. It is much more appropriate to look at the policies and programmes of different homes and the success or otherwise that these have in determining the well-being of those who live there.

I have already referred to the work which has been done in setting down guidelines for the promotion of good practice in the registration of residential homes, and to the similar pointers to good practice which have also been devised for the care of those suffering from severe dementia. However such checklists or notes are not designed to measure, only to guide.

The majority of work on measurement has come from projects carried out in the USA. One such project has devised a comprehensive set of assessment scales under the title of the 'Multiphasic Environmental Assessment Procedure' (Moos *et al*. 1979, Lemke and Moos 1980). This has a range of different scales which includes, for example, a scale for looking at the policy of and programmes in a home. This covers, among other things, the way residents are selected, what they are expected to be able to do for themselves, how well eccentricity is tolerated, how much say residents have in the way the home is run and the availability of social and recreational facilities. This scale alone consists of 150 items in total so we can see that measuring these things is no quick and easy matter. Moreover there is as yet no similar British scale. For the moment this sort of study can therefore only give us guidance as to what areas to cover rather than a tried and tested instrument for routine use.

This may be rather frustrating but it worth noting that just reviewing things in a systematic way can help to bring about improvements. Perhaps the biggest danger in working in any institution for any length of time is that you become blind to its faults. Taking a careful and systematic look at what is going on can be a great stimulus to change.

Such a review is also important in looking at the progress of residents. We are not very good at seeing things change when they change slowly. Few of us, for example, can say that we actually see trees and plants grow nor do we see ourselves ageing. Similarly if we are to be alerted to gradual change in the abilities or well-being of residents it is valuable to take stock at regular intervals to see if things have changed and to decide how best to provide care. It is a good idea to set aside specific time for such a review, which for any one resident might only be necessary every few months.

Such a review might cover that individual's present physical abilities, his or her mental and social functioning and contact with people outside the home. It can cover things like clothing, activities and interests to see whether any of these have changed or might benefit from improvement.

The outcome of care

When it comes to assessing outcome things are more difficult still. In the case of older people in any kind of residential care many will be suffering from progressive conditions such as arthritis, Parkinson's Disease or dementia. The fact that someone has deteriorated may be no sign that the care they have received has been inadequate. Moreover a home which takes lots of very frail people will have more who decline, or even die, than one which takes only the relatively fit and healthy. Comparing such homes it may look as if the one is doing very much worse than another unless we take such variables into account.

It is possible however to predict at least approximately how people might be expected to be in, say, 6 months' time from a detailed knowledge of their present problems. One fairly radical suggestion, again from the USA, has been that this could form the basis for relating the reimbursement of private nursing home fees to the quality of care (Kane *et al*. 1983).

The notion is that each resident would be assessed at regular intervals. On the basis of this assessment some prediction would be made about how that person should be getting on when next assessed. The actual outcome would then be compared with the predicted. A home where the residents consistently did better than expected would get paid a bonus. One where residents did less well would get only a basic fee. This of course is much better suited to a system where private care is the norm but should not be dismissed as irrelevant elsewhere. It might have many problems in terms of practical implementation but would at least avoid the situation where it pays those running homes to provide care for the most able rather than those who really need such care.

In particular we can learn a lot by just considering the ways in which such outcome has been assessed. Success in care has been defined in terms of residents' abilities to think and remember, their satisfaction with the care, the residents' mood, their physical state and their level of social activity. Making some regular assessment of these could surely do much to improve the quality of care for many older people in institutions.

The idea of principles of good practice is, of course, much more widely applicable than just to homes and hospital. Doing the best possible job is something which should concern us all. I shall now look at changing ourselves.

References

Gilleard, C. J., Pattie, A. H., and Dearman, G. (1980) Behavioural disabilities in psychogeriatric patients and residents of old people's homes. *Journal of Epidemiology and Community Health* **34** 106–110.

Kane, R. L., Bell, R., Reigler, S., Wilson, A., and Kane, R. A. (1983) Assessing the outcome of nursing home patients. *Journal of Gerontology* **38** 385–393.

Lemke, S., and Moos, R. H. (1980) Assessing the institutional policies of sheltered care settings. *Journal of Gerontology* **35** 99–107.

Masterton, G., Holloway, E. M., and Timbury, G. C. (1979) The prevalence of organic cerebral impairment and behavioural problems within local authority homes for the elderly. *Age and Ageing* **8** 226–230.

Moos, R. H., Gauvin, M., Lemke, S., Max, W., and Melven, B. (1979) Assessing the social environments of sheltered care settings. *Gerontologist* **19** 74–82.

Simpson, S., Woods, R., and Britton, P. (1981) Depression and engagement in a residential home for the elderly. *Behaviour Research and Therapy* **19** 435–438.

Further reading

The Centre for Policy on Ageing (formerly called the National Corporation for the Care of Old People) has published a number of reports relevant to the principles of good practice in the care of older people. These include:

Home Life: A Code of Practice for Residential Care (1984)

The report of a DHSS working party which includes guidelines used in the registration of private residential homes in Britain.

Rights and Risks: A Discussion Document on Civil Liberties in Old Age (1980) by Alison Norman

This identifies the need to balance individual freedom against the possible risks to safety for frail older people.

Severe Dementia: The Provision of Long Stay Care (1987) by Alison Norman

Reviews the national specialist provision for the mentally frail elderly, describes in detail 14 establishments providing high quality care and gives a checklist of good practice.

Winslow Press publish a number of books suggesting activities for frail older people including:

Norris, A.   *Reminiscence.*
Cornish, P. *Activities for the Frail Elderly.*
Holden, U. *Thinking it through—A Handbook for Those Working with the Elderly.*

Section III

Professional Issues

Chapter 9

Who Cares?

So far we have been looking at the ways in which psychological knowledge about ageing can help us to provide better help for older people. The focus has been on understanding the processes of ageing, the effects of life events common in late life and how the environment influences people's behaviour. We have seen how to apply a knowledge of the psychology of ageing to older people. But it should already be clear that in order to do things better *we* have to change. As we are people too, we can also use psychological knowledge to advantage concerning ourselves.

Changing ourselves

If what is in this book is to mean anything in terms of improved care for older people it has to achieve a change in what people, namely you the readers, do. I therefore make no apologies for spending this chapter setting down some suggestions for doing just this. The model that I am using is very much the same as the goal-setting model which I have described earlier. The aim is to help you answer the following questions:

1. What are the aims of the care or help that I and my colleagues provide for older people?
2. What skills do we need to achieve these aims?
3. What sort of a person am I? What skills do I already have?
4. How can I best improve my skills to match those identified in question 2?

Exercise

Very briefly try to put down at least one short answer to each question. (Do not worry if this seems difficult. It should be a bit easier when we have looked at each question in more detail.)

What are we trying to do?

Before we can change, we need to look hard at the way we do things now and why we do them. I have not so far said much about how caring for older people depends on the attitudes and expectations of the carer, thinking here particularly of 'professional' carers, i.e. those who get paid. Why do people do this sort of job? Is it just a job like any other or does it tend to attract special sorts of people? Perhaps like being an explorer or a missionary it even requires one to be have a particular sort of personality. Certainly the rewards are in many ways different from those of other jobs.

You may already be aware that this is not as easy to answer as it may seem. It depends both on the kind of care which you are trying to provide, where you work and what is your idea of the needs of older people. One way to illustrate this is to consider a few remarks about the needs of older people and their families.

Old people are just like children. All they need is ... warmth, comfort and affection. They are vulnerable and need protection and looking after.

Old people deserve to be looked after because they have done their bit for society in the past.

Families have a duty to care for their elderly relatives.

If old people can't manage on their own they ought to go into a home.

Now you may not agree with any or all of these but I hope you would accept that there are many people who would agree with at least some of them. Even when these sorts of things are not expressed directly they may be believed to be true and influence what people do. There are moreover many other examples of similar statements and attitudes which show how people think about older people and the implications of growing older.

It is not appropriate here to go into the many different attitudes to ageing and the implications of all the stereotypes. However it is useful to look at a few recurring themes. One is that older people are frail and need looking after. They are not seen as choosing the sort of care they need but as needing this to be chosen for them. Similarly they may be seen as being somewhat like children or for some other reason having simpler, more basic needs than other people.

Another unwritten 'law' for some people is that families are the right people to care for old people and that anything else is second best. Others may think that when older people become frail the 'best' thing is for the person to go into a home. If there is no family to provide the care, and remember that nearly one in three of those aged over 75 has no surviving children, then is it the duty of the state to provide care instead?

Attitudes like this are not just important in so far as they are held by those directly concerned with helping older people. Attitudes of this sort are also reflected in the way 'the public' expects older people to be cared for and I shall now consider two examples of this. One is the way in which items of news relating to older people are reported on the television and in the newspapers. The other is what people say to you at parties.

The media and ageing

Because it makes much better 'news', it is only the more dramatic examples of what happens that get into the media. Thus it may not be until a tragedy occurs that there is any mention of older people at all.

However when we do read of the response in the press to a tragic case such as where an older person has died at home and lain undiscovered for some time it is not hard to pick out a sense of public outrage. 'Something should have been done' would probably sum up most of the reports of this nature.

Of course in cases where things genuinely did go wrong such outrage is quite right and proper. It can go a long way towards preventing similar problems arising in the future. However this outrage seems to apply whether or not something *was* done. Even if help had been turned away by that old person there is the lingering feeling that 'something *more* should have been done'. The assumption from the start is that such cases happen because the services failed rather than because the older person did not really want help. Older people are rarely credited with the power to decide for themselves.

One example of this I saw very recently on the television news. The item in question was based on a recent report from Age Concern England highlighting a shortage of nursing homes. The short picture sequence included pictures of a lady in her nineties who was making a cup of tea despite her poor sight and arthritis. The commentary went something like 'Mrs Jones has been told by her doctor that she should no longer live on her own but should go into a home ....' No mention of what Mrs Jones wants, only what her doctor has said she should do. When you consider that no organisation is more committed to older people being independent and able to choose for themselves than Age Concern, the style of reporting was perhaps unfortunate to say the least.

Party talk

One other way to find out how people feel about old age is to notice how they react when you say that you work with older people. The usual response is something like 'How do you put up with it?—I couldn't do that sort of work.—Doesn't it make you depressed seeing all those old people?' It is not very often that you get a reply such as 'That must be really exciting. Do tell me more about what you actually do.'

In extreme cases admitting to an interest in older people can bring the conversation to a total standstill and leave you with the impression that they

feel sorry for you having to do such a dreadful job. Being the envy of all
your friends is not one of the obvious rewards of working with older people.
Nevertheless we all need rewards for what we do and for most of us this
should mean more than just money. We need to know what we are trying
to do and that sometimes at least we succeed in achieving this.

Doing our best

In order to know that we are doing our best we must first ask the question
'How do we define success in helping older people?' Is it just in terms of
how long someone lives or can it also include how *well* they live? Are we
trying to provide as much care as possible for an older person or do we
need to think about helping them to help themselves? If there are risks in
not having help can we allow them to say no? Allowing people to exercise
choice is never very easy, especially if there is any hint of some degree of
dementia. It can be very hard to decide that the best thing to do is to do
nothing.

The same sort of problems can arise in the care of an older person who
is very frail and seriously physically ill. How much should we be expecting
every possible medical intervention to be tried in order to prolong life?
Are other circumstances when it is better to refrain from treatment and 'let
nature take its course'?

As we saw in chapter 5, the definition of what is 'success' in providing
care depends very much on the setting in which you work, as well as, hopefully, on the needs of each individual older person. In an acute geriatric
hospital the emphasis will be on identifying and treating medical problems.
A measure of success here might well include the number of illnesses correctly identified and successfully treated. This might then be reflected in the
success in discharging people so that the limited resources, especially hospital beds, can be used to treat as many people as possible. There would,
all being well, be general agreement among patients, relatives and staff as
to what each was trying to achieve. Also the success of acute treatment is
usually fairly obvious as the patient goes from being very ill to being well
again. Not only this but after successful treatment the grateful patient often
leaves expressing his or her gratitude for the care given. This sort of care
has its own rewards built in.

Even so in acute care there will be some cases when all treatable conditions have been excluded and in such cases there must be a shift towards
concentrating on the relief of symptoms. The right measure of success here
is the extent to which pain is relieved or other distressing symptoms controlled and the adjustment of the patient and family to the fact of dying.
A dignified death is a perfectly reasonable definition of success for terminal
care.

Where rehabilitation rather than treatment is required the priorities may
be rather different. In this case success may be measured in terms of some-

one's return to independence and self-care. The idea of being a patient here is rather different and the process is much more one of partnership. This can be quite a shift away from the aims of acute care even though both involve people called nurses and take place in places called hospitals.

This distinction may be a bit easier if the hospital, ward or clinic specialises in this but of course in many cases active rehabilitation must be an integral part of care on an acute ward. Are the nurses there to provide all care or are they there to promote recovery and independence? Is it possible that the patient sees things one way and the staff have quite a different view? Do the staff all have the same view about what they should be doing? These sorts of differences can make it very difficult to be consistent and thus to provide the most effective care.

There may be even more scope for differences of opinion in a continuing care hospital or in a residential home. I have already suggested that the 'hotel' model does not fit very well with a programme to encourage the maximum level of individual independence. Neither is the idea that those receiving care are 'patients' correct either. But if they are residents who have a right to decide what happens to them, how do we deal with a situation when we think they are making the wrong decision? What happens if their choice interferes with the freedom of others? So many questions. Let us now try and look for some answers.

What are we trying to achieve?

It may well be that any attempt to define the aims of care is bound to fail. However having at least some idea as a starting point does seem to be worthwhile. We might begin by defining our aim as being

to provide such care, help and attention as enables older people to have the best possible combination of physical health, emotional well-being and social integration.

This is still rather vague, after all it is hard to see many people disagreeing with this. We can take things a stage further and look at some of the things that are important in achieving this. Examples of aims and objectives would include:

1. Treating people as individuals, respecting their need for privacy and dignity.
2. Understanding the effects of common disabilities and how people can cope with these, e.g. what is it like to be
     hard of hearing
     partially sighted
     immobile
     without language/speech
     very forgetful and disoriented

3. Giving people choice and control about what happens to them, e.g. where they live, how they spend their day, what they eat, what they watch on television and so on.

Because these things are a bit more specific it is easier to see how we can monitor what is going on and how well we are doing. As I mentioned before, one useful rule of thumb can be 'Would I like to live like this/be treated in this way?' or perhaps 'How would I feel if that were my mother?'

Exercise

Add at least two more items to the list of aims and objectives. Try to be specific. Can you think of ways of measuring your success (or failure) to achieve these?

Just asking this sort of question should alert us to the worst of the things that we do. The problem is that most of the time we are too busy to stop and stare at others let alone hold up a mirror to our own behaviour. I am sure that if we did do this regularly then very few old people would have to sit on the toilet with the door open or use the commode in the sitting room where everybody else is having tea. I use both of these as examples because both were observed by a colleague of mine last week just as I have seen similar incidents in the past.

Having defined some of the aims and objectives we can now go on to consider what sort of skills and resources we need to achieve these.

What skills do we need?

It is important first of all to recognise that real skills are required. It is no good just relying on common sense. This is not to say that some people are not very good as carers even though they may have had no formal training. We all have different skills and talents some of which will of course be very relevant as a person caring for older people. However just because I enjoy gardening and may have quite a bit of experience of this, it is not right to assume that I could easily run a commercial garden centre. Some of the skills may be the same. Certainly my interest in this area will help but the two are really very different tasks.

Similarly it has tended to be assumed in the past that anyone who has brought up a family or who has looked after an elderly relative is well qualified to work caring for older people. This is not necessarily the case. Some people with this sort of experience are indeed very good at this sort of job but that may not be so. Certainly as any relative will testify there is a very big difference between being a paid carer for, say, 40 hours per week and being the main supporter all day and every day.

Nor is it enough just to do the job for the money, especially since the pay for caring jobs is generally significantly below that for other jobs in, for example, business or commerce. If you have neither good pay nor job satisfaction then you are unlikely to be very happy. A good part of job satisfaction can come from the feeling of having done a job well or with a high degree of skill. The task may only be a simple one, for example listening to someone tell you about how worried they are about their daughter who has had to go into hospital. However if it is done well then that person will feel much better afterwards than if it is done badly. We have all had the experience of trying to tell someone something which is important to us but feeling that person is just not interested in what we are saying. They may appear too busy, bored or whatever but we are likely to be left feeling pretty unsupported at the end.

Thus having the right skills is important not just for the person we are trying to help but also for ourselves. What are some of those skills?

Caring skills

Obviously many of the skills that we need to help older people are practical things like lifting or bathing. Exactly which skills you need depends on what job you are doing. A home help does different things from a district nurse. However the need for interpersonal skills is common to all carers and this can be where psychological approaches can help most. In fact we have already mentioned many of these interpersonal skills in connection with specific types of problems. For example back in chapter 3 we considered the importance of empathy and of being a good listener. It is nonetheless worth summarising a number of interpersonal skills here and considering briefly what makes for a high level of skill in each area.

Listening	Talking
Observing	Ignoring
Enabling	Waiting
Being flexible	Respecting and accepting

Listening

One of the many useful results from detailed studies of social interaction has been a better understanding of what we do when we listen. One particular difference between listening and talking for example is in where we look. The person who is listening looks mostly at the person who is talking but not the other way around. Important 'messages' are given by facial expression and these must be attended to if we are to 'receive' as much as possible. Being a good listener means using your eyes as well as your ears. Even the way you sit depends on whether you are being the listener or the talker. The listener tends to adopt the same sort of posture as the talker, for example.

Moreover good listening depends on taking in both the words that the person is saying and the tone of voice that he or she is using. Being a good listener involves keeping distractions to a minimum. Some of these are obvious things like trying to avoid having to listen to someone in a busy corridor or dining room. These distractions are external. Others are internal, for example worrying about what time the next bus goes or whether your spouse got the job he or she was being interviewed for that morning.

Being a good listener is therefore a complex process which most of the time we take for granted. It is however something that can be improved if we work at it, just like any other skill. It is certainly very important in whatever our caring role whether as a nurse, care assistant or any other carer.

There are several examples of how knowledge of social skills such as listening can be applied to various types of jobs. This includes not only such things as nursing but also jobs like being a probation officer or a personnel manager. I have listed a relevant example in the reading list at the end of this chapter.

Talking

Of course much of what I have just said about listening also applies to talking. How we say things depends on much more than the words we use. In the case of older people however it is especially likely that the person to whom you are talking will have some problem of hearing or possibly even of language. It is important to make the most of all available means in getting your message across. The person should not only be able to hear you (are you sitting near enough, is his or her hearing aid switched on etc.?) but he or she should also be able to see your face as we can all to some extent lip read.

For someone whose language is impaired it may be content or style rather than volume which matters. The effect of a stroke or dementia, for example, is not to make you deaf but to slow down how quickly you can understand what people are saying. Speaking slowly and using simple sentences is likely to be much more effective than shouting. It is also important to check that what you have said has been understood since, memory problems apart, what has not gone in cannot come out.

Observing

Perhaps of all the things that psychologists do the most particular is the observation of behaviour. There is an old joke that the definition of a psychologist is someone who goes to a strip-tease club to watch the audience. Certainly the study of human behaviour does involve watching very closely what people do. This may need to be done in a very careful and systematic manner, perhaps recording what is happening every few minutes or counting how many times something particular happens in a given period of time. For most purposes however a careful record of less finely detailed observations is sufficient.

What is important is to separate the observation from the interpretation. We may see someone behaving in what we take to be an odd manner but we must think carefully before deciding why they are doing this. It may turn out to be for an unknown reason which we cannot determine but in lots of cases it will be understandable in terms of who they are, what has happened in the past and what is going on at the time.

Of course not just psychologists need to observe behaviour carefully. We all depend very much on observation in almost everything that we do although in the case of working with older people it may require particular care. I was impressed recently by what was said by a medical colleague when giving a talk to a group of students. He showed a picture of a hand which had been quite severely deformed by arthritis. He pointed out how important it was to look beyond the deformity to what that person was still able to do.

Once again this means doing more than just following 'common sense'. The first reaction on seeing anybody is for us to notice what is odd or unusual about them. We readily observe how they differ from our expectations. This is another example of how we are sensitive to things that change and this can stop us looking at what is ordinary about that person. Looking for the ordinary can be very difficult if someone is very disabled but it is essential if we are to see the whole person.

Ignoring

In some circumstances it may be important to observe but not to react. We know that many of the things that people do depend upon the reactions of others. Most of the time this just means that appropriate and reasonable social interaction is maintained. However it can happen that someone behaves in a way which gets lots of attention but which is unreasonable in some other way. It is necessary sometimes to be selective in how we respond with attention so that we encourage people to behave in ways which are better for them. This has to be very carefully thought through since bad practice must always be avoided.

Indeed there is a very important difference between ignoring inappropriate behaviour and ignoring the person who is behaving in that way. The latter is not desirable. Indeed if this sort of strategy is to work it is vital that the person be helped to do other, more appropriate, things. This means, overall, giving the person more attention not less.

In the case of those who are suffering from some degree of dementia such 'ignoring' takes a rather different form. Here it may simply be that a behaviour which is inappropriate but which is doing no harm to anyone is allowed to continue until it stops spontaneously. Thus if someone is carefully rearranging the chairs in the dining room into neat rows, trying to stop him or her may provoke confrontation. Just leaving them to get on with it may mean having to rearrange them later but is better in the long term.

Whatever the situation it is often very hard indeed to ignore things even when we have agreed that this is the right thing to do. It depends very much on everyone supporting one another and recognising why one person may get lots of attention for doing something which is taken for granted in other people. Anyone can wreck such approaches if they are not consistent with the rest.

Enabling

The same can also be said of enabling, by which I mean the alternative to taking over. It is often much easier to do something *for* somebody rather than do it *with* them. This is not special to old or disabled people, it can apply to one's children or spouse as well. However in the case of children they are usually very determined to be independent so that they insist on trying to do things for themselves. Thus they learn to do things for themselves despite us if not because of us. In the case of spouses, moves towards equality achieve the same ends. For example you may object greatly if your husband or wife keeps all the bills and never lets you know how much money is in the bank. But there are some people who are quite happy for another person to take this on and so may never learn to balance the household budget. This is fine so long as there is someone to do this for them but things often go sadly wrong when widowhood comes along. I have previously noted what a good thing equality is for the future well-being of widows and widowers.

Likewise it will be better to help someone to dress or walk themselves rather than to dress them or push them in a wheelchair. However being 'enabling' does tend to take longer and may be much more demanding in terms of having to be persistent and persuasive. There is no doubt here that this skill is good for the person being helped but hard work for the helper.

Waiting

There are lots of times when patience is important. Being in a rush to get things done and insisting that such-and-such happens *now* can be a disaster. This is particularly true for those who are suffering from dementia when a tolerance of the individual matters most. It can be hard, for example, to remember that although this person has said, no they do not wish to do something now, they might respond quite differently in 5 minutes' time.

Over a rather longer time scale, patience and persistence are important in many aspects of rehabilitation and recovery in older people. That change is slower with advancing age is one of the few universal facts of ageing. We generally have to wait and work longer to achieve the same results.

Flexibility

This is essential if we are to treat people as individuals and we have already seen how older people tend to be especially different from one another. It is no good having a few standard solutions to problems and then just picking the one that seems to fit best. This might not work too badly for younger people but it is no good for those who are older. This can be more than a bit frustrating and does not at all help us to feel like an expert. After all an expert is someone who can look at a problem and say 'I know what's wrong here. What you need to do is ....' It is not someone who says 'Well I think I know what may be wrong but first of all I need to know a bit more about you. What do you think we should do?'

In fact it may take much more *expertise*, which of course is just another word for skill, to deal with things in the second way rather than the first. It also takes more effort to be flexible in this way because you actually have to think about each instance separately. We all recognise that individually tailored suits cost more than those which you buy off the peg. They are more difficult to make but they do fit much better. To carry the analogy a bit further, we might think of older people as being much less likely to be a standard size. We should not be surprised if, when we try to squeeze them into a suit that is the wrong size, everything falls apart at the seams.

Having a flexible approach will mean that we are able to give people more choice though even that is sometimes not as easy as it seems.

Respecting and accepting

Finally in this brief list of skills are those skills which involve recognising that older people are adults and should be treated as such. We may well have to put up with people saying 'No' and not doing what we think is best for them. We probably do not find it so difficult to say 'No' to them if we think that this is the right thing to do but can we cope with them saying it to us? If an older person is in any way mentally frail it can take great skill to decide what decisions that person is able to make for him or her self. It can be so much easier to take the decision, any decision, on his or her behalf. It may be hard to accept that someone may have been accustomed to a very different daily routine from that which we accept or, more likely, that which we might try to impose upon them. The choices that they make may, we think, be foolish but we may have to accept them nonetheless.

As I suggested earlier, we have to look beyond the frailty and age to accept and respect the person beneath.

The professional approach

All of these skills, as well as many that I have no doubt you can add to the list, are part of the range needed for helping older people. Before going on to look at how we might measure up to these, it is as well to remind ourselves of a couple of general points about being 'professional'.

First there is the matter of being dependable. We all have had the experience of being let down by someone. It may have been a repairman who did not turn up or someone who failed to keep a promise. Whatever the situation it does not feel good. Thus it is very important to promise to deliver only what we can achieve and to do so when we say we will. One Age Concern training officer I know always tells volunteers working with older people to be sure and keep their appointments. If you cannot go when you said you would, let the person know and try to go sooner than you had arranged rather than postponing the visit. This seems to me a very good practical example of trying to ensure that we are dependable.

Secondly many of the things that we do to help older people are very personal. They may be personal in the sense of involving close personal care, for example dressing or toileting, or in that we are told things which are very private to them. In either case we are the guardians of confidences and must be relied upon to be confidential. The people we help must be sure that we will not be gossiping about them or taking their confidences lightly. This is every bit as important as keeping written records confidential.

What kind of person am I?

The next step in setting down a personal programme is to decide what are one's own particular strengths and weaknesses. This can be divided into two stages, general motivation and specific skills.

First of all you need to ask the questions (a) 'Why do I want to work with older people?' and (b) 'Why do I want to do better?'

Exercise

Write down one or more answers to the two questions above.

The sorts of answers you might give could include for (a) finding older people interesting, seeing this sort of job as very worthwhile, enjoying a challenge or reckoning that this is an area of growing demand where there are prospects for the future. Perhaps you might also have included some reference to how you feel about growing older or wanting to 'repay' those of an older generation who brought you up.

These are the sorts of things that you might reply to the person who says to you 'I don't know how you could do that job' and they may also say something about your attitudes to ageing and older people. Of course the answers could also include just having a job and just doing it for the money. However I reckon that if you have got as far as first picking up this book and then getting to chapter 9 you must have more than a purely financial interest in ageing.

For (b) you might have included just wanting to do better for its own sake, because it could help you get a better job or because somebody else said you ought to learn more about looking after older people. It might be because you find some particular aspect of your job difficult and you would find it less stressful to be better skilled.

For both questions you are likely to be able to find many answers although as this is not something we do very often it may not be easy to think of them at first. It really helps here to have someone with whom you can discuss the questions and your attempts to answer them. If you are reading this book as part of a course then you will most likely have other people on the course who can help you with this.

The second stage is to identify what you are good at and some specific skills which you think could be improved. These could be in the list that we looked at earlier in the chapter or from your own list that you compiled to add to it. Once again it is much better to do this with someone else. Again it could be someone on your course or it might be someone in the place where you work. In either case not only can they help you to 'think aloud' but they may also be able to stop you being too hard on yourself.

This is important because we do not always recognise that we tend to be our own harshest critic. It can be a bit discouraging if you come up with lots of problems or things you would like to improve but very few strengths. The idea of this personal plan approach is to help you, not to drive you into the depths of depression. Sharing this task with somebody else and helping them to do the same is a good way of keeping things in perspective. Just as I do not expect you to have got this far if you only do your job for the money, I am quite sure that you do your job quite well. This kind of personal review is simply a way of helping you to do even better.

We all have some ways we would like to improve and none of us could cope with changing everything we would like to change at once. So the other thing that must be done is to try and put your aims into some sort of order. This order should not mean putting the most difficult things first but the easier ones. Again it may be tempting to say that you find doing something particularly difficult and if only you could get that right the other things would be easy to change. Unfortunately it does not seem to work like that.

Presumably the biggest changes are the biggest precisely because they are the most difficult. If they were easy you would have sorted them out ages ago. If you set a very difficult task first you are quite likely to fail to achieve it and leave yourself with no improvement. In fact you will be thoroughly discouraged and so even worse off than you were before.

Far better to set a reasonable task first and achieve that before going on to something more difficult. Of course it is also important to set your sights high enough since there is little satisfaction in doing something very very easy. Just as with using goal- setting to help other people, the trick is to get the goals just right, neither too difficult nor too easy.

Exercise

1. Draw up a list of the skills which you have in helping older people.

2. Draw up a list of skills you would like to develop and improve. Put them in order from the easiest through to the most difficult.

The final part of setting out to change things is to see what there is to help you. You might immediately think of some sort of training course, indeed you may already be reading this as a part of just such a course. However this is only one way of going forward. Other examples include:

seeing how other people work
inviting other people to come to where you work
going to study days/conferences
meeting with your colleagues
reading relevant books and articles

Few of the problems which we face are new or unique. We may feel as though there is something special about our own circumstances but there is almost always much in common with what other people are trying to do. Just exchanging views with them may be a very useful way of getting ideas as to how we might do things differently. What is more, we ourselves may have found some way of solving a particular problem which is potentially useful to somebody else.

For this reason most of the things on that short list above involve finding out from other people. But this can be easier said than done, especially if you see yourself as being at the bottom of some great big organisation where you may get told to do things but do not get listened to. Hopefully this is not the case. If you do feel that way then perhaps it is a worth trying some ideas out just to see if it is really true!

Certainly there are several opportunities for short or longer periods of 'training'. It is perhaps as well to remind ourselves of some of them here. With regard to study days and short courses organisations like Age Concern England (ACE) and the Kings Fund regularly run study days, courses and conferences (for addresses see the reading list at the end of this chapter). ACE has its own training centre which puts on a full programme of courses each year. There may be other more local courses run by local Age Concern groups and you can get their address from ACE.

If you are not able to get to this sort of thing, or perhaps just want to start with something you can take at your own pace then you would do well to look at the various courses organised by the Open University. They produce a wide range of material including a course entitled 'Caring for Older People' and specific study packs on such topics as 'Working with Mental Health Problems in Older People' as well as study packs produced jointly with the Health Education Council.

These sorts of courses include both written material and audio or video cassettes. I have alredy referred to the material which they have produced for older people themselves such as 'Health in Retirement' and these too can be very valuable to carers.

If you work for a large organisation such as a social services department or a Health Authority then your employer will have a training department. This may not be very visible, especially if it has a small budget and is situated in some rather remote corner of the town in a building no one else wants to use any more. However they do exist, and exist to do the sorts of training that people need. We are all so used to school however that we tend to expect to be told what we need to learn and to have someone summon us to learn it. However, if you think of how many things you learned in school and have now forgotten, this does not seem to be very effective. When we are trying to improve practical skills it may be much better for the consumer to decide what he or she needs to know. I have yet to meet someone running a training department who is not delighted to be given some idea of what sort of training would go down well for a study day, training course or similar.

Of course this does suppose that you know enough to have some idea what you do not know. Any reasonable amount of experience will, however, give you some ideas on this. If you follow the steps I have outlined for a personal plan you should have no problems getting at least as far as seeing what you would like to improve.

For those who belong to particular professional groups there are a range of opportunities from national courses, such as those run by the National Health Service Training Authority, to local courses leading to recognised qualifications such as the Certificate in Social Care.

Even if you do not seem able to track down such formal training to suit you, there is always the possibility of simply meeting with your colleagues to discuss how to do things better. In fact this is just as, if not more, important than formal training since it helps to change things in the real workplace. Just like reading this book and doing nothing, it is not much good going on a course and then slipping back into the same old ways back at work. Some sort of regular self-review is essential to keep things at their best.

An example of a personal plan

The following example is intended to summarise what I have been describing in this chapter. It is fictional, that is to say I have made it up, but hopefully realistic. I have imagined the situation of someone working in a residential home for elderly people called Autumn View.

1. What is Autumn View trying to do?

   (a) Look after the residents in their old age.

       This means: helping residents with dressing, bathing, walking, shopping etc. depending on need.

It also means: providing meals, making beds, washing clothes

(b) Help the residents to enjoy their remaining years.

This means: letting them do what they enjoy doing, listening and talking to them, providing recreational activities.

2. What skills do I need to do this?

Lifting/transferring a person from bed to chair etc.
Knowing how much each resident can do for him/herself.
Talking.
Listening.
Knowing what each resident likes.
Dealing with 'confusion'.

3. What skills do I have?

Practical skills, e.g. bed-making, washing.
Enjoy talking to people.

Good at calming people down when they are upset.
Find older people interesting.

4. What do I find difficult?

(a) Talking to the residents who are hard of hearing.
(b) Dealing with a resident who is confused about where he/she is.
(c) Knowing what sort of recreational activities residents like.

5. How can I improve the things in 4?

(a)   Go with Mr Jones when he goes to the Hearing Aid Clinic and ask their advice.
(b) (i) Ask if we could have a talk in the home by the community psychiatric nurse who visits Mrs Smith.
     (ii) Obtain a copy of appropriate Open University pack.
(c)   Try to have a chat with up to five residents and find out what their main interests have been. Organise ONE activity based on these and see how it goes.

As you can see none of these is in itself very dramatic but each is geared to what that person sees as important and can reasonably manage to do. YOUR programme will probably look nothing like this, just because it is yours. It will have the items important to you but the outline should be the same. For now that is as far as I can take you, getting the plan together is up to you.

Further reading

Hargie, O., Saunders, C., and Dickson, D. (1981) *Social Skills in Interpersonal Communication*. Croom Helm: Beckenham

A book aimed at helping professionals use social skills knowledge to improve their interpersonal skills.

Courses

A number of organisations run short courses, study days and workshops on topics related to health and social care of older people including:

Age Concern England
Bernard Sunley House
Pitcairn Road
Mitcham
Surrey CR4 3LL

Kings Fund Centre
126 Albert Street
London NW1 7NF

Open University
PO Box 76
Milton Keynes MK7 6ANT

Chapter 10

What Next?

At the beginning of this book I referred to the changing pattern of the ageing population. We have already seen large increases in the proportion of older people in our society and we know that more changes are on the way. More people are living longer and many are retiring earlier. Those who are preparing for retirement in the late 1980s need to reckon that they could spend as long in this phase of life as they did in their working life. Being retired is no longer just a short period of our lives between working and dying.

However the growing numbers of very elderly people and our improved life expectancy are by no means the only things that are likely to be different in 10 or 20 years' time. In this final chapter I am going to take a look at some of the other things that seem likely to affect the way older people are helped if they are no longer able to be fully independent. Because this involves looking to the future, the particular topics I have chosen are mostly some of those that seem most interesting to me. The excuses for indulging in this speculation are first that I hope you might also find these interesting and second that these thoughts might set you thinking still more about the future challenge of ageing.

A changing society

It is said by every generation that 'things are not what they used to be'. This is usually taken to imply that there are falling standards, rising discontent and that generally society is in a state of decline. However, whilst this could prove to be the case, early disintegration of modern civilisation does not seem very likely and we perhaps need to think carefully about what the real changes have been and what are mirages seen through the blue haze of nostalgia.

The numbers of older people have certainly changed and continue to do so. I do not need to repeat the figures here. But lots of other aspects of society are also changing. We have seen, for example, a steady rise in the number of marriages ending in divorce such that we know that one in three marriages now ends in divorce. We also know that if we look at the care of older people in the community, spouses tend to be those who succeed best in looking after frail older people at home. For those who are in their eighties today this means almost always their first and only spouse. The care is given against a background of having been together for 40 years, 50 years or even longer.

Can we necessarily expect the same pattern of determined self-sacrifice for the sake of someone who is the carer's second, third or fourth spouse? Where people remarry there are often children from a previous marriage and the likelihood of someone having a step-parent is much higher than it used to be. Is looking after a step-parent any different from caring for one's own blood relation? Certainly there has been some suggestion that there can be differences between natural and adoptive relationships but as far as I know we still await any systematic study of any effects associated with divorce or remarriage. It would be very wrong indeed to assume without careful study that there is any truth in the 'wicked step-mother' stereotype so often found in fairy tales.

Similarly we know that there have been changes in the attitudes of society to being a single parent and that very many children today will have been brought up by only one parent. Will this mean changes in the support which children will give to their parents?

Note that I am avoiding here any suggestion that any of these changes is likely to have an effect in any particular direction. It would be very easy to suggest, for example, that they will mean less care commitment by families. It is just as possible that the flexibility in relationships implied by, for example, a high divorce rate could enhance rather than diminish care patterns. Admittedly the present evidence for divorce seeming to have generally negative effects on those involved would not suggest this as the best bet but it is important not to prejudge this. It is not at all unknown for there to be problems in a marriage in late life which one feels might have been prevented if the individuals concerned had found it easier to get a divorce 40 years ago.

One example where positive change does seem likely is, as I mentioned back in chapter 5, in the gradual extinction of the helpless widower. Seeing how devastated some widowers are by being faced with taking on unfamiliar domestic skills there does seem much to recommend a greater sharing of domestic responsibilities. Of course this also applies to widows, though generally less so and for different skills. Practical household maintenance can be every bit as important as cooking, shopping and cleaning. Indeed the need for a broad range of skills is seen in those who are having to cope not with being alone following bereavement but with the task of caring for a frail spouse who can no longer carry out his or her contribution to day to day activities.

In terms of population shifts there may be quite big changes over the longer term in the balance between the numbers of older men and older women. One of the changes which we are already seeing is a tendency for women to adopt some of the unhealthy activities, such as smoking, which have for so long been an important factor in the shortened life expectancy of adult men. At the same time men have been tending to give up smoking and there is a steady growth in the number of people taking up regular exercise to keep fit. This could mean that in the future the imbalance between the numbers of older men and women is greatly reduced. It will be a long time before this shows any effect on the balance of sexes in the very aged but perhaps we should not be too surprised if changes do occur.

Associated with the changes in the respective roles of men and women are marked changes in people's incomes and standard of living. One of the reasons that older people are among the poorest in society is because they do not benefit directly from improvements in pay and conditions (neither of course do the unemployed but this is a book about ageing rather than unemployment). However some changes do work their way through eventually. For example we might anticipate that the move towards changing the arrangements for pensions could have a big effect even if it takes 40 years or more for these to be fully appreciated.

Changes in the proportion of older people who own their own home also tend to influence the pattern of care. I noted in chapter 8 that the sort of housing that you are used to will influence what you expect from residential care. But having a house or other financial assets will also mean that your relatives are likely to be much more interested in your will and whether you are mentally competent to spend money which they might otherwise inherit. This question will also be more pressing if you have several sets of children and step-children rather than a more traditional set of descendants.

The fact that there are more home owners is just one example of the rise in consumerism. As we buy bigger and better things we become more and more aware that it is important to get good value for money. This affects not only things like refrigerators and washing machines but services like travel and education. It is often said that older people today are reluctant to claim benefits to which they are entitled. The idea persists for many of them that many of the benefits which are available are charity rather than a right to which one is entitled. If, like my wife and I, you have been used to claiming child benefit, then it is not so great a step to claiming other benefits if you are entitled to these. When today's readers of *Which?* arrive at retirement they are likely to take getting value for money as a senior citizen very seriously. They are not going to put up with anything that they might see as a meagre second-rate service.

Treatments and technology

The problems of rising costs in health care is not, of course, just a matter of changing expectations. It is also very much due to advances in the technology of health and the treatment of disease. We already have many more techniques at our disposal to deal with a whole variety of medical problems. On the whole the advances tend to be in the treatment of acute illnesses rather than the disabilities of old age. Better surgical techniques mean shorter stays in hospital and advances in drug treatment mean that many conditions are nothing like as dangerous or disabling as once they were. Some of these do affect older people; for example the successful amelioration of Parkinson's Disease has meant many more years of independence for very many older people. Other common conditions such as chest disease and stroke have perhaps changed less or where there has been change it has been due to successful prevention arising from improvements in working conditions and general health rather than new medical treatments.

Stroke is perhaps a good example of the complex way in which different changes come about and how difficult it can be to say what will happen in the future. In terms of treatment of the condition itself it is fair to say that progress has been limited. Once someone has suffered a stroke there are some things that can be done medically to enhance recovery but the development of rehabilitation services is probably just as important and the results of treatment are significant rather than dramatic. It is much better of course to try and prevent someone having a stroke in the first place and this illustrates the importance of changing behaviour. We know now that having high blood pressure is bad for you in lots of ways, including making it much more likely that you will have a stroke. This means that it is important to control blood pressure when necessary.

The major efforts in this regard have been in two main ways. First there is the detection and medical treatment of high blood pressure. It is no good waiting to pick this up when someone has their first stroke, early treatment is what works for prevention. The case for treating high blood pressure is now well established in younger people and there is some evidence that it also works for older people. But no treament is without side effects and the focus now is also on preventing the high blood pressure, that is going one stage earlier. This means persuading people to eat differently so that they are not overweight, encouraging people to give up smoking and getting them to take more exercise.

Taking this sort of approach is a very long-term matter and the benefits in terms of a decreased number of strokes might not be seen for many years. There may be special resistance to these approaches among older people or those who care for them in that it is seen as being 'too late' for them to change. However the extent of this is probably over-estimated and it is attitude rather than fact which works against helping those who have already reached late life.

It is very hard to see what will be the long term effects of such changes in people's health behaviour. It seems plausible to suppose not that we will live very much longer but that we will stay healthier until later in life. One of the arguments used by those who resist a more healthy lifestyle is that of saying 'Well, you have to die of something, so why should I bother to....'

In fact the aim is to reduce illness and disability rather than make everybody live much longer. If you work with those who are frail in late life you will be able to see how perhaps dying from a heart attack in your sleep at the age of 90 is no bad thing. Being crippled by a stroke for the last 10 years of your life is, I would suggest, far worse. But when we think of 'being healthy' we tend to focus on avoiding the fatal conditions rather than the disabling ones which are in many ways the more tragic.

This may be one of the reasons why it has taken so long for there to be very much research into finding a treatment for dementia. Although dementia does shorten the sufferer's life span it is not acutely fatal. People do not die of dementia but rather of illnesses like heart failure or broncho-pneumonia which go with being very frail and disabled. Because of the stigma attached to mental illness it is much more acceptable to say that your parent or other relative died of pneumonia rather than from senile dementia.

Fortunately this is all changing now and there is a good deal of effort going into looking for a treatment for dementia. This of course means mostly dementia of the Alzheimer's type since it is likely that the best hope for the prevention of multi-infarct dementia lies in the prevention of stroke.

It is important to realise however what might be the implications of there being a treatment for this dreadful disease. First it is most likely that the treatment would be one which slowed down or even stopped the progression of the disease. It is most unlikely that there will be any treatment in the foreseeable future which will reverse the cerebral atrophy of moderate or severe dementia. It is much more possible that there will be a treatment which postpones decline in early cases. Alzheimer's Disease is like Parkinson's Disease in that it is associated with deficiencies in brain chemicals in certain parts of the brain. It seems reasonable to suppose therefore that an effective treatment will work in the same sort of way.

If this sort of treatment is going to work then it will be very important that people are diagnosed and treated early on in the disease. At present we have no way of regularly monitoring the general health, let alone the mental health, of older people. There is no one system which sees all older people in the way that schools, for example, do for children. Health Visiting for the elderly takes on a whole new meaning if this sort of screening is required.

Whatever sort of screening might be devised there are always likely to be some cases which are missed. If the treatment slows the progression of the disease then giving it at a late stage may be to prolong the period of disability compared with the present situation where there is no treatment. The alternative, namely withholding treatment from those not detected until the condition is advanced, has ethical rather than practical implications.

Likewise at present we rely on the fatal effects of dementia to provide the resources, for example beds in hospital, for those who require them. Put bluntly, being on a waiting list for a long-stay hospital bed means waiting for someone already in hospital to die. If a treatment prolonged the life span of those already with severe dementia the effects on the need for resources could be considerable. The benefits of there being fewer people who need to come into hospitals or residential homes could be balanced by those who do come in needing care for longer.

The fact that those who suffer from dementia often have little or no insight into their problems adds to the complexity. This could be even more the case if the treatment has nasty side effects. Are you likely to agree to taking a tablet which makes you feel sick in order to treat a condition which you do not think you have?

It may be that this all seems a bit unlikely but in fact is very near the truth for some existing treatments. For example at present some people find that they get side effects from the drugs used to treat high blood pressure. The high blood pressure may be very easy to see when the doctor measures it but may not give the patient any symptoms. Some people may therefore choose to run the risk of a stroke rather than put up with the effects of the treatment. All I have done in looking forward to the future is to add in the extra problem of a condition, namely dementia, which itself affects your ability to understand what is happening and to evaluate risks and benefits.

Finally it is even more difficult to say what might be the effectiveness of any treatment in the longer term. It is only now some 10 to 15 years after the discovery of an effective treatment for Parkinson's Disease that we are seeing the problems of what happens once the treatment is no longer effective. The benefits of the treatment are immense but there is still a need to provide other care once this is no longer effective. Treatments for common disabling illnesses in older people are unlikely to be so effective as to eradicate the need for care.

Technology

Because of the problems of insight, there are difficulties with applying technology like sophisticated alarm systems to those with dementia. However for those who are mentally alert these already offer much in the way of benefit. It is now possible to have an alarm in your home which alerts a central control and gives them your name, address and various medical details. It is usually possible for the person on the other end to speak to you and to find out what the problem is before sending the right sort of help. The alarm can be triggered by a small transmitter carried by the older person so that he or she can push a button to summon help wherever needed within the house.

This sort of technology might easily be expanded to operate anywhere just as now happens with the portable telephones which the advertisers say every busy executive must now have in his or her car. The limits here are probably going to be those of cost and acceptability rather than ingenuity. Busy executives are much more likely to be able to afford new technology and to adopt eagerly each new advance. It may be necessary for some time yet to concentrate on seeing that all older people have an inside toilet and an adequate, safe heating system rather than look for solutions at the frontiers of technology.

Nonetheless the costs of such new technology do tend to fall quite rapidly once a real mass market develops so some impact is to be expected sooner rather than later. Once again these changes are likely to highlight the variety of needs of frail elderly people. For example, having an alarm which you can activate anywhere if you need help works very well if you are physically frail but mentally alert. It is not such a great advance if you are physically fit but mentally frail.

Changing services

Bringing about changes in the way that help and support are provided to older people is likely to be much more important than any advance in the way in which computers are built and designed or other advances in high technology. I may live to see the management of incontinence revolutionised by the micro-chip bladder but I have my doubts. Introducing more flexibility and choice seems to me as much of a revolution as we are likely to bring about.

This sort of change is already beginning to happen. There is a good deal of talk, and rather less in the way of planned development, aimed at improving the level and range of services to older people in their own home or in their local community. There are examples of special programmes which aim to give care to people when and where they need it. The care can be tailored to meet their particular needs rather than selected from a limited range of choices none of which is quite right for them.

Apart from the implications for resources, the most important change required for this is in the attitude of the carers, especially the ones that get paid. All too often good ideas fail because people find it difficult to work in different ways. It can be very hard if you have spent many years training to do one job to accept that really you need to do something rather different. You may not even have the same thing to do every day and you may find that some of the time you are doing the same thing as someone who was trained to do something completely different.

Similarly it can be very hard to get used to seeing people in their own home rather than in a home (or hospital or wherever). It is quite a bit harder to feel that you are in control if you do not know your way around and the other person does. Residents and patients have been having to put up with this for years as they are bemused by an institution and the unwritten rules followed by the staff. If care is to be tailor-made then we have to give the customer what he or she wants not some left-over outsize garment from last year's collection. I am not at all sure that we are yet ready for customer choice but I am sure it is on its way.

Note here that I am referring to 'choice' rather than to any particular type of service. The idea of older people as 'individuals' has recurred throughout this book. Helping individuals means having a range of choice and flexibility to meet individual need. Nevertheless I do not think that we will ever see the end of the old people's home or the extinction of the continuing care hospital ward. There will always be some people for whom high quality, high dependency care is the right choice.

The emphasis on community care rightly shifts the balance to the needs and wishes of the majority. It is quite wrong to suggest that people ought to have to go into a home when they become frail, in later life. But some may wish to and others may do so because that is the best way of meeting their needs. The residential and nursing homes to which they go will hopefully be very different from the converted workhouses which we use today. They will offer both better physical surroundings and truly individual care. Such homes will cater for the very frail, not those who had to come in because there were not the services available to them at home.

Principles of care

The theme of individuality is one of the principles that can be used to guide us in how we help older people. This can be seen, for example, in the guidelines for residential care which I referred to in chapter 8. I would suggest that three more general criteria can be used to assess how good is any particular help or intervention. High quality care should:

1. Reduce the extent of the problem for the older person.
2. Enhance the older person's independence and dignity.
3. Reduce the strain on carers.

You can test this out for yourself against all sorts of different interventions. By way of example let us just consider the problem of an older person who suffers from Alzheimer's Disease and who is wandering. Consider how just three of the many different strategies we might use measure up to these principles.

A. Using drugs to sedate the individual.
   1. Dubious how much it helps the patient. He or she may be less 'at risk' from wandering but could have side effects, for example be more prone to falling.
   2. Practically not at all.
   3. The only real achievement.

B. Providing a 'safe' environment such as a secure residential home or hospital.
   1. Does quite well in some ways but can be distressing or disruptive in that it means moving to a new place.
   2. Rather limited but not too bad for the more restricted environment.
   3. Very good except for the carer's probable feelings of guilt.

C. Providing individual home care workers to the person and his or her carer at home as needed.
   1. Good.
   2. Good.
   3. Good.

Exercise

Use the same criteria to evaluate four other problems and possible strategies. You might include problems such as a language impairment following a stroke and urinary incontinence.

Now you may just be saying, well yes this is obvious, but what about the cost? It is easy to come up with some wonderful scheme if you have unlimited resources. Naturally this is true and in the real world we do have to compromise.

Nonetheless it is usually true that even within such limits there is more than one way of doing things. There are two things which such an evaluation helps us to do.

The first is to choose the best option given what we have available now. The second is to identify what we could do if things were different. Things might be different if we had more of the same but what we can also identify is when we need things that do not exist at all at present.

We may not have the power ourselves to decide what resources are available. We do however have a responsibility to make the best use of what we do have and to tell those who do control the resources what else is required.

Looking forward

The examples I have given are just some of the many changes likely over the next few years which could have quite far-reaching effects on attitudes and behaviour of older people, their relatives and on the pattern of care which is considered appropriate and acceptable. Change of this sort can be both exciting and threatening but it does not need to be sudden. Indeed it is usually much more comfortable for all of us if our attitudes can change slowly rather than suddenly.

We know now that things will be different as each succeeding generation grows older. We can take on the challenge of preparing for this ourselves or have the change thrust upon us at the last minute. Changing services for the better must surely be a good objective. Better still would be so to improve the help we offer older people that they become the standard others seek to achieve, not the service people hope to avoid.

Index